PRAISE FOR RICHARD B. SCHWARTZ

Proof of Purchase
It's like this guy is just channeling Raymond Chandler on every page. . . . The ending . . . would make Mike Hammer proud.
— Jochem Steen, *Sons of Spade*

In this engaging hard-boiled mystery, one of three in Schwartz's Jack Grant series (Frozen Stare; The Last Voice You Hear), the seasoned California PI looks into the disappearance of an ex-girlfriend at the request of the woman's husband. When her mutilated body turns up in the woods, Grant makes it his mission to track down her murderer. With the assistance of Lt. Diana Craig, an attractive fast-riser in the San Bernardino police department, Grant follows leads that point to his client, as well as to a consortium of underworld bosses who are branching out into a mega-real estate project. The pair find time, between car chases and gun battles, to begin a relationship. . . . Fans of Robert Parker will enjoy encountering Grant . . . .
— *Publishers Weekly*

The Last Voice You Hear
It's not often that an author's second book is as good as the first, and even less frequent are the instances when an author . . . top[s] it with an extraordinary second . . . deliver[ing] a walloping good tale as well. Richard B. Schwartz has done just that. In *The Last Voice You Hear*, Mr. Schwartz places himself on par with our finest contemporary murder-mystery writers. This is a book you won't want to miss. . . .
— Alan Paul Curtis in *Who Dunnit*

The author . . . writes vividly, putting the reader right into the scene. Schwartz explores the meaning of right and wrong, crime and justice.
— Mary Helen Becker in *Mystery News*

The story rockets along . . . a fast-moving, well-told story with a surprising conclusion that blurs the line between crime and justice.

Jack Grant, the Vietnam vet and Pasadena-based PI who debuted in Frozen Stare (1989), returns in this engrossing sequel by Schwartz, author of several scholarly studies of Samuel Johnson. Schwartz knows his London, but surprisingly he evokes California with equal ease, mainly with vividly etched strokes. An apparently maniacal killer is on the loose in London, someone strong and very practiced at impalement. So far, so nasty. But when a victim is dispatched in similar fashion in Disneyland, of all places, Jack Grant is called in. He discovers the killer's identity, but there's a problem: there's a method to the killer's madness. Moreover, Grant has an ethical problem of his own: he's plagued by his conscience, since he understands and even sympathizes with the murderer's cause. The cinematic climax takes place high above the floor of the California desert, and Schwartz squeezes every last drop of suspense from his setting. . . . The result is a high-tension thriller awash in sanguinary detail. Paper towels, anyone?
— *Publishers Weekly*

Frozen Stare

I welcome Richard Schwartz to the club. It's been a long time since I've seen two more engaging characters entering the series scene.
— Sandra Scoppettone

Grant and White play nicely off each other and the switch-on-a-switch works well.
— *Kirkus Reviews*

This tale, in the California private eye tradition, has a rousing finish and is an enjoyable read.
— *Publishers Weekly*

A new author devoted to the hard-boiled tradition. . . . Schwartz has the hard-boiled formula down pat. . . . Schwartz does not break any rules in Frozen Stare. . . . He writes crisply. The narrative moves at a slam-bang pace as bodies

pile up. . . . As a dedicated student of the hard-boiled school of detective fiction [Schwartz] has learned his lessons well.
— *The Washington Post Book World*

Gives a whole new meaning to the phrase 'cold-blooded murder'. . . . This is a quick read with plenty of action. Schwartz's first novel is a winner!
— *Sarasota, FL Herald Tribune*

This is a delightful tale, full of amusing touches, and the relationship between Grant and his good cop friend, black Frank White, is a joy. I hope that Schwartz can keep this standard up for a long time to come.
— *The Armchair Detective*

Nice and Noir: Contemporary American Crime Fiction
Opinionated but always fascinating, shrewd and smart, but always readable. . . .
— *The Thrilling Detective*

BOOKS BY RICHARD B. SCHWARTZ
FICTION
The Jack Grant Novels

Frozen Stare
The Last Voice You Hear
Proof of Purchase

The Tom Deaton Novels

Into the Dark
The Survivor's Song
Nightmare Man

CRITICISM

Samuel Johnson and the New Science
Samuel Johnson and the Problem of Evil
Boswell's Johnson: A Preface to the Life
Daily Life in Johnson's London
After the Death of Literature
Nice and Noir: Contemporary American Crime Fiction
The Wounds that Heal: Heroism and Human Development
(with Judith A. Schwartz)
ed. The Plays of Arthur Murphy, 4 vols.
ed. Theory and Tradition in Eighteenth-Century Studies

MEMOIRS

The Biggest City in America: A Fifties Boyhood in Ohio
Accidental Soldier: A Reserve Officer at West Point in the Vietnam Era
Postwar Higher Education in America: Just Yesterday

EBOOK

Is a College Education Still Worth the Price? A Dean's Sobering Perspective

A TOM DEATON NOVEL

NIGHTMARE MAN

RICHARD B. SCHWARTZ

DARK
HARBOR
BOOKS

NIGHTMARE MAN

Published by Dark Harbor Books
First Edition 2021

Cover design: Jana Rade

ISBN: 978-1-7374748-6-9 Paperback Edition
       978-1-7374748-7-6 Hardcover Edition
       978-1-7374748-8-3 Digital Edition

Library of Congress Control Number: 2021920461

Author services by Pedernales Publishing, LLC
www.pedernalespublishing.com

10 9 8 7 6 5 4 3 2 1

Printed in the United States of America

xx-v6

For Kirsten and Jonathan, *munera domini*

Now he goes along the dark road,
whence they say no one returns.

Catullus

ONE

When the lockdown came it brought as much relief as the pocketful of lint-covered percocet he had hoarded (and then traded) from his last two trips to the infirmary. It was an art really—hiding them in the back of his mouth but also keeping them dry enough that they remained intact and could be put to later use . . . dusting off any powdery edges and metering them out one by one in return for services rendered or violence postponed. In this case he had been able to immunize himself for a month, distributing each of them carefully, even when it meant foregoing release from the migraines and the stomach spasms which always seemed to make their joint visits when his fellow inmates had become restive and his other protective options had shrunk.

Two bloody fights in the yard and the related slashings of a belly and a throat with sharpened spoon handles had been enough to cause the lockdown, the second in three months. He wished it had come a week sooner. The shorter you got the more you were shoved, tripped, and cut—anything to provoke a response that would keep you inside longer.

Two days before the lockdown he had been cornered in the north shower by an east L.A. defective named Montalvo who was wearing a thin-lipped grin and carrying a long piece of green soap. "It'll be just your size," he said. The incident was interrupted by a jumpy lifer named Biggs, who threw Montalvo to the cold, stained tile floor and kicked him in the face, groin and kidneys until it was clear that he would not be able to get back up on his bare feet. The word was out about the percocet and Biggs promptly demanded six pills as payment. By then, unfortunately, there were only two left and Biggs was long on need and short on patience. He was also angry because the shower had gotten a few drops of water on his thick, black hair, which he never washed because he believed that soap and prison water had the power to sap him of all of his manly strength.

Biggs accepted the two pills as a down payment and gave him 48 hours to either get more or prepare for something much worse than a slow soapy shower with Ramon Montalvo. The only way he could get any pills in so short a time was to approach the few individuals he trusted and see if they had any dope or prescription painkillers they were willing to deal for the carton and a half of unfiltered Camels he had already promised to the Puerto Rican they called Chugger. If he was caught even attempting such a trade he could kiss away any thought of his parole, but he was desperate and he had to try something. He couldn't use the packs to deal directly with Biggs. Biggs wouldn't use them. He had broken three fingers and the right wrist of a con named Slipper when Slipper approached him in the yard, and the wisps of secondhand smoke from his cigarette made their way into Biggs's face and hair.

Two hours and two minutes before his scheduled meeting with Biggs the south-block Aryans had suddenly gotten tired of the damp, hot weather hanging over the bay and the greasy, congealed glop laying cold across their breakfast trays. To pick up their spirits they decided to go hunting for spics and spooks with their edged spoons. The second the blood began to run the lockdown came and he was able to buy valuable time.

Turning on his side in the dark he accidentally bumped his elbow against the thick rounded lump in the top bunk that was Chelton's ass. Its broad cheeks were hanging above him like an overloaded longshoreman's net hovering above an open cargo hold, stretching the four-inch mattress and nylon rack directly into his chest and face. Turning back in fear, he felt the taut pull of his collar button against his throat. He always wore his shirt to bed and he always buttoned it to the neck, as if that might somehow protect him against the sounds and creatures of the night.

"Lay still, you fucking little pissant," Chelton said. "You touch me once more and I'll come down there and break a few of your fingers a joint at a time. Maybe pull off one of your fucking ears. You know I'll do it too, don't you, Snack?" It was a statement, not a question.

At 10:00 the guard came to awaken him and tell him he'd return in an hour to out-process him. He gathered his things as quietly as he could but Chelton woke up again, leaned over, and slapped him hard on the left side of his head. His ear burst with pain and red-black light flashed across his eye as his right shoulder slammed into the cell door. Chelton told him not to get too goddamned comfortable on the outside. He called him *Snack* over and over, knowing how much he hated it. "You'll be back, Snack; you know you will, you little prick. You'll be out there just long enough to get a taste, just long enough for you to start to get used to it; then it'll all be over in a second. You'll fuck up the way you always do and you'll be back here with us . . . and you know what? We'll all be waiting for you . . . and the next time we won't make it so fucking easy on you."

Once when he was fourteen, looking for things to steal and people to hurt—anything that might impress Jimmy and Wes and his other older friends—a rich woman in west L.A. had told him to stop loitering outside her house. When she threatened to call the police he shoved her back through her own gate, squeezed and pinched her tit hard, told her to go fuck herself, and began to take a long, satisfying piss in her swimming pool. Before he finished, she had opened the back door of her house and sicced her Rotty, T-Bone, on him. The dog took his left testicle in the first snap-and-pull and when he screamed and tried to jab his left index finger into the dog's right eye, T-Bone took it too, along with the front of his right sneaker and the better part of two toes. The first time Chelton saw the complete results in the shower he laughed uncontrollably and called him *Snack*. "What *you* are, *Snack*, is a fucking dog's breakfast," he said, and the name took.

Chelton had called him other names too, but he would forget them all as soon as he stepped across, into the outside. When the guard came, he put the carton and a half of Camels at the top of the yellow and black plastic bag with the thin drawstrings that he had been given for his things. The door locked behind him and he didn't turn to glance back. When he and the guard approached Chugger's cell he slipped the Camels out of the bag, gave the guard a chance to inspect them (a *gift*, he said), and then slid them along the floor under the bars, giving them a final shove to put them out of anyone else's reach. It was the payment for their deal, their *contrato*. Now he knew he could never come back to San Quentin. In return for the carton and a half of unfiltered Camels Chugger had promised to cut off Chelton's ears.

TWO

"Sit your ass down there and wait until your name is called," the guard said, pointing to a short pine bench on the opposite wall. He then locked the steel door behind them, and disappeared through a double-locked oak door to the left of the property clerk's window.

There was no sign of the clerk, but the fluorescent lights inside his cage were flickering and there was a dead-caramel smell of burned coffee over a layer of thick cigarette smoke.

After ten minutes the clerk approached the window, brushed the hair back off of his forehead and said in a bored voice, "Harris, Earlon G. Number 06538527."

Harris approached the window and stopped at the yellow plastic strip that had been glued to the gray-flecked vinyl floor. "Stand up straight and look like you're half awake and intelligent," the clerk said. When he tried to change his expression and his posture the clerk said, "Shit, boy, back in the 'Nam you would have lasted about a minute and a half before we'd see skinny-ass parts of you flying past our fucking heads."

Harris stood straighter still and refocused his eyes, trying to avoid blinking. The clerk dropped a brown plastic folder on the counter, unzipped it, and removed a narrow sheet of pink paper itemizing the contents. He put on a pair of smudged glasses, raised the paper toward his eyes, and read.

"One plastic wallet containing seventeen dollars . . . three loose dimes, one nickle, and six pennies . . . one plastic keychain with boxed green plastic dice and two automobile keys . . . one purple-striped man's handkerchief with initials **EH** . . . one yellow tin of Bayer aspirins containing three tablets . . . two concert tickets for a show at the Los Angeles Forum, December 6, 2012. These aren't gonna do you too damned much good now, boy," he said, laughing.

"I want 'em anyway," Harris said.

"What the fuck did you just say to me?" the clerk asked.

He forced the words through his tightened lips. "I said I would like to have the tickets, sir."

"You got a time machine or something, fuck?"

"No sir, I don't."

The clerk paused, enjoying himself. "You're a devious little son-of-a-bitch. Maybe you could change the date, find some dumbass to buy them off of you." He took another look at them, laughed and lit a cigarette. Harris noticed he was chewing gum while he smoked. "Go on and take them," he said, adding them to the pile. "Frame the goddamned things. Wipe your ass with them. I don't give a shit. They're yours . . . and there sure as hell ain't much else in that folder to help you launch your new career."

He put the slip down, turned it abruptly toward the window, and put a pencil stub next to it. "Third line from the bottom, Harris. Autograph the sumbitch for me. You know how to write your name?"

"Yes, sir."

"Do it for me then."

As soon as he signed the slip and took his things the guard reappeared and took him to a holding cell. "You got twelve more minutes, Harris. I hope you can sit there with your mouth shut and not fuck that up, 'cause your ass is still ours 'til 12:01."

The cell was small, with a bare toilet filled with crumpled cigarette packs, a three-foot bench bolted to the back wall, and a black plastic chair. Harris sat down in the chair, opened his yellow bag, and checked the other contents: a toothbrush and paste, a red plastic comb, a pack of letters, the most recent three years old, and a sheaf of yellowed pages torn from a school tablet, covered with notes and scrawls. He looked at the first ten pages of his notes, reading them slowly and thoughtfully; then he counted the rest of the pages, folded them carefully, and returned them to the bag. He picked up the letters, pulled the top one from the pack, took it out of its envelope, and read:

March 13, 2017

Dear Earlon,

I still do not know why it is that you had to be
caught when I know that you were doing it all for
me. You know that my heart is with you every day
and that when you get out things will be just as
they were before. There is nobody else but you and
I am waiting for you to come back to me so that you
can love me as before and I can make you happy. You
asked me about Roy and I told you that he doesn't mean
a thing to me. Well he doesn't. You've got to believe
that. Roy just helps me out from time to time. It's not
always easy here. He is just a friend. When you meet
him I'm sure that you will like him. I better say good-
bye for now. I have to leave because my boss gets angry
if I am late. I am trying to put away some money so
that we can take a trip together when you get out. I
will be here waiting for you.

I love you, Earlon.

Lorna

There was a tear welling in his sore eye as Harris read the last words. "You'd better be waiting for me, Lorna," he whispered, as he folded the letter carefully, returned it to its envelope, slipped it back into the pack and returned the stack of letters to his bag, "or I'll find you and make you very sorry that you weren't."

THREE

The giveaway prison suit was tight and scratchy and the change he had left after ten years of bribes and buy-offs was barely enough to get him across the bridge and into town for breakfast. He pulled off the plain brown tie, crumpled it in his hand and threw it into the weeds. Then he opened up his collar, checked to make sure that he had buttoned his wallet pocket and started to walk. Jesus, who would wear a wool tie in California? They must have bought a couple hundred thousand of them as part of some goddam kickback scam. Met the terms of some phony fucking law, pocketed a hefty piece for themselves, and screwed the ex-cons at the same time. Things hadn't changed at all since he went inside.

Two and a half hours later, walking along the side of the 101, he found a nervous citizen with a dead Volkswagen sedan. It was a late 1980's model that seemed as if it was trying to look like some kind of sports car. Some of the parts had been chromed and it was painted a shade of candy apple red that Harris had never seen before on a Volkswagen. It *evoked* the feeling of a hot rod or sports car; that's what Loyal would have said. *Evoked*. This guy evoked the feeling that he could easily be separated from his money, if in fact he actually had any.

Harris approached him, shook his hand, told the man his name was Barry, and offered to help. The guy was dressed in what looked like a Sears or Penney's suit and a pair of brown Thom McAns. Jesus, Harris thought, I should have saved that tie; I coulda sold the ugly son-of-a-bitch to *him*. It might have drawn some attention away from the fucking glare coming off of the seat of those polyester pants. When he first looked at Harris, carrying a plastic bag and walking beside the freeway, he was apprehensive, but he was desperate enough to take any help he could get at that hour of the morning.

"Maybe *I* can get it started…" Harris said, doing his best blue-collar wizard impersonation. "No charge if I can't," he added, smiling.

After a quick check of the car's vital signs (battery, starter motor, air, and fuel all OK, just no spark) Harris asked the man if, by any chance, he happened to have a nail file.

"I think so . . . yeah . . . here," he said, sliding a miniature file out of one of the inside pockets in his wallet.

Harris got a serious look on his face, did a lowkey Ed Norton, wiggling the fingers of his right hand, made a series of passes through the ignition points to take off the accumulated grit, and told the Sears man to try to start it up. When it coughed and then fired, the man smiled in wonder.

"There you go," Harris said. "Just took a little magic touch…"

"What do I owe you?" the man asked.

Harris paused a second before answering. "What do you think a garage would have charged you at this time of the morning?"

"Probably around 85 or 90 bucks."

"If you were lucky. Tell you what, I'll take a ride into the city and forty bucks in cash," Harris said, turning over thoughts in his mind of what he might do if the guy refused.

"Deal. Do you mind giving me a receipt for the forty?"

"Of course not," Harris said, taking a sheet of paper from the guy, writing on it very formally and signing it *Barry A. Emerson*.

The driver was an office supply salesman from Novato, making a courtesy stop at an all-night service station in the city and then catching breakfast and a dawn flight to a sales conference in Anaheim.

"Pretty early to be going to the airport," Harris said.

"I always get there early," the man said, checking his watch. "Really only one road. If there's a problem, you're really stuck."

"Not much chance of a problem at this hour," Harris said.

"You never know," the man said. "Strange things can happen sometimes, especially around here."

"You may just be right about that," Harris said, smiling.

He dropped Harris off on Lombard, between Pierce and Steiner. He walked around for about fifteen minutes until he found an all-night hole-in-the-wall where he ordered eggs, ham, home fries, biscuits, coffee, and extra ketchup.

"You just get out?" the waitress asked.

"Yeah. You can tell that easy?"

"I seen suits like that before," she said. "Seen 'em in all sizes. Always the same suit. Summer . . . winter . . . the same. Want to trade it? I know a guy who might be interested. He sells 'em to the illegals."

"What for?"

"Jeans, a sweatshirt, maybe a plastic windbreaker."

"Levi's?"

"Probably not," she said. "Maybe Lee's if you're lucky. Here..."

She gave him a piece of torn cardboard with an address on Fillmore. "Don't wake him up yet. He'll be in the store about 7:00. You wake him any earlier and he'll be meaner than cat dirt."

"You think that's mean?" Harris asked.

He walked around the Marina district, disappointed that he couldn't see more damage from the recent quake. Probably wasn't half as bad as the fucking TV newsmen made out. He checked the time on a clock in a shop window and went down to the wharf to watch the fishermen pull out. The people who sell postcards and geegaws were setting up their tables and registers. He saw a banjo player tuning up, an assortment of beggars, and an old man in a blue uniform with an open cigar box and three dogs dressed in human clothes sitting on a stained wool Army blanket. One dog was wearing strapped-on sunglasses; another had a baseball hat tied to the top and bottom of his collar; the third had a plastic cigarette glued to the side of his mouth. They didn't look as if they were looking forward to their day. By 7:00 Harris was back on Fillmore, hitting the painted-over doorbell on the secondhand clothing store. A light came on and the owner opened the door. He was licking the brown filter on an unlit cigarette and running his left hand through his unwashed brown hair. He was badly hung-over. When he breathed, Harris could hear things moving around in his throat and sinuses.

"What have you got, a Q-suit?"

"Yeah. What can I get for it?" Harris asked.

"I don't know . . . I got a shitload of 'em already. What do you want—jeans, a shirt?"

"Yeah, and a jacket and shoes," Harris said.

"I don't have shoes. You might be able to buy some knockoff gym shoes from one of the guys in the park. What kind of jacket? A sport coat or something? The suit's not worth that much to me."

"Something light."

"How about this?" the guy asked, turning the cigarette over with his tongue.

He held up a purple nylon jacket with a large ad on the back for a Union station in Petaluma: *Ed's All Service*.

"I'll take it," Harris said.

"The jeans I got may be a size or two too big, but they've got a lot of wear left in 'em. You can have your pick of tee shirts. There's some in the back there without any sayings on them."

Harris caught the dawn bus with the tired maids and baby sitters and made it to Washington Square by 7:45. A scraggly bum with a pint bottle in a wrinkled brown bag looked at his jacket and asked him if he was really from Petaluma. He smelled of body odor and store-label gin. Harris checked his size and then told him that if he cared any about his health he ought to shut the fuck up and not talk to people he didn't know.

The bum shuffled off and Harris sat down in the park and opened his plastic bag, making sure everything was still there. After a few minutes he began to feel the chill in the air. A dying Saab pulled up on Stockton and the driver started unloading card tables and setting up a display of knockoff Gucci and Fendi watches. He was tall and looked like he'd rather be sitting on the beach with his fingers wrapped around a bottle of something strong. Harris got up and walked over to him.

"How much for that one there, the one with the gold band but without the colored stripes?" he asked.

The salesman looked Harris up and down and then said, "Forty bucks."

"You got to be fucking kidding," Harris said.

"OK, since you're an old friend . . . thirty five."

"How about five and I promise not to call the goddamned cops?"

"Piss off," the salesman said, reaching into the Saab's trunk for some lookalike Gucci purses.

"What happens if you sell a watch and the son-of-a-bitch suddenly stops working?" Harris asked.

"I guarantee all my stuff," the guy answered. "I'm here at this location every day."

"Bullshit," Harris said.

"Look," the guy said, "you want a watch, right?"

Harris didn't answer.

"And you want something good that's also cheap. Something that works."

Harris just looked at him.

"Take a look at this one," he said, taking off the watch on his left wrist. "It's the same as the others, except that it has a plain dial."

"Bullshit. Look at the strap. It's stained from your goddamned sweat," Harris said. "How long have you been wearing it? A year? It's probably ready to wear out any minute."

"So? What does this look like," the man said, gesturing at the card tables, "fucking *Tiffany's*? You're buying from a street corner, Ace, and you're trying to buy cheap. This is *my* fucking watch. The stain means I been wearing it for awhile and it still fucking works."

"How much?" Harris asked.

"Ten."

"Five and I don't call the cops."

"Take the son-of-a-bitch," the guy said. "And have a nice day . . . somewhere else."

Harris wiped the back of the watch and the inside of the imitation leather band against his pants leg and put it on his left wrist. It was 25 minutes after 8:00 when he crossed Columbus Avenue. "Now to make some money so I can get the fuck out of here," he said.

FOUR

He walked to Chinatown, searching the streets for a peddler, a guy with good stock, the kind who might also trust him. He looked for one his own age, one with the same blank eyes. He found a thin man in a faded red polo shirt with four tables of knockoff Vuitton, Prada and Dooney and Bourke purses with reversed initials, a box of Totes umbrellas, a half-smoked cigar with a wooden tip, and sallow arms covered with bad tattoos. Harris looked for a public phone and then called the police.

"Officer?" he said, politely. "My name is Bowen . . . George Bowen. I'm here in San Francisco on vacation with my wife and family and I want to report a crime . . . yes, sir . . . a serious crime . . . a man tried to take indecent liberties with my little girl . . . yes, sir . . . right on the street . . . she's only *eleven* years old; if you don't do something to him I *will* . . . yes . . . let me see here . . . I have to check the signs . . . he's at the corner of Powell and Clay. Yes, it's just terrible. We knew that San Francisco was . . . well . . . different, but we didn't expect anything like this. The child is still crying . . . something like that had never happened to her before . . . he just put his hands on her and started to rub all over her. The man is also selling counterfeit purses. I know; I operate an accessory shop in the largest mall in Des Moines and I know the prices of purses. Yes . . . thank you very much. We're staying at the *Meridien Hotel* and I'll be happy to press charges. That's *George Bowen*. I have to get my little girl out of here now. I'll wait to hear from you."

Harris hung up the phone and approached the peddler. "Nice purses," he said. "How much?"

"Thirty-five bucks," the guy answered, relighting his cigar. The smoke smelled like old leather and burnt cherries.

"They look just like the real thing. My girl needs a new purse too. She's got a denim one that's OK for everyday stuff and all, but she needs a really nice one for good."

"Thirty-five each, two for seventy," he said, exhaling and chuckling.

"I like your tattoo," Harris said, "the one there with the snake curled around the girl. I got one too but it's nothing like yours. I got kind of a shitty job."

Harris pulled up his left sleeve and exposed a ballpoint-and-safety-pin prison tattoo that read: **LOYAL FOREVER**. There were rough marks along the edges and what looked like the remains of infection.

"Christ," the guy said, "who did *that* to you?"

"A friend of mine."

"You must have quite a group of friends."

"I do," Harris said, smiling.

Just then a black and white cruiser arrived and two Asian cops got out, setting their nightsticks in their belts and flexing their fingers around the handles as if they were anxious to test them on a forehead or groin. As they approached the peddler he put up his open palms and started to try to talk his way out. They spun him around and bent him over his card table, crushing his purses. When the smaller of the two cops cuffed the peddler and grabbed his arm to take him to the cruiser, Harris asked him what was wrong.

"Why don't you just shut up and stay the hell out of this," the taller one said.

"I don't want any trouble," Harris said. "I just wondered what was happening . . . why you were arresting this man."

"You want to come along too?" the short cop asked.

"No, officer," Harris said. Then he turned to the peddler and said, "Hey, is there anything I can do?"

"You could take my stuff," he said, "and put it in my car. It's right around the corner, the blue sedan. The keys are in my left pocket."

The cops were getting impatient. Harris reached into the peddler's pocket and took out his keys.

"Just throw the keys in the trunk," he said. "I've got another set at home."

"Sure thing. I'm glad I was here to help. Good luck…" Harris said, his voice trailing off at the end.

As the cruiser pulled away Harris collected the inventory on the ground and table and walked around the edge of the building to the peddler's car, a rusty Datsun with a back seat full of trash food wrappers. He opened the trunk and found dozens of loose umbrellas and six boxes packed with purses, all jammed together and tied with cheap green ribbon. He closed the trunk, drove to Union Square, and unloaded the boxes on the street. He found an old pen in the tire well, tore off a piece of cardboard, and lettered a sign:

SPECIAL SALE: $15 FOR PURSES, $3 FOR UMBRELLAS, TODAY ONLY

The purses were all sold in 45 minutes, the umbrellas in 30. Harris got back in the car, tied a ribbon around $1200, kept $426 loose, and drove the car back up to Clay. He opened the trunk and tossed the keys into the tire well. Then he looked around, poked the blade of the tire iron through the lock, replaced the iron, and let the trunk fall shut.

"Thanks," he said. "That wasn't hard at all. Too bad some thief broke into your trunk…"

He walked a block or two, found a bar with blackened windows and a scuffed, steel door called *The Happy Times* and drank four rum and cokes. He sat in the center of the bar, running his finger tips around the moist rim of his glass, then lifting it in the air in a silent toast as he talked to himself and smiled. The tired regulars on either side of him leaned over their beer and shot glasses, paying no attention at all.

An hour later he walked back to Union Square and caught the airporter van at the St. Francis. He stared through the business people who were looking at his clothes and commenting quietly to one another. Thirty-five minutes later the van pulled into San Francisco International. A porter asked Harris if he could help him with his luggage. "This is all I have," Harris said, lifting up his yellow and black bag. He entered the terminal, noticed the people checking themselves in at the self-service kiosks, wondered what the fuck that was all about, and got into the line for the United check-in counter.

"Where are we traveling today?" the clerk asked. Harris looked at him closely and thought he could see some clear polish on the man's fingernails. "Jesus," he said to himself.

"Give me a ticket to Burbank," he answered. "One way."

"Enjoy your time here?" the clerk asked.

"Some of it," he said, as he counted out the $279.30 for the fare, "but I got to go south . . . got to finish up a few things."

"Enjoy your flight," the man said. "Thank you for flying United," he added, as Harris walked toward the security check point.

FIVE

Roy Haggerty stood in the bathroom of Lorna's apartment, soaping up the gray washcloth he was going to use to wash her smell from his face and body. He tried to keep from splashing water on her hair dryer and curler box even though he had seen the rust rings from her deodorant can on the back of the sink and seen how she had thrown her cosmetic brush in the same paste-stained glass as her toothbrush.

She was pulling the sheet off of her bed and wondering whether or not she would have to wash the mattress cover this time too. "I'm sorry . . . I should have told you this earlier . . . you have to stay away for awhile, Roy," she said.

"Why the hell is that?" he answered.

"Because Earlon's getting out of prison and if he finds you here with me or even thinks you've been here with me he'll be very angry. I don't want him that way. He might do something terrible."

"You haven't said anything about that crazy son-of-a-bitch for years," Haggerty said. "How in the hell was I supposed to know he was coming here?"

"They just now called me," she said, "the people from the state. They told me he was getting out. He gave my address to his parole officer. He expects me to be here waiting for him."

"You've got to tell him about us," Haggerty said. "Tell him that what the two of you used to have before he went away is gone now; tell him things have changed and he's not a part of any of it anymore."

"You don't understand, Roy," she said. "Earlon doesn't think that way."

"I don't give a good goddamn how he *thinks*," Haggerty said. "Tell him how it *is*."

Lorna took the sheet into the bathroom, opened the hamper, moved some dirty towels out of the way, and shoved the sheet beneath them. She walked over behind Haggerty, pressed against his back with the tips of her breasts, put her arms around his waist, and slid her hands over the front of his belly. "I'm sorry, Roy, but you're going to have to stay away for awhile. Just try to be patient. I'll see you again soon enough, but I can't do it while Earlon is here. Do you have any idea what he might do if he thought I was sharing myself with somebody else?"

"So you're gonna take up with him again, then. Is that what you're telling me?"

"I didn't say that," she said. "I have to be here when he comes back. I don't have to be here with him forever. He's been in prison for over ten years, Roy. I can't just dump him out on the street. How would you feel if you were him? How would you feel if you were treated like that? I can't abandon him at a time like this."

"Why the hell not? He's a goddamned criminal and a fucking lunatic. If it was me I wouldn't even let the crazy son-of-a-bitch in my house."

"Don't talk that way, Roy. He *loves* me," she said, trying hard to believe it. "At least he *thinks* he does. He *says* he does. I have to at least give him the chance to try to prove it to me."

"Shit. He doesn't even know what the word *love* means."

"And I guess you do, Roy," she said.

"Hell yes," he answered. "Of course I know what love means. What do you think we just did, Lorna?"

"I don't see any gold rings or wedding cake around here," she said. "All I see is a wet spot on the bed and you trying to wash away the memory of me."

"I didn't hear any complaining ten minutes ago," he said. "I heard a lot of other things though. Maybe you've forgotten already."

"I think you better leave, Roy," she said. "I think you better leave right away."

SIX

Harris settled into his shuttle seat next to the window and flipped through the airline magazine. He looked at the section in the back, listing the artists and songs that were taped for long flights. "Who in the fuck *are* these people?" he asked his seat mate, who promptly got up and took an open seat on the other side of the aisle. "God *damn*," he said to himself, not noticing that the woman was gone, "they play that black shit on the airplanes now too." The flight attendant asked him to attach his seat belt and he did it without answering her.

As the plane broke through the light cloud cover over the south bay Harris loosened his seat belt, leaned forward and reached under the seat in front of him for his yellow and black plastic bag. He took out his pile of notes and a pen he had broken away from its holder in the lobby of the St. Francis. The skies were ice blue and clear but he didn't look out. Instead, he studied his notes and clutched his pen, turning the ribbed end between his teeth and flicking the bit of remaining metal chain with the tip of his tongue. He read seven passages in his notes under his breath:

> **There are few pains so grievous as to have seen, divined, or experienced how an exceptional man has missed his way and deteriorated.**

> **God created woman. And boredom did indeed cease from that moment—but many other things ceased as well! Woman was God's second mistake.**

For believe me: the secret for harvesting from existence the greatest fruitfulness and greatest enjoyment is—to live dangerously.

How people keep correcting us when we are young! There is always some bad habit or other they tell us we ought to get over. Yet most bad habits are tools to help us through life.

In heaven all the interesting people are missing.

Morality is the greatest of all tools for leading mankind by the nose.

The higher a man gets, the smaller he seems to those who cannot fly.

"You're goddamned right," he said. "Fucking A." Positioning his pen carefully between his fingertips he drew a rectangular block around each quote and in the margin of the sheet wrote:

LOYAL FOREVER

He thought awhile and turned to the next sheet in the stack. He looked at the statement at the top of the page:

In revenge and in love woman is more barbarous than man.

"Sorry," he said, "but even *you* can't get it right all the time."
The Asian flight attendant worked her way down the aisle from the

front of the plane, stopped and locked her cart next to his seat, and said, "Snack?"

"What? Who the hell are you?" he said.

"I beg your pardon," she said, her accent heavy. "I asked if you would like a snack."

"Oh yeah, sure," he said, taking a small bag of pretzels from the basket.

"Can I get you something to drink?" she asked, guardedly.

"Uh, yeah. Have you got any of that Mountain Dew stuff?"

"I'm sorry," she said, "We don't have that on this airline. I've got Sprite."

"Just give me a Pepsi," he said.

"I'm sorry, sir. I can offer you Coke, Diet Coke, Vanilla Coke, and Coke Zero. Or anything else . . . juice . . . bottled water . . . did I say Sprite? . . . and, of course, beer and wine . . . Bloody Mary mix . . ."

"Just give me the plain Coke," he said, cutting off her spiel.

She handed him a cup of ice and the full can and quickly released the cart and pushed it down the aisle. He poured some of the Coke, waited for the bubbles to settle, and then tasted it. "Damn," he said, "I should have asked if she had some of that Mr. Pibb shit." The woman who had vacated the seat next to him looked over at him from across the aisle, shook her head, and then turned her back to him, sliding as close to the seat on her left as she could.

He turned back to his notes and the passage that read:

In revenge and in love woman is more barbarous than man.

He took his pen and slowly drew a right diagonal line through each letter of each word. Then he drew left diagonal lines, crossing each letter of each word with a perfect **X**. Then he drew vertical lines, then horizontal, until each letter was covered with a black asterisk. Then, holding the sheet up toward the window, he paused for a second and drove the point of the pen through the paper five times, stopped, folded the sheet neatly, returned it to his plastic bag, and looked at the time on his new watch.

SEVEN

After the 737 landed in Burbank Harris pushed and elbowed his way through the aisle of the plane and hurried past the passengers already on the tarmac. He felt the difference in temperature between the Bay area and the Valley and removed his windbreaker, carrying it over his arm. When he got inside the terminal, he went directly to the metal rack of ragged phone books beside the Pacific Bell booths. He tore out the page with Lorna's address and number and then flipped to the yellow pages. He found the page he wanted, tore it from the book, and went into the men's room to take a quick leak and run a comb through his hair. As soon as he finished he folded up his plastic jacket and shoved it into his bag. He looked in the mirror a second time, patted his hair nervously, and walked outside.

He got in a Burbank Checker cab with a Latino driver. His license card said that his name was Norberto. The photo i.d. was dated but recognizable. Harris couldn't make out the last name. "You speak English, Norberto?" he asked.

"Of course," the driver answered.

"Good. Look, I've got a problem. My car crapped out on me last Tuesday right before my flight out. The battery was shot and I was running late, so I had to take a cab all the way in from the east Valley. I want you to take me to the Pep Boys store in San Fernando to pick one up and then drop me off at my home in Sylmar. Don't worry, I'll put the battery in the trunk; that way I won't mess up your back seat."

"Do you know the name of the street that the store's on?" the driver asked.

"Yeah," Harris said, unfolding the corner of the torn page from the phone book but keeping it out of the driver's line of sight. "It's on the main drag there—Brand."

"I think I've seen it," the driver said. "It's the one a few blocks east of the Mission."

"Right, whatever," Harris said, trying to get comfortable as the driver slalomed through the airport traffic.

When they got to the store twenty minutes later the driver pulled in, facing its front window.

"Why don't you turn around and back in," Harris said. "Pop the trunk latch. That way I can put the battery right in the trunk when I come out and I won't have to walk so far. Those damned things are always heavier than they look."

The driver shrugged, turned the car around, pulled the trunk release, and picked up a Spanish language newspaper. He left the meter running.

Harris walked up to the counter and asked if he could speak to the manager. The clerk called out "Lou" and a tall, thick, and fiftyish man with a shock of white hair and a pocket full of mismatched ballpoints came out from behind an unpainted pine and wire cage. He walked up to the counter and said, "What do you need?"

"My name's Chelton," Harris said. "I work for Branson Electric over in Pacoima. Old man Branson's kid brother just picked up a fleet of used vans and we need a shitload of parts, mostly tires, batteries, alternators, and water pumps, but other shit too. We'll put together the order and call it in but when I come to pick it up I'd like some help loading it. I got two steel pins in my back now and I don't want to have to go in for another set."

"No problem," the manager said. "When do you need the parts by?"

"We'll check everything out today and tomorrow and call you . . . probably be either Wednesday night or Thursday morning."

"Good. If we haven't got what you need in stock we can get it for you in two hours. Max."

"Do you mind if I take a look at your loading dock?" Harris asked. "I've got to decide what truck to bring and I want to make this as easy as I can for everybody."

"Come on, I'll show you. It's right out back."

Harris followed him through the store, walked out the back door, and looked at the dock. "No sweat. This one will be easy. I'll bring our big Chevy."

"Just give us a call when you're ready," the manager said. "And thanks. We appreciate the business."

"Fine. Thanks a lot. I think I'll walk back along the side of the building and check widths and clearances, all that shit…"

"Suit yourself," the manager said, and went back into the building.

"Don't worry, I will," Harris said. He walked down from the dock, pulled his jacket out of his plastic bag, put it on, and walked around the side of the building. He saw the cab idling in front of the store and laughed. Then he cut behind the Texaco station next door and walked away.

A block and a half north he found a place called *Al's Fine Wines and Liquors*. The only wine he saw was Central Valley screwtop, but Al had nine different brands of tequila. "What the fuck happened to all the Americans?" he said to himself. The clerk wore a plastic name tag that read **JUAN**.

"Hey Juan, you got any American whiskey?" he asked.

"Sure," the clerk said. "What do you want, bourbon, rye, what?"

"How about some Grand Dad?"

"Pint? Fifth?"

"Give me the biggest you got," Harris said. "I'm going to a reunion."

EIGHT

Lorna was running late. Her boss, a balding B-School grad from Cal State-Long Beach, was loosening his belt after a carb-laden, desktop dinner and a day spent inventorying merchandise in his independently-owned cooking utensil store. Located in leased space in a Tujunga strip mall, the store—*Crouper's Kitchen Works*—specialized in teak salad sets, stainless steel cutlery and tables of various sizes and shapes constructed of butcher block laminate. He scooted uncomfortably in his chair. He felt bloated and could taste the acid bubbling in his stomach and esophagus.

"Lorna," he said, "where in the hell are the mini- cutting boards? I ordered three dozen and I can't find a damned one except the display model."

"They only sent fourteen, Mr. Crouper," Lorna answered, "and we sold the last one this morning. I reordered yesterday. They said we should have a new shipment in forty-eight hours."

"Goddamned computer error probably," he said. "How many did you order?"

"Three dozen, Mr. Crouper."

"If they only send fourteen when you order thirty six, we should order more. Call New York. No, wait a minute. It's almost 10:00 o'clock there. There won't be anybody in the warehouse except the night guard and he'll be racked out on the boss's Barcalounger . . . or worse."

"I'll call first thing in the morning, Mr. Crouper," Lorna said.

"Yeah, yeah, OK," he said. "By the way, whatever happened to those big salad forks with the carved Easter Island heads on the end of the handles? The mahogany ones."

"There's just that one in the window, Mr. Crouper. We're taking orders for more."

"Goddamnit, why are we always running out of things?"

"I guess because we're always selling them."

"I *know* we're running out because we're selling them," he said. "Why in the hell aren't we reordering on time?"

"We *did* order those forks, Mr. Crouper," she said, "but the warehouse was out of them. We ordered right away. We've been waiting for them now for a month and a half. Like I said, we're taking orders for them."

"Shit. Where are those things made?"

"Just a second," she said, walking over to the window and picking up the fork from the display. She turned it over, looking for the tiny gold sticky. "They're made in . . . I can never pronounce it right . . . Sri Lanka."

"Fucking Sri Lanka. Now I know what my father meant when he talked about the good old days when everything came from Occupied Japan. You're too young to remember that."

"That's right, Mr. Crouper," she said. "I don't remember it. *What* part of Japan did you say it was?"

"Jesus. Never mind," he answered.

By the time she got on the 210 the traffic was light. She pulled into the parking lot of her apartment building on San Fernando Road at 8:20. There were two ramshackle carports at the end of the lot. One had an open space but she would have had to move a drain pan of used oil and a kid's Big Wheel in order to drive into it. She checked her watch and decided instead to park outside.

She opened the door, entered her living room, turned on the light and found him sitting in the corner on her green, nylon couch with his left arm wrapped around his yellow and black plastic bag and his right hand wrapped around what was left of the bottle of Old Grand Dad. "Why in the hell did you stop writing to me?" he said, his eyes heavy and bloodshot.

"Earlon?"

"Of course. Who the hell did you think it was—your old *friend* Roy?"

"When did you get out, Earlon?"

"What do you care? You still haven't answered my question. Why didn't you write to me?"

"I couldn't."

"Why the hell couldn't you?"

"I just couldn't."

"Why? Wouldn't Roy let you?"

"Quit talking about Roy, Earlon. I couldn't write because I couldn't stand it."

"Couldn't stand what?"

"Don't talk to me in that mean tone, Earlon. It hurts my feelings."

"OK, how's this—what is it that you couldn't stand?"

She paused, staring at him, searching his eyes.

"I couldn't stand writing to you and hearing from you—feeling that close to you when I wasn't able to see you and touch you."

"Bullshit."

"It's not *bullshit*, Earlon," she said, "and I don't like that kind of language. What I said—it's true. Every word of it is."

"If it's so damned true what are you doing standing there on the other side of the room? You don't look like you've missed me at all."

"Earlon, I just walked in the door. You surprised me. The last time I saw you was years ago, and when I did it was through a piece of prison glass. I had to talk to you over a telephone. They wouldn't even let me be alone with you. All those people around me . . . watching me . . . listening to me. Give me a second to get used to you being here. Let me look at you."

"Come over here," he said.

As she approached he carefully placed his plastic bag on the table at the end of the couch. He smiled at her as lovingly as he could manage. She smiled back, sat down, kissed him long and deep, and put her arm around his waist. He offered her the bottle and she took a small sip without wiping off the top.

"I know you were in there all this time because of me," she said. "You wanted things for me. You wanted to do things for me. I understand that. I know how you felt."

"That's right," he said.

"You wanted to take me new places, take me away from here. Take me someplace where we could be happy, maybe even have our own home."

"That's right, Lorna, I did. I still do, and I will. I just have to do some things here first. I've got . . . work to do . . . a couple of things I got to straighten out. Get my affairs in order. It won't take long. Then it'll be our time. I promise."

"It *is* good to see you, Earlon," she said. "You look good. You haven't changed very much."

"Thanks," he said. "I try to take care of myself. You look good too."

She smiled at him without speaking.

"There's one thing I've got to ask you, though. Why are you still living in *this* place? It's all gone to hell. It used to be pretty nice. It's all spics and dog shit and broken glass now. It didn't use to be this way."

"I don't know, Earlon. I just never moved. If I had, you wouldn't have been able to find me."

"Not if you'd written to me," he said.

"Now stop saying that," she said. "Why don't you stop thinking about the past and come into the bedroom and love me? Now that you can finally do it, don't you want to?"

He replaced the cap on the Old Grand Dad, picked up his plastic bag and followed her to the room at the end of the hall. She was slipping off her blouse and skirt. He stretched her elastic bra and pulled it over her head without undoing the catch.

"Careful," she said. "You could hurt me. We've got plenty of time, Earlon." She lifted up his shirt and kissed him on the chest; then she reached down to slip off her underwear.

"Where'd you get *those*?" he said. "They look like something a French whore would wear."

"That's what they all wear now," she said. "That's the new style. Some men would be glad they were around long enough to see it."

As she pulled off her underwear, folded it, and put it in the laundry basket on the floor of her closet, he picked up his plastic bag. "I want you to do something for me," he said.

"What, Earlon? What do you want me to do?"

"I want you to read to me while we do it," he answered.

"What do you mean?" she asked.

"Just lay on your stomach," he said, opening his plastic bag and looking for his notes.

"What are you going to do?" she asked.

"I'm not going to do anything. You're going to read and I'm going to love you."

"You want me to *read*?"

"I'll tell you which ones to read," he said. "These are my notes from Loyal."

"Who's Loyal?"

"My guide. Here. Just read this page."

As he penetrated her she tightened around him and said, "You're sure you want to read and not just love?"

"Just read it," he said, moving slowly inside her.

"OK," she said, running her finger down the page and laboring with the words.

The release of aggression is the best palliative for any kind of affliction. The wish to alleviate

pain through strong emotional excitation is, to my mind, the true physiological motive behind all manifestations of resentment.

"Pal-li-a-tive, ex-ci-ta-tion," he said. "Phy-si-o-log-i-cal."
"What does that all mean, Earlon?"
"Just read," he said, "don't worry about it now."

All good things have at one time been considered evil.

Let us ask once more: in what sense could pain constitute repayment of a debt? In the sense that to make someone suffer was a supreme pleasure.

"I don't like that," she said, pushing the papers away. "I don't want to do this."
"You're not supposed to like it. You're supposed to learn from it," he said, moving faster and deeper. Now keep reading."

To behold suffering gives pleasure, but to cause another to suffer affords an even greater pleasure . . . . There is no feast without cruelty, as man's entire history attests.

"I'm not going to read that kind of thing. It's not right," Lorna said.
"Just one more," he said, breathing hard and moving rapidly.
"That's all I'm going to read," she said, her eyes welling with tears. Finally she breathed deeply and continued.

An artist worth his salt is permanently separated from ordinary reality.

"Read that last one again," he said, breathlessly. When she did, she felt his spasms intensify with each word.

Later, as they sat in the center of her bed, he held her breast in the palm of his hand, kissing it gently.

"Earlon, I didn't like that reading. I want you like this. Gentle. Sweet. That wasn't right."

He continued to kiss her as he ran the tips of his fingers down the center of her back and under the cheeks of her behind.

"You shouldn't be frightened by Loyal," he said. "All geniuses scare us sometimes."

"But it's not normal," she said. "You don't want someone reading while you're loving them. You want them talking to you . . . talking to you with their own words."

"Of course it's not *normal*," he said. "Don't you see? That's the whole point. I don't want to be like some goddamned *normal* person. There's plenty of them already. Too damned many of them. I want to be different. Don't you understand? I want to be like Loyal."

"You want to hurt people? You want to give people pain and get pleasure from that?"

"I have to," he said. Her expression fell and he said, "Don't worry; I'd never do it to you, Lorna, not if you loved me and stayed by me."

"I don't want you to hurt *anybody*," she said. "If you do that they'll put you back in prison and then I'll *never* see you. I want to be with you here. I want to be able to love you. I don't want you gone from me again."

"Don't worry," he said. "They're not going to put me back in there. I just have some things I got to do here and then we can go away. We'll go wherever you want."

"You promise me you'll never ask me to read like that again?"

"I think you could learn to understand it," he said, "maybe even enjoy it someday."

"I don't want to understand it. I just want you; I want you the way you were before you were sent away."

"I can't be that way, Lorna. I'm better than that now. It's like I finally opened my eyes and saw things the way they really are. You wait and see. Sit up here on me and love me again while I tell you what I'm going to do."

She looked into his eyes before she moved. At first they were blank. Then he curled his lips into the beginnings of a smile. "Come on, darlin', he said, "I haven't changed all that much." She kissed him on the cheek, and put her arms around him as he lifted her over his knees and legs and penetrated her. As she tightened her arms around his neck and began to move her hips he stared across the room at a mark on the wall, his lips a flat slit, his eyes blank again.

NINE

"Happy Birthday, Chief," Tom said, handing Chris Dietrich a bottle of French red wine. "I skipped the card and put the extra $3.99 into the wine. I didn't want to be presumptuous, but I thought that . . . being the generous person that you are . . . you might share it with me."

Chris smiled and then laughed. "Thanks, Tom. You didn't have to do this. I'm impressed that you even knew it was my birthday; it's not something I usually make a big deal of."

"Julie told me," Tom said. Julie Li, Chris's executive assistant. "She keeps a list of important dates like that in her appointment book. Seriously, I hope you *are* planning to do something to celebrate."

"I hadn't planned much, really," Chris said. "I've got some more paperwork to clean up here first. Then I thought I'd have a quiet dinner and turn in early. Want to join me? I was thinking maybe a steak . . . at **Westie's**. After all, I've got to celebrate a little."

"Sounds good," Tom said. "I've got some stuff to do too. Call me whenever you're ready."

"I'll set a thirty minute limit," Chris said. "Otherwise we'll both be here all night."

Westie's—the popular steakhouse in Newport Beach—had been operated by the same family for three generations, beginning when Newport was the home to real fishermen with working vessels rather than sport fishermen with 65' Hatterases and homes in the low eight figures. Tom's father Wayne, the now-retired harbor master at Newport, had taken Tom to **Westie's Steak and Seafood** when he was a boy and Tom introduced Chris to it soon after Chris took the job of Chief of the Laguna Beach PD, relocating there from L.A.

"I actually come here for the potatoes," Chris said to Tom, as they were shown to a table in a quiet corner. "All the good restaurants in southern California have corn-fed Midwest beef, but none of them have these man-sized baked potatoes. The only place I've seen them this big and this good was in a small town in Ireland. I'm sure they don't get them from there."

"Probably Idaho," Tom said. "Sometimes I have two and skip the salad. My mother hated it when I did that. She always said you should eat something green at least twice a day."

"I miss your mom," Chris said. "Nobody expected her to go before your dad like that. She was always so fit . . . so alive…"

"Yes," Tom said, "she was."

"Anyway, this isn't a time for tears," Chris said. "I've got some news for you. It may be my birthday, Tom, but this is a big day for you as well. I'm promoting you to Lieutenant. Carl Gable came in this afternoon and told me that he's retiring; you're my best detective, so the decision was easy. If anything, this is overdue. Congratulations."

"Are you sure you want to do that, Chief?" Tom asked.

"I've never been surer of anything," Chris said. "Don't tell me you've got reservations…"

"No, I don't, Chief," Tom said. "I appreciate your confidence in me. I just don't want *you* to ever have regrets."

"Simplest decision I've ever made," Chris said. "And before you say anything . . . you're not buying dinner."

"But it's *your* birthday, Chief," Tom said.

"We'll celebrate your promotion. It's much more of an accomplishment to close cases the way you've been doing than to simply be a day older."

Tom smiled and thanked him again.

"Here," Chris said, reaching across the table and handing him the lieutenant's badge, "your new shield."

Although **Westie's** was in a light industrial section, near the harbor, they could still see the sun setting over the Pacific. The few remaining clouds were tinged with streaks of orange and gold as the sun rested on the edge of the horizon. "Quite a sight," Chris said. "I never get tired of seeing it. I wish more people *could* . . . you know—get off the freeways, get away from the graffiti and the gangs, the dealers and the urban decay, the smog, the razor wire..."

"The South Bronx with palm trees," Tom said. "Fortunately it's not all like that, especially in the O.C. The only problem is that nobody can afford to live down here."

"Right," Chris said, as the waiter approached.

"Hi guys," he said. "How about that sunset?"

"Not bad at all, Harry," Chris said. "Could you open this for us?" he asked, lifting Tom's gift bottle up from behind the table leg.

"Sure, no corkage fee for regulars like you," he said.

"We'll put it in your tip, Harry," Chris said.

"An officer and a gentleman," the waiter said.

"Most of the time," Chris said. "Say good evening to my newest lieutenant."

"Really? Congratulations, Tom. The boss's got good judgment."

"Thanks, Harry," Tom said.

There was a newsbreak on the flat-screen TV above the bar. Nothing big—a pileup on the 405. It was already being cleared.

"I like that woman on ABC," Chris said. "She's feisty."

"That's Hector Campo's sister," Tom said. "Estella. She married a lawyer; now they've become the rich side of the family."

"Hector's come a long way from his gangbanger days," Chris said. "I know you've got a lot of confidence in him. You think he's ready to become a detective?"

"He's an excellent officer," Tom said. "I can't compare him with all of the others that you might be considering, but I'm sure Hector could do the job."

"Let me give it some thought," Chris said. A moment later he felt the twitch of his cellphone. He took out his phone, checked the caller i.d., and said, "This might be good for a laugh." He held the phone between them and hit the speaker button.

It was Bill Engle, the desk sergeant. "I know you're at dinner, Chief, and I knew that your phone would be off, but I wanted to send along some dessert. I swear to God you're not going to believe this one..."

Chris muffled the sound with his right hand. "Bill is my chief informant for news of the weird."

"O.K. Malone, Chief . . . he peed in his pants and nearly electrocuted himself..."

Chris muffled the sound a second time. "Bill will get to the point eventually..."

"You remember O.K.; he's a minor celebrity—the skinny black kid at Venice Beach, the one who wears the power pack and amplifier on his back. He roller skates up and down the beach walk, playing his electric guitar for the tourists. There's no way you could forget O.K., Chief. He's the one who wears a metallic gold suit and pilot's goggles. The wires run all through his clothes. That way he can look all cool and sleek and keep skating without tripping himself. Anyway, when O.K. saw Johnny he was so shocked and scared that his bladder gave out and he peed all over himself. He shorted out his amplifier cord and started dancing wildly as the sparks were jumping up his back . . . And Chief . . . you know Clara, the one they call the Cat Lady? She's the one with the two scruffy Burmese who're trained to sit on her shoulders and not lick or eat or leap to the ground unless she tells them to . . . When Clara saw Johnny she screamed, jumped, and came down with an instant case of the walking farts. That scared the daylights out of the two cats and they started chasing each other around her neck and clawing the fabric off of her cape. They looked like cats in an old cartoon. You know—running in circles so fast they started to turn into a blur. Anyway, she yelled at them to get down, but she must have somehow screwed up the command and confused them, because one jumped on O.K., felt his body convulsing, and then jumped back on Clara. The other one must have somehow picked up the electric vibe from O.K. because he immediately jumped up on Clara's head. He took the high ground. It was a three-ring circus, Chief. Maybe four. And we're not talking the *Cirque du Soleil* here. This was a good old-fashioned circus, complete with unruly animals, ripe smells, gawking tourists—the entire nine yards. And just as things are quieting down, this kid that operates the local roach wagon, Manuel—the one they call Manny the Master Chef—he's so damned upset he pulls his hands out of his pockets and accidentally pours hot coffee into two wax paper cups instead of two cardboard cups. Then he gives them to these two tourists who are suddenly holding handfuls of scalding coffee, shredded paper, and melting wax. The husband starts threatening Manny with legal action, Manny gives him the blank look and the *no comprende* gesture, and the guy's wife suddenly cracks her husband across the ear and tells him it was *his* idea to come to L.A., that *she* never wanted to come here. *She* wanted to go to the Wisconsin Dells. The husband's ear is red as hell and the anger is starting to move up his face like a United Way progress thermometer. He says 'Screw L.A. and screw the Wisconsin Dells double,' and this tie-dyed kid standing next to him—who looks like he just hitched a ride down from Berserkly—stops smoking his joint and watching O.K. and Clara and instead starts laughing uncontrollably. Clara finally sees the humor in the situation, starts laughing, and farts again. By now the only one who's not laughing is O.K., who's finally stopped shaking. Instead he's reaching down his pants, checking his chobes—just like the Jewish guy in the joke. You know the one, Chief . . . the two Jewish guys in the car crash. The one is making frantic motions that look like the sign of the cross. The other says, 'So . . . Izzy, one crisis and so soon you change your religion.' 'Not at all, Morris,' Izzy replies, 'I vas only checking my valuables . . . spectacles, testicles, vallet, and vatch.' Anyway . . . it was *Johnny Richetti*, Chief, the songbird who rolled over on Tony Lupinelli. You were right all along. He *was* in way over his head. *He* started all this. He washed up on the beach in a rubber boat. *Sears best*, Chief. None of that toy store plastic junk. Somebody killed him and his girl friend Angela Scottori somewhere out in the bay, put them in the boat, and let the tide bring them in. Johnny's mouth was slashed open from the corners of his lips to the lobes of his ears, and then back down along the jaw line. His teeth were exposed—two little white rows of Chiclets in a gory red puddle. Angela had a large calibre round in her forehead, Cyclops-style. Probably from a .44 mag. Curious. The mob usually goes for something smaller, like a .22. Anyway, her mouth was frozen open and she was wearing a white tee shirt with an arrow pointing toward Johnny and four words across her chest, all written in his blood:

I'M WITH BIG MOUTH

They were laying there, side by side, like two sleepy sunbathers floating around on a summer afternoon. Apparently O.K. was playing some kind of heavy metal version of 'How Deep is the Ocean,' when the afternoon tide delivered Johnny and Angela. He never finished the second verse. By then his pants were already wet and he was four steps into his electric-crack dance. So there it is, Chief. I only have one question..."

"What's that, Bill?"

"How much do you miss the LAPD?"

"Not a lot, Bill. Thanks for the update."

"I thought you'd want to know. Anyway . . . happy birthday, again."

"You're . . . irreplaceable, Bill," Chris said, as he clicked off the phone and turned to his new lieutenant.

"They're all out there, Tom. They're driving and they're voting…"

"And a lot of them are armed, Chief," Tom added.

TEN

"Bill means well," Tom said. "He's got the smarts and the skills. He just can't speak in sound bites. He's like the story tellers in that old drama series, **Roots**. They can't just tell you what happened the day that Kunte Kinte disappeared. They have to begin with the creation of the world and come forward. And Bill *is* funny. He just hears a different drummer . . . and he gets his food from a different caterer . . ."

"I know," Chris answered. "We just had a retirement party for one of the local council members, a guy named Megglethorpe. You were in San Diego. They put out a nice spread: wine with corks, unidentifiable orange canapes (probably some kind of imitation salmon), coffee in small cups with handles . . . the whole bit. Bill took a look at the food and started rooting around in his jacket pockets, looking for something more interesting. I think he found a can of smoked oysters. It could have been a tin of kipper snacks. Anyway, he starts working it, breaking off the little metal key that's attached to the bottom of the can and then carefully rolling the nib on the side until the can is fully open . . . lifting the lid cautiously and dropping it onto a tray with empty drink glasses . . . and then he goes into his pocket again and comes out with a plastic toothpick . . . he starts spearing the contents and freeing them from the mustard sauce or linseed oil or whatever it was that they were floating in and popping the pieces into his mouth, which he's using like a moving basketball hoop. After he's finished he disappears for awhile and a few minutes after Megglethorpe's farewell speech and the mayor's toast he comes out of the men's room, complaining about how hard it is to get certain things off of your hands and out from under your fingernails."

"He's the best, but for some an acquired taste," Tom said.

"I agree. What time is it now?" Chris asked.

"Just about 8:00," Tom said. "Make it 7:58."

"I should be getting home soon. Laura's always good about having the kids call me on my birthday. I need to talk to her a little too."

Tom nodded and smiled without commenting. Chris and Laura had split when he was working for the LAPD. Never knowing whether he'd come home or not, they had held off on having kids until he was promoted to Lieutenant. Now the girl was in her late teens and the boy was just turning sixteen.

He and his wife had stayed friends. There had never been any anger or acrimony, just the slow disintegration that results from long, uncertain hours and lengthy separations. She kept their house in the Simi Valley and now that the kids could drive they visited him in Laguna on the weekends. Sometimes Laura came with them. It was very sad to see them together because their affection for one another was still palpable.

"We've got to start thinking about what to do with the house," Chris said. "Jen's going to live on campus at UCLA next year and Will's going to be looking at college options this fall. Laura doesn't really need that much space and now that she's working in South Pasadena she'd like to be closer."

Laura taught special ed students. There was a story about her in the Pasadena *Star News* the previous year. She had received a grant for a special project on autism; Chris had shown it to him. Tom had only met her once. It was at least two years ago—before he had been hospitalized. She had come by the office to drop something off to Chris and pick something up from him. Tom had seen them kiss before they parted.

"I'm a little concerned about her," Chris said. "Not that it's any of my business, but I worry about her. She's dating some guy and it sounds as if he wants to move in with her, but I haven't heard any talk about an engagement, much less about a wedding. Like I say, it's her business, not mine, but I don't want to see her hurt. I met him and he's nice enough. I don't worry about him treating her or the kids badly. Besides, the kids will both be in college soon . . . I just don't want to see her hurt."

"I understand," Tom said. "She's very nice. I only met her once, but she was very warm. I'm sure that she's wonderful with the kids that she works with…"

"Yes," Chris said. "She's great with them. It's not just that she's so patient. She's made the effort to understand the challenges that they face. She probably knows more about some of their conditions than the average doctor would. Anyway, I better get going. If you want to stick around and have some dessert or anything, feel free…"

"That's all right, Chief. Thanks for the offer. I'm going to stay on my boat tonight and get an early start tomorrow."

"We'll do something in the office. I'll bring in some rolls or donuts or something and I'll pull the available officers together and announce your promotion."

"Thanks, Chief. Please don't feel the need to go to any great trouble. You know that the more you do the more they'll needle me."

"Hey, it's what they do," Chris said. "They'd be disappointed if they lost the opportunity. We won't have any dancing girls or marching elephants…"

Tom checked his watch as Chris left. He needed to call Sarah and didn't want to wait until it was too late. The waiter collected the signed, restaurant copy of the bill and said good night, wishing him well.

"Take care, Harry, I'll probably see you again soon."

"Say hello to your dad, Tom."

"Will do," Tom said, and walked out into the cool evening air. There was moisture in the wind off the marina when Tom walked to his car. As a retirement present the members of the marina club allowed Tom's dad to keep his executive parking place there and Tom was able to use it whenever his dad parked in the members' lot. It was a great perk, but the members all knew that Wayne Deaton knew things and could solve problems that were well beyond the abilities of the man who had succeeded him—a nice fellow but primarily a manager, not—like Wayne—an expert on everything from naval architecture to marine biology. They still called on him for help and Wayne was happy to provide it. He moored his own boat there (letting Tom stay in the small family house in the Laguna Hills) and had a vested interest in the marina's longevity and prosperity.

As he drove down the coast Tom called Sarah. He had put her number on his speed-dial list. His father (always Sarah's most devoted advocate) had noticed the fact and been encouraged by it. Tom and Sarah had once dated regularly but split just prior to his hospitalization. The separation had not resulted from his condition; they had simply drifted apart. She visited him after his surgery but he could tell that her feelings had changed. She was there as a friend, doing her duty . . . visiting the sick.

Her phone rang twice and then rolled over to a message center. "Sarah," he said, "it's Tom. Just checking in to make sure that we're still on for tomorrow evening. I'll pick you up at 7:00. If there's any change, just give me a call. Good night."

Sometimes she turned off her phone when she had had a long day at the emergency room. Perhaps she had done a night shift or a series of night shifts. A highly-skilled nurse, she was always in high demand, protecting patients from green interns and overconfident residents.

Her specialty was assisting with heart catheterizations, though she was good with domestic violence cases, having trained and worked in L.A. She could remove bullets and broken glass and cleanse and close a knife or razor wound with the skill of an experienced surgeon. On a Saturday night or the Sunday night of a holiday weekend the waiting room for the ER at County Medical Center looked like a field hospital at Gettysburg or Antietam. The only difference was the absence of the smell of ether. That's when the best training occurred—when the docs were few in number and otherwise occupied and the patients were too sick to notice or complain about who was working on them. "That's why they call it a medical *practice*," she once told him.

When he got to his boat at the Dana Point Harbor Marina, Tom checked his landline answering machine and the answering machine at his home in the Hills. No messages at either location. He removed his keys, his wallet, his comb and his coin purse. Sarah had bought it for him years before. She thought it might protect him, since the sound of loose change could make some perp aware of his presence. He also removed his credential folder and looked at his detective's shield. He removed it and replaced it with the lieutenant's shield that Chris had given him at dinner.

He thought about his mother and how proud she would have been, called his father, said that he hoped he wasn't calling too late, and then told him that he had been promoted.

"No announcements though," he said. "The Chief is going to tell everybody tomorrow."

"That's great, Son," Wayne said. "I'm very proud of you and so is your mother." He didn't say, "I'm sure your mother *would* be too." Katharine Deaton was still present for her husband. "We'll have to celebrate," he added.

"I didn't know it was coming," Tom said. "Today was the Chief's birthday. We went to **Westie's** and suddenly he reached in his pocket and pulled out a lieutenant's shield."

"Terrific. That's just grand," Wayne said.

"I've got even bigger news than that," Tom said.

"Oh yes? What, Son?"

"I'm just kidding you, Dad. Sarah and I are going out for dinner tomorrow night. I knew you'd be pleased."

"I *am* pleased," Wayne said. "You know my feelings on that subject, Tom."

"Yes, I do," Tom said, wondering if his father could sense that he was smiling.

"Having a wonderful woman in your life . . . it's very important," he said. "It changed mine."

"I know, Dad," Tom said.

"Anyway, thanks for calling and telling me. Let's get together this weekend. Pick a night."

"Sounds good. I'll call you back on that. I've got to see what the Chief has planned for me. I'm replacing Carl Gable and I don't know how many cases he was working or how far along he was on them."

"Any time, Son. I'll be here," Wayne said.

"OK, Dad," Tom said, hanging up and checking his cell phone for missed messages before turning in.

ELEVEN

Tom got into the office at 6:55. Chris planned to announce his promotion at 7:30. That gave Tom a few minutes to celebrate and be teased before he had to drive to Irvine and give a deposition at 8:30.

The deposition was on behalf of Officer Hector Campo, who had recently been verbally attacked and threatened with legal action by a Los Angeles Councilman. The problems had begun with a sleazoid realtor, who had been suspected of plotting to torch a property on the PCH between Irvine and Laguna Beach. Hector caught the case and followed him for three months, from Escondido to Northridge, cooperating with all of the local jurisdictions along the way. The case came to a head in L.A., where Hector was introduced to Patrick D. (for Dennis) Burton.

Councilman "Pat" Burton had once been antiwar activist "Red Denny" Burton. Anxious to throw pig blood on anyone in uniform or public office in 1969, he was now casting urgent glances at a congressional seat and whatever might lie beyond it. He buttered up his followers with all the right words and moves and though the local party braintrust held their noses whenever his name came up in conversation, they still had to deal with him as a political presence.

The long-term aftermath of Hurricane Georgina—in particular its racial overtones—were his current fixation and though he had been criticized for accomplishing next to nothing for the tiny number of minority constituents within his own district (that district a tidy 2,740 miles from Miami) he continued to say the most inflammatory things to the hungriest media outlets from the most visible platforms. Red Denny had always known how to attract the cameras, the spotlights and the microphones.

Hector's personal contretemps with him had occurred two weeks earlier on a smoggy Thursday afternoon. After following the realtor, Harry Lapin, the length and breadth of the southern California coast, Hector was staking out a faded-glory mansion in Holmby Hills. The platinum-triangle property had been listed as a possible tear-down by Lapin's single-salesman company. His buyer was a suit from West Hollywood who had just sold his two-bedroom condo in a rapidly expanding neighborhood that the local realtors are fond of calling "Beverly Hills Adjacent." The buyer and likely co-conspirator—a lawyer named Terry Eton—was suddenly flush with walking-around money, but despite the new spike in his money-market account numbers, it was clear that it would take some serious stretching for Counselor Eton to be able to afford what he wanted in the triangle.

Lapin's seller was a Beverly Hills plastic surgeon named Badri Ghomar, who specialized in chin implants, ear tucks and blepharoplasties and whose *L.A. Magazine* advertising bills alone made Hector's annual salary look like a teenager's pocket change. His newest venture was a lipodissolve clinic in Azusa. Property-wise, he was ready to move on to something grand. The problem was that his flaking mini-mansion had been sitting on the market for fourteen months with no takers. Then Harry Lapin appeared, arm in arm with Terry Eton.

To the LAPD and LBPD the deal smelled. It smelled for at least three reasons. First, the buyer didn't appear to have the necessary cash to swing the deal. Second, all three of the players had been seen in each other's company on several occasions in a West Hollywood bar called **The Local**. Third, Harry Lapin had been involved in a tear-down transaction a year earlier and the house had burned to a small pile of charcoal and cinders under very suspicious but very convenient circumstances. Though he was never convicted, the allegations were enough to put the LBPD on its guard when Lapin was seen inspecting light-industrial property on the PCH at 2:30 a.m. on a Tuesday morning. Chris had called Tom and Tom had recommended Hector, who was both notoriously patient on stakeouts and fully up to the task if and when things became physical.

Lapin's newest venture would have made for a very attractive deal. Houses in the triangle sit on land worth three to four times more than the buildings themselves, more still, the closer you get to the heart of Bel Air. With a tear-down the house is already history; the seller doesn't care about its condition and neither does the buyer. If the building should happen to burn after the contract is signed, the insurance company bears the full brunt of the loss. In this case *State Farm* was looking at a 3 mil package with a 1 mil house. If the house was torched and the deal was prearranged the buyer could take the property for 2 mil and the seller could grab the third mil from the insurance company (minus Harry Lapin's commission), a cumbersome way to do business but a very convenient and lucrative way out when the property had been gathering dust for months and its asking price was discouraging all of the buyers who could handle a legitimate deal. A private arrangement would make everybody happy, with the insurance company unwittingly tapped to play facilitator/fall guy. If Harry Lapin *was* masterminding the scam to make this happen, as Chris, Tom, Hector and the LAPD feared, he would also be taking something additional back on the side to make it worth the time and the considerable risk involved.

That's why Hector was sitting in Holmby Hills, under a row of Canary Island date palms, in the most modest car on the street, drinking black coffee and waiting to be relieved by his LAPD counterpart, Dave Boiardo. He had been hoping to catch one of the principals in the act of being himself, most likely Lapin. Ten minutes before Boiardo was due, Hector saw him. He was wearing an out-of-character baseball cap over his eyes and sidling around a eucalyptus tree, carrying a large container marked **Roundup** on the side. Since it was unlikely that a realtor would be moonlighting as a gardener Hector's interest was immediately aroused.

He waited until Lapin doused the living room carpet and drapes with accelerant before calling a halt to his plan by flipping on his flashlight and making it clear to Harry that the Glock 17 aimed at the bridge of his nose was in fact his service weapon and not a prop. He also told him that he didn't want him playing with matches in a room soaked with what smelled like diesel fuel.

Lapin froze, thought for a second, began to act docile, mumbled something conciliatory, and then threw the fuel container at Hector's face. Hector ducked and Lapin broke, figuring correctly that Hector wouldn't pull the trigger while he was surrounded by volatile fumes. Lapin ran for the back yard and Hector followed. Even with Lapin's modest head start Hector was able to get to him before he was able to circle around the side of the house and return to his car.

He had holstered his weapon when Lapin began running and tackled him a few seconds later in the backyard of the estate. Lapin squirmed and kicked, and temporarily made it to his feet. The two of them waltzed around Badri Ghomar's tennis court for awhile until Lapin managed to loosen the steel net crank and take some healthy swipes at Hector's face and body. He eventually caught him in the chest and left shoulder and Hector decided it was time to end the exercise. He grabbed the crank with his left hand and kicked the edge of Harry's right shin with the point of his shoe. Twice. Before he could go for the third, Harry collapsed and Hector drew his gun.

"This time I'll shoot you until you stop moving," he said. "Believe it."

Lapin tossed some leaves and dirt in the general direction of Hector's face and started to scramble to his feet. Hector shot him in the fleshy part of his right thigh and Harry sat down promptly, tearing at his pants leg and making plaintive sounds like an anguished pet with an indifferent master.

Dave Boiardo arrived just in time to verify enough of Hector's story to keep him from being slapped with police brutality charges. The Assistant D.A., a man named Blechman, made some noises about

Hector's shooting an unarmed man, but they were mostly for the benefit of the press. There was never any thought of prosecution, particularly when it was shown that Lapin had cracked one of Hector's ribs as well as bruised the hell out of his left shoulder. An X-ray of a small fracture or a doctor discoursing with a light pen and a PowerPoint screen doesn't mean much to a tired jury, but a 16 x 20 color glossy of bloodied and badly discolored flesh somehow always manages to speak volumes.

Everyone seemed reasonably satisfied with the outcome of the case with the exception of Councilman Burton, who immediately took to the streets in search of TV reporters and cameras. He turned the event into a case of vigilante brutality and anti-gay violence (though Harry—notoriously silent on his sexual interests lest they jeopardize his potential for attracting the largest possible client base—was, at least on the surface, a twice-divorced father of three). Hector pointed out that he was a twelve-year veteran in law enforcement, a legal, lifelong resident of the state of California and an officer protecting a reputable, respected company (and all of its customers and investors) from what was little more than a cool million dollar rip-off. That tack was immediately criticized by Red Denny as a defense of money and business over 'people'. Hector also pointed out that Harry Lapin was now under arrest and a plausible suspect in a case of assault, battery, attempted arson, reckless endangerment, and, potentially, attempted murder. None of these had anything to do with his sexual orientation. As Hector said, when the microphones were shoved at his mouth, "All I saw was someone swinging for my face and head with two pounds of steel."

Burton's immediate response was to attack Hector's credibility by pointing out that he was a former gang member, noting in passing that the members of street gangs are notoriously homophobic. In the peroration of a speech later reprinted in full in a local gay newspaper he referred to Hector as a *troglodyte*. That served to encourage Hector's fellow officers to attempt to defuse the emotional situation by telling Hector that they had never had any doubts about his personal sexual orientation.

That was good for a moment's laugh, but when the LAPD and LBPD said that they were happy with the manner in which Officer Campo had conducted himself and that they considered the case closed, Lapin attempted to use the threat of a criminal complaint to plea bargain himself down to simple battery. That went nowhere, despite Burton's private urgings. When the event moved from page three to page thirty-seven, Burton tried to reinvigorate it by issuing a press release in which he announced that he was considering filing a civil suit.

At that point Chris Dietrich decided that it was time to gird their collective loins for a legal battle, hoping that the evidence that they were prepared to offer would be sufficient to dissuade Burton from taking the matter further.

"He'll pay much more attention to the current headlines than to the facts of the case," Chris said, "but I think we should start with some simple depositions."

Tom testified to the fact that he had known Hector for years and that his service had been exceptional. "It *is* true that he was a member of a youth gang when he was very young," Tom said, "but he was never arrested on any criminal charges, he was never indicted, and he was never convicted of a crime. As soon as he began to mature he left the organization, completed high school, attended community college and then Cal-State at Dominguez Hills and joined the Laguna Beach Police Department. He was an outstanding police cadet and he has been an outstanding officer."

Tom also noted that his handling of the Lapin case had followed all relevant police protocols, both for the LBPD and the LAPD. "This was strictly by the book," he said. "I would have done it exactly the same way. Under the circumstances he used minimum force to subdue a very dangerous man in the process of committing a series of felonious acts."

Privately Tom thought to himself how grateful he was that Hector had actually drawn his weapon and fired a single round into the perp's thigh. With all of their squirming and wrestling Hector might have been tempted to use one of the knives that he usually carried with him. While that might have caused less ultimate damage than the 9mm round, it would have reinforced the image that Burton was trying to peddle— that Hector, in his heart, was still a savage gangbanger, thirsting for the opportunity to carve up a harmless civilian.

As he completed his deposition Tom thought to himself that this was likely to be the first of many. Lieutenants worked the lawyers and the courts as much as they worked the streets. The department lawyer, Gerry Lanham, who had taken him through the process, ticked off Tom's name and said to the court stenographer, "OK, who we got next?"

When Tom returned to the station he collected his personal effects in a cardboard box and carried them down the hallway from his work station to his new, lieutenant's office. Holding the edge of the box against the door jamb, he turned the knob with his left hand, and entered. There was a collection of commemorative gift items on his desk, ranging from a plastic, Kaiser Bill helmet to a toy riding crop.

OK . . . Tom thought to himself. This isn't so bad. When Bill Brighton made lieutenant he was given a set of sex toys and an anonymous note whose principal theme involved overcompensation. Then Tom turned and saw the two stacks of folders that represented Carl Gable's current caseload.

TWELVE

Carl's portfolio was fairly generic for Laguna, with a preponderance of drug cases and grand theft/autos. The southern California thieves' choice had long been the Toyota Supra but in the O.C. the tastes were more exotic. The high end Beemers and Lexuses jockeyed for first place. They were sold whole, while the middle market Camrys and Civics were instantly cut up and sold for parts. The trick in dealing with professionals was to find the middle men who handled the sales or operated the chop shops, since this sort of operation was well organized and the piecemeal search for a single vehicle was no more likely to yield satisfactory results than the hunt for a perpetual motion machine. The amateur thieves, on the other hand, were strictly smash-and-grab, targeting radios, Garmins, cell phones, laptops and any freestanding items that could be sold for ten cents on the dollar and converted to ready cash or a packet of a controlled substance, the latter being the ultimate goal of the great majority of the thieves anyway.

The drug enterprises were also well organized and highly disciplined and nearly all of them crossed multiple jurisdictional lines. The key here was to form networks and alliances with other departments and agencies and use those connections to isolate the weaker links that were capable of leading you to the organizational center. Carl had worked every corner of the county, with special relationships with law enforcement agencies in Orange, Anaheim, Tustin and Santa Ana.

Conventional shrinkage and loitering at Costa Mesa were handled by the mall police, but the South Coast Plaza was a major crossroads for illegal trafficking of various kinds and Carl had logged a considerable amount of time there in consort with officers from other jurisdictions.

Domestic burglaries occupied a portion of his time, though most professionals marketed their goods through established fences, flea markets and other structured outlets. The trick for law enforcement was to build solid, detailed lists of missing items and move as quickly as possible on their recovery. After two days the more attractive items would begin to disappear; after five they would have vanished into the ether.

Violent crime was rare, though road rage increasingly qualified, particularly when those throwing tantrums were also DUIs. There was only one open homicide case in Carl's stack of folders. The victim was a woman named Rachel Henderson; the prime suspect was her ex-husband—again a generic case. There were two alleged rapes, each involving previously-known individuals, both of whom were pleading that the acts had been consensual.

Three males, all relatives of the respective victims, were under investigation for child molestation and one recidivist was set to go on trial for car-jacking. A pharmacist at a big-box store was under investigation for stealing stock and marketing it to street dealers and a trucker based in Irvine had just been indicted for consorting with highjackers working back streets and canyon roads to channel an occasional set of auto parts or appliances to the black market.

The most interesting case concerned an identity theft/credit card scam masquerading as a website for a 'concerned and caring' non-profit. The agency purported to be saving children in Guatemala, but when the donors received the pictures of the infants they believed that they were sponsoring they also received bills for items which they were inadvertently purchasing for the scammers. The trick was to target zip codes where the monthly MasterCard and VISA bills were three-four pages in length and an item or two could easily be overlooked. The success of the operation turned on the scammers' willingness to resist quick scores and instead bleed the unwary a little at a time. The purchases were smaller items—flash drives or video games, items in high demand that could be turned over quickly. All of the 'purchasing' was done through a central 'company'; when and if the victims complained, the 'company' issued immediate apologies and corrected their accounts. Meanwhile their personal information and credit card numbers were filed and eventually sold to another scammer as this particular putative non-profit dissolved and was re-formed under the banner of a totally different but apparently equally worthy cause. Carl had worked the case for a year and a half and the two principals, both pimply slackers working toward the purchase of a Maserati and Lamborghini respectively, had been indicted two weeks ago.

Carl had also left a note for Tom, indicating his willingness to meet with him and discuss his gallery of snitches, several of whom, he said, could be particularly helpful in handling the drug and auto theft cases. He left both a cell number and an email address and Tom made a note to himself to contact him as soon as he had studied the files thoroughly enough to be able to sit down with Carl and present him with a complete, coherent set of questions. Better that than to keep returning to the well and irritating the person who could help him succeed in closing the cases.

As he moved from folder to folder he was interrupted by an occasional detective or patrol officer who had been unavailable for the morning meeting and wanted to offer congratulations and best wishes. Late in the afternoon he received a delivery from his dad, a bottle of 12 year-old Glenfiddich with a note card reaffirming his congratulations and the statement "Take two as necessary and call me in the morning."

He checked his watch and suddenly realized that he had forgotten to eat lunch. He walked down the hall to the vending machine room, picked up a salad that still looked reasonably fresh, a container of yogurt and a bottle of iced tea. Two hours later he was satisfied that he had a good sense of Carl's caseload and he began to plan the allocation of his time on those that were most pressing. Then he went into the men's room, washed his hands and face, combed his hair, and left to pick up Sarah.

She was removing her mail from the lobby box when he arrived at her apartment building. "Hi," she said, "I just barely made it. Come on in; let me change my clothes and we can go."

She slipped out of her nurse's whites and into a silk dress with a light floral design. "That looks comfortable and cool," Tom said.

"Yes," she said. "I've had enough starch and bobby pins for one day."

They drove to Dana Point. "Food or view?" he asked.

"Food," she said. "I've seen the ocean every day for weeks now."

"So have I," he said. "Let's go to **Littlenecks**."

Littlenecks actually specialized in shrimp, crab and scallops rather than clams. She ordered a shrimp salad; Tom ordered scallops with linguine. Each passed on the appetizers and went straight for the bread and wine.

"It's been a long time since we've done this," Tom said.

"I know," she said. "Too long. I was glad when you called."

"And you're at Saddleback now?"

"Yes, for about four months."

"Where were you when I was in there for my surgery?"

"South Coast."

"Oh yeah, that's right. I was pretty loopy when you came by."

"Carving up the brain has a way of doing that," she said. "How are you now?"

"Never better," he said. "I highly recommend having brain tumors removed. You really don't need them."

"No, you don't," she said. "How's your dad?"

"Great. Just talked to him last night. He's very happy; his son just got promoted to lieutenant."

"Really? That's wonderful," she said.

"Thanks," he said.

"No, I'm serious. That's terrific."

He just smiled at her. "So, are you still in the ER?"

"Yes, most of the time. I don't know why but I can't imagine being anywhere else. It may be ignorance or it may be that I've become addicted to the activity level. Sometimes, when there's a break or a change in the rotation, I do med/surg."

"The day goes quickly in the ER . . . or the night..." Tom said.

"Yes, even when it's ten or twelve hours long. Sometimes I do three or four long shifts and trade that off against a shorter work week. You're too tired to do much anyway. Better to concentrate the work."

"Right," Tom said. "How about your personal life? Anything interesting going on there?"

"I thought there might be . . . it was about six months ago . . . but it didn't pan out."

"I'm sorry to hear that," Tom said, "that is, if you wanted it to. Maybe you were lucky and escaped something."

"Maybe," she said, noncommittally. "It's hard to say when you get to be our age."

"We're not ready for the rest home yet," Tom said.

"No. What I meant was that people in their early twenties are often impulsive; sometimes they make bad decisions. By the time they're in their early thirties they start to establish patterns. They're not as flexible. If something good happens . . . so be it, but if it doesn't . . . well, they're ready to deal with that eventuality. It takes some of the passion out of things."

"'The Triumph of Life'," Tom said.

"What do you mean?" Sarah asked.

"It's a Shelley poem. People get ground down. Actually it's not usually as bad as Shelley makes out, certainly not for people at our age. At least I hope it's not."

"I envy you that," she said.

"What do you mean?"

"When I was in school we practiced sticking needles into oranges; you read poetry."

"Not all the time," he said.

"No, you're really educated, Tom. You *are*, really. I read about some of the cases you've solved. It wasn't just police stuff that enabled you to do that."

"Thanks," he said. "The police stuff is important too, very important."

"I know," she said, "but you're special. I'm not just saying that. So what are you going to do as a lieutenant?"

"Pretty much the same sort of thing I usually do—try to find people and things that have been lost, try to protect people from getting hurt, physically . . . and financially, try to keep bad people from selling things that they shouldn't and taking things that aren't theirs, protecting the elderly and small children…"

"I do *some* of that," Sarah said.

"You do a lot of it," Tom said. "You're cut out for that kind of work. I admire the way you do it."

"Thanks," she said.

"How's your salad?"

"It's good. How are your scallops?"

"Fine," he said. "Not quite as good as some that I had in Sicily . . . I was there recently, working on a case, actually."

"Really?"

"Yes. It wasn't all that exotic—not international jewel thieves or anything. I needed to talk to some people who had lived in California. I saw them there."

"That sounds exciting," Sarah said. "Next time you should take me along with you."

"I'd be happy to. You would have enjoyed it. And I would have enjoyed having you there with me."

"Really?" she said.

"Really," Tom answered.

She took a sip of her wine. "This is very good," she said.

He nodded and said, "I'm glad you're enjoying it."

"So do you think we should do this again sometime?" she asked.

"Do what? Have dinner? See each other?"

"Yes. All of the above."

"*I'd* like to," he said.

"So would I," she responded.

"We were pretty good at it in the past, as I remember," Tom said.

"Yes, we were. The best. How about you and *your* personal life, Tom?"

"There's not really much of one," he said.

"Really?"

"No, there isn't."

"I'm glad," she said. "Not that there's no personal life . . . but that maybe there's room there for one."

"There's plenty of room," he said.

"And time?"

"That's always harder," he said. "I think we'd both need to work on trying to change that."

"Here's my schedule," she said, taking a small booklet from her purse. You show me yours and I'll show you mine."

"Sounds like an offer that would be hard to refuse," Tom said.

"I certainly hope so," Sarah answered.

"It's not just the quantity anyway; it's the quality," Tom said.

"There was always plenty of quality," Sarah responded.

Tom sipped his wine and looked into her green eyes. She was looking back, seeking answers.

"How about some dessert?"

"I've got some dessert *wine* at my place," she said. "I was in Temecula a couple months ago. I tasted it and decided to buy a bottle. I've been saving it for a special occasion."

"That's *good*," he said.

"What's that?"

"That you consider this a special occasion."

"I absolutely do," she said.

THIRTEEN

The infirmary trusty carried a 50-count box of packaged syringes to the safe and was waiting for the guard to set the lock when they brought Chelton in on the gurney.

"Jesus Christ, Chelton, what the fuck happened to you?" he asked.

Chelton didn't answer until the guards left.

"What the hell's the matter with you, Ebo?" Chelton said. "You think I'm gonna spill in front of the fucking guards?"

"I forgot, Chelton. I'm sorry. It's just . . . you look like shit, man. How much fucking blood did you lose? It's all over you."

"You think I look so fucking bad? You should see that greaseass Chugger. That son-of-a-bitch tried to cut off my goddamned ear."

"Your *ear*?" Ebo said.

"Yes, my *ear*, asshole. Is there something wrong with your fucking hearing?"

"No, Chelton," Ebo said, looking at the blood-soaked, makeshift bandage that began at Chelton's shoulder and ran across his chest and down to his waist.

"Fucker jumped me in the library. Slashed at me with a homemade edge. I got my head out of the way but he still cut my goddamned chest open. Then he went for the other ear and damn near took out my right eye."

Ebo pulled back the bandage and put some peroxide on a cotton ball. "This'll help prevent infection and you won't feel anything," he said, swabbing the gash across Chelton's nose and the deep slice across his chest. "It bubbles and shit but it don't hurt and it's the best way to clean the wound." He then put some butterfly bandages across the slashes to hold them in place until the doc could stitch them up properly.

"Why the hell did he do it?" Ebo asked.

"Contract," Chelton said.

"Somebody here?" Ebo asked.

Chelton gave him a look that said mind your own fucking business.

"So he admitted it?" Ebo asked.

Chelton gave him the look again, but spoke anyway. "I broke his wrist and he dropped the fucking blade," Chelton said. "Then I told him, 'You should have tried it the easy way,' and I grabbed his left ear, pulled the sumbitch off, and shoved it in his fucking pocket. Then I said, 'You want to try for the right one too, asshole, or do you want to tell me why the fuck you did that?'"

"You *pulled his ear off?*"

"Fuck yes. It's a lot easier than you think."

Ebo's mouth had fallen open. "I bet he was ready to talk then, huh Chelton?"

"He was ready to talk all right. His body was starting to turn different fucking colors and he was shaking all over. Yeah, he was ready to talk."

"Look, Chelton, anything I can do for you here, you just let me know."

"What have you got for pain?" Chelton asked.

"I can't give you anything like that," Ebo said. "That shit's all controlled by the docs. One of them should be here soon. You want a pillow or something?"

"Sure," Chelton said. "That'd be good."

Ebo slipped a pillow in a throwaway paper case under Chelton's head. "I didn't know you could do that," he said.

"Do what?" Chelton asked.

"Just pull off somebody's ear like that."

"You can pull off a lot of things if you really want to," Chelton said.

The prison doctor took his time getting there. He looked at Chelton, shrugged, and then flipped on the intercom and called for a nurse. A few minutes later, after he got a cup of coffee, he told the nurse to throw away the bandages and clean the wounds a second time; then he finished his coffee, slipped on some plastic gloves, deadened the areas, and put in the sutures. He looked at the nurse, a black man with arms the size of drain pipe, and said, "He can have a little morphine now and some 500mg aspirins later. Make sure he takes each one of the pills. Make him swallow each of them and then open his mouth and show you that they're gone. I don't want him hoarding them and then selling them later. Change the bandages every six hours or so. If he starts to ooze, let me know."

"Right," the nurse answered.

"What?" the doctor said.

"What do you mean?" the nurse asked.

"Don't you say 'Right, *Doctor*'?"

"No, not usually," the nurse said. "I can if you want me to."

The doctor shrugged, said something under his breath and went to get a fresh cup of coffee.

After they left, Ebo walked over toward the bed where they had put Chelton. He found him laying on his back, smoking a cigarette. Ebo checked to make sure that there was nothing flammable nearby. He noticed the oxygen tank standing next to the wall beyond the bed and moved it to the other side of the room. Then he returned and spoke to Chelton.

"I guess it's time for some payback on that guy who put out the contract, right Chelton?" he said.

Chelton gave him the look again and Ebo left. Chelton took a long drag on his cigarette, crushed it against the side of the steel bedpost, and dropped it on the floor. He tried to put his hands under his head to relieve some of the pressure he felt on his chest but he felt the pull of the sutures and stopped. Whatever it was that that quack prescribed for him didn't do a whole hell of a lot of good, since his face and chest still hurt like a son-of-a-bitch. He thought about what Ebo had just said. The little shit was right. It *was* time to have somebody pay that little fuck Snack Harris a visit. Deliver some major payback. Let him know what happens when you get in way the fuck over your head. Maybe *start* by pulling off *his* ears . . .

FOURTEEN

Carl's chop shop snitch was a kid named Nemo. "No relation to the captain and no known address," Carl said, "but he hangs out around the beach in Laguna. He's a spotter now. He watches people drive in for the day, looking for parking places. When the metered spaces are filled as well as the local pay lots he follows them into the highways and by-ways. If they're ten minutes from the beach he's got twenty minutes at least to call his playmates and give them the chance to boost the vehicle before they return.

"Nobody returns in twenty minutes and everybody stops for ice cream before they return, so the spotter's job is easy. Nemo used to steal the cars, but he's gone down too many times now and he's looking at a serious bounce if he ever gets caught at it again. Still and all, it's in his blood. If somebody else owns something, he's gotta have it. I picked him up for reaching into a car window and helping himself to what he thought was a purse but turned out to be a diaper bag. He's a dumbass, Tom. I didn't write him up for it, but I told him I can do so at any time. That's when he became my go-to guy.

"I'll be happy to introduce you. He won't be there yet, but he'll be there in a couple of hours. He's a man of leisure. I don't know where he sleeps, but wherever it is he likes to sleep late. By the middle of the day when the tourists are arriving in significant numbers . . . he'll be there."

"I appreciate it, Carl," Tom said. "We got another stolen vehicle report late yesterday afternoon."

"What kind?"

"A new Corolla."

"Not enough sex appeal," Carl said. "They'll chop it up for parts. What time is it—8:45? They're probably a third of the way done already. I'll take that box of stuff from the desk home and come back in two hours. We'll go down to the beach. I'll introduce you to your new best friend. If he's not there yet we'll have a fresh cup of coffee."

"Sounds good, Carl. I appreciate your help."

Gable left and Tom completed setting up his office. He had pictures of his mom and dad in joined, facing frames and put them on the shelf behind his desk. He also had an old picture of Sarah. He had put it in a desk drawer after they split up and found it yesterday below a pad of note paper and a box of paper clips. He looked at it, remembering the blouse that she had worn the day that it was taken. He thought about putting it on his desk or shelf but decided not to push his luck. He put it in his top, right-side desk drawer and emptied the rest of his box of personal items, distributing them among the drawers of his new desk. This one was oak laminate rather than plastic and except for a small stain that had been worked and reworked with Pledge, Carl had taken good care of it.

The IT tech, a man by the name of Hal Bender, brought in Tom's computer and transferred the public files from Carl's machine to Tom's hard drive. "I stripped out the personal stuff and put it on a flashdrive for Carl," he said. "He thought you might be able to use the rest of the files. I'll put them on your desktop and you can use them or lose them. I figured you'd want to keep your same machine, but I can transfer your stuff to Carl's if you prefer. It'd only take a few minutes."

"That's all right," Tom said. "I'm used to mine and it works fine."

"Virtually the same model anyway," Bender said. "And they've both been kept clean and given a lot of TLC. We'll get you a new model next year when we work through the rotation cycle; this one should be fine for now."

"Right. Thanks, Hal," Tom said. While he was waiting for Carl he made copies of the most recent stolen vehicle reports. If they *were* able to hit a chop shop, the formal records might be useful in persuading whoever they found there to start telling their life stories.

Chris Dietrich stuck his head in the door a little while later, asked Tom if everything was copacetic and then left for a meeting with the mayor and a group of concerned citizens. "You've got the best job here, Tom," he said. "Real policing and minimal politicking."

Carl returned at 10:40 and they went to the beach, which was already crowded. "Another perfect day," Carl said. "Perfect for sun and sand, perfect for boosting the turistas' vehicles. I don't see Nemo yet. No, wait a minute, there he is now, even if a little worse for wear."

He was dressed in downscale casual—a baseball hat with tears around the edges of the bill, except that these tears were the result of age; they didn't come like that from the Polo factory. The tee shirt was stained, as were the pants. They seemed to be a mixture of old paint dribbles and dried spackle. "That's interesting," Carl said. "Nemo's never worked an honest day in his life. He must have stolen those clothes from somebody." The gym shoes were old Converse Chuck Taylor All Stars. "Good for running away," Carl said. "Tell you what . . . Nemo's lazy; he'll lean against that shelter house for hours. You go around the right and I'll come at him from the left. If he tries to run, grab him."

He didn't run, but his face sunk when Carl approached him. "Happy Wednesday, kiddo," he said, "let's take a little walk and have a little talk. Meet Lieutenant Deaton. He's the new sheriff in town and your ass is now—as of this very moment–his."

Nemo muttered something under his breath and accompanied them to a picnic table in the shade.

"It's like this," Carl said. "I'm retiring. It's something that people do who have worked for a living for several years. Look in the dictionary some time and check it out. I'm being replaced by Lieutenant Deaton. Unfortunately, he's not a very nice man. In fact, he's dedicated his life to making the lives of people like you a living hell. He's got all the paperwork on your last theft and if you don't work with him I can promise you that he will not hesitate to send you back inside. You know: to the big house with the itty-bitty rooms and the playmates with hair everywhere but on their heads."

"Shit," Nemo said, under his breath.

"Yeah, that about covers it," Carl said. "Now Lieutenant Deaton has a question to ask you and I would advise you to answer him honestly and completely."

"Chop shops," Tom said. "I gather you understand the concept. Who? Where?"

"They move around all the time," Nemo said. "They never tell me where."

"Look," Tom said, "I'm not in the business of letting people waste my time. Give me something now or I'll give you twenty-four hours to come up with something. And that's with a tracer bracelet on your ankle, so you won't be able to take off without adding another couple years to your sentence. And I don't know about you, but if it was me and I was sniffing around, asking questions, I wouldn't want to do it with an ankle bracelet on. After all, you don't look like a coed in a poodle skirt to me…"

Nemo stared at him blankly.

"The long and the short of it is that you're going to help me find the people who stole these cars," Tom said, holding up the reports. "You don't have any choice on that."

"I heard a rumor…" Nemo said.

"Rumors are good . . . sometimes," Tom said. "What did you hear?"

"Out on the canyon road…"

"Yes?"

"There's an old Quonset hut, about half way to 73."

"On the left side of the road as you're driving away from the beach," Tom added.

"Right."

"It's being remodeled," Tom said. "I saw some painters there yesterday."

"Right, but it isn't that building. Back behind it is a garage. Three, maybe four car. It looks abandoned. Try there."

"I will," Tom said, "but I'll hold off on my thanks until I've checked it out. In the meantime, you're coming into the station."

"What the hell for?" Nemo asked.

"Oh, just to talk and visit for awhile," Tom said, "and to keep your idle hands away from cell phones and landlines."

Tom went in with Hector Campo and three uniformed officers. When they approached the building they saw that the garage windows were painted black, but the paint job was amateurish. There were multiple gaps along the edges, where they could see the flash from an acetylene torch.

"Don't let him use that as a weapon," Tom said.

"Don't worry, I won't get that close," Hector said.

There was a door on the left front of the building and one on the right rear. "They have to be able to get in and out somehow," Tom said, "but the space is relatively small. They may have junk piled against the back door. It didn't look as if it had been opened recently. Let's put two of the uniforms back there; the other three of us will go in from the front. They'll be surprised and they won't have any weapons other than the tools they're working with. These will be tech guys, not muscle. That's the theory at least."

"Works for me, Lieutenant," Hector said.

Two minutes later they went in. They found three men, one with a welding torch, one sorting parts on a brick-and-boards shelf, and one removing parts with a socket wrench from the engine of a small sedan. Tom was right; they weren't muscle. When he yelled "Freeze," they froze. The welder nodded first for approval, then turned off his torch and set it gently on the cement floor. Hector cuffed each of them and instructed them to each sit down and shut up.

"My, my," Tom said. He was standing by the sedan, reading the serial number on the firewall with the help of a small flashlight. "What's left of this Civic is the property of Mr. James Stringer of Huntington Beach, California. Here's his theft report." Tom bent over and held the sheet of paper in front of their eyes. "Mr. Stringer is a lawyer and he knows, just as I know, that grand theft auto is a major felony. That means hard time. Lots of it. Understand?"

Two of the men hung their heads; the third responded in Spanish that he didn't understand English. "Not a problem," Tom said, turning to Hector, who repeated Tom's words in Spanish. "We'll do this in tandem," Tom said, continuing in English and pausing for Hector to repeat the same statements each time to the third man.

"What we have here are three mechanics who went for the quick money rather than the honest money," Tom said. "There's always *more* of the quick money, but there's also always a problem. When you get caught there's no money at all. What there is is a long time in prison to think about how stupid you were." He paused to allow Hector to repeat what he had just said in Spanish. "Now here's what we're going to do. All three of you are coming with us—each in a different car—and then each of you is going to a different interrogation room. We want to know who stole these cars. If you cooperate with us we'll work with you to limit the punishment for your crimes. If you don't, you'll take the fall for all of the people who've been using you. It's real simple."

While the uniforms put them into their cruisers, Hector said, "That was easy. Congratulations on a successful start to your new work as a lieutenant."

"Thanks, Hector," Tom said.

"Only one problem," Hector said.

"What's that?" Tom asked.

"What do I call you now that you're so far up in the hierarchy?"

"That's no problem," Tom said. "When we're alone like this you call me Tom. When we've got other officers around us you call me Lieutenant."

"I'll try," Hector said. "It may be tough for me to call you by your first name. Anyway, Lieutenant, again, congratulations. I think the Chief made a good decision on this one, and you know, I'm not a kiss-up. I only speak the truth."

"I know. That's why I appreciate the kind words," Tom said, patting Hector on the shoulder as they left the garage.

FIFTEEN

Harris was half-way into a fresh pint of Old Grand Dad, reading through the notes he had spread out on Lorna's coffee table, and jotting down his thoughts on a sheet of *Crouper's* office letterhead. He heard the footsteps on the stairs long before the knock came at the door. He wasn't expecting anyone and he definitely wasn't expecting anyone friendly. He looked through the venetian blinds in the front bedroom window, saw the man, called out, "Just a second, please, I gotta get dressed," then picked up a steak knife from the kitchen counter and slipped through the kitchen window and around the balcony to the front of the apartment.

The man was short, white, and heavily muscled. He had tattoos on his forearms and he appeared to be holding something in his hand inside his right pants pocket. It was too narrow to be a gun. Maybe a gravity knife. He was tapping on the door with his left hand. Harris sucked up his courage and walked by nonchalantly as if he was going to the next apartment. Then he suddenly pivoted and drove the point of the steak knife into the man's right forearm. As his eyes fell open in shock and pain, Harris grabbed the man's left arm, holding it in place, and kneed him hard in the groin. The man fell to the ground, all doubled up and breathing hard. Harris stood there, shaking with surprise at how easy it had been.

"Take whatever you've got out of your pocket," he said, pushing the point of the knife into the center of the man's throat. "Carefully."

His hand shook uncontrollably as he tried to move his hand in and out of his pocket. Harris pulled the knife across his throat, drawing blood with the point. "God damn it; I said *carefully*."

"You stabbed me in my fucking arm," the man sputtered. "I can't control it."

"Bullshit," Harris said, and put the knife blade against his throat. "Either control it or I'll cut your fucking throat open and pull your tongue through it."

The man took a panic breath, straightened his arm, and forced his hand out of his pocket and over his waist. He was holding onto the concealed object with his fingertips.

It was a ball bearing sap, small but nasty.

"Well, Roy," Harris said, "what were you planning to do, eliminate your competition?"

"Who the hell's Roy and who the hell are you?" the man said. His eyes were blurry and his voice was hoarse as he choked out the words. The blood was soaking his shirt and trousers, running down his arm and oozing through his fingers as he clutched at the wound with his left hand.

"Let's go inside and have us a little chitty-chat, fuckhead," Harris said, looking around the apartment area to see if anyone had been observing him.

When they went into Lorna's apartment Harris pulled back the aqua rug in the living room and told the man to sit down on the bare floor. "Try not to bleed so fucking much," he said.

"What were you going to do with this?" he asked, dangling the sap in front of the man's eyes.

"Fuck you," the guy snarled, his voice recovering. Harris' face froze. He tightened his grip on the sap, leaned back, and then smashed it across the man's mouth. When his eyes flashed with pain Harris hit him a second time. "How did that feel? Was the second one as good as the first?" he asked, as the man fell back, gurgling and spitting up blood and pieces of teeth.

"You got to understand something, fuckwad," Harris said. "I don't like to be talked to like that. Especially not by some little faggot like you. Now what should we try next? Maybe a couple more swats in what's left of that mouth of your's. The first two times were fun . . . wait, I got a better idea . . . He held the knife above the man's body and dropped the point into his chest between his throat and waist. "I'm heading south," he said, raising the knife again, "and you know what that means. You ever want to see your balls again you'll have to come visit them . . . I'm thinking maybe a clear glass jar, a big one, so you could see them floating there . . . maybe I'll put it up on my mantel . . . make you part of my permanent collection. They'd sure as hell make a nice conversation starter, don't you think?"

The man's voice was faint after gagging and spitting. He tried to turn to his side so he could breathe. "A guy sent me . . . to deliver a message."

"Oh? A *guy* sent you. And what was this *guy's* name?" Harris asked, holding him down and dragging the knife point across his belly as his back arched in pain and the edges of his sliced tee shirt dampened with fresh streaks of blood.

The man tried to talk faster. "He's a friend of another guy, a con."

"Really, a con?"

"Yeah . . . some guy named Chelton." The words were coming harder.

"Chelton wanted to send a message to me? And what did he want you to tell me?"

The man was silent. "Here we go again then," Harris said. He smiled as he pulled the knife point across the man's belly and over his crotch and started to probe and jab.

"Please," the man said. "He wanted . . . he wanted me to..."

"He wanted *what?*" Harris said, the smile gone along with his patience.

The words came out slowly. "He . . . he . . . wanted me to pull off both of your . . . ears."

"*Pull* off my ears? That wouldn't have been very nice," Harris said.

"And you were gonna use that sap first to soften me up. It was more than just the ears. You were gonna break my nose, knock out some of my teeth, maybe. You coulda blinded me, you piece of shit. I bet you had all kinds of plans. Well, I'll tell you this much; your fucking plans don't seem to be working out too well. And you were really looking forward to trying them on me, weren't you?"

He paused, put his knee down, hard, on the man's heaving chest, and thought for a moment. "I've got an idea," he said. "We'll send a message back to Chelton. You know, I never really did like him. I bet you haven't even met him, have you?"

The man mouthed the word *no* as he tried to move his head from side to side.

"So what the fuck are you, some kind of hired muscle or something? I'd say you were pretty shitty at it. Well, I'll fill you in about Chelton. What he is is a bully. And when he's in a situation where all that counts is strength he can be very mean. But it's not like that out here, is it? You're mean and strong too and you even had your weapon, but now you're laying on Lorna's floor, all cut and bleeding. You've lost some of your teeth, your right arm isn't worth a shit, you're having trouble talking, and you're afraid that you've made me so angry that I might do something to you that would cause you a whole lot more pain. You're really worried I might cut off your balls, aren't you? That's good; you *should* worry. Maybe I won't *display* them though; maybe I'll just shove them down your throat one at a time instead. Watch you while you choke on your own pills . . . and that could just be for starters. . ."

The man was quiet, his body convulsing.

"Well, I'm not going to do that. Instead I'm going to take you somewhere where you can make a call to Chelton. Would you like that?"

The man seemed to nod.

"Very good. I thought you might prefer that."

Twenty minutes later they were on the Angeles Crest Highway, driving through the forest up the narrow road that led to Mt. Wilson. The road snaked along the mountain, sometimes paralleling itself at different altitudes.

"Pretty deserted today," Harris said. The man was silent, his hands tied in his lap and his bloodied right arm tied loosely to the armrest on the passenger side of Lorna's car. Every time they had hit a rough spot in the road the man had winced in pain. Harris had covered the knife wounds with some duct tape to keep him from bleeding out.

"Here we are," Harris said, pulling into a turnout. He untied the man's forearm and pulled him out of the car and over to the edge of the mountain. Below them was the segment of the highway they had just driven over and a system of power and telephone lines.

"Isn't it beautiful up here? It's one of my favorite places in all of California. I thought you might like it too, what with the sun shining so brightly and all. This has really been fun and I wish we could spend more time together, but unfortunately I've got work to do, so I'll have to say goodbye now. Oh yeah, one other thing. Remember to say hi to Chelton for me," Harris said, pushing the man over the side and watching his body land in the wires below, jerking back and forth with the electrical surge as one of the cables snapped.

He picked up Lorna at 6:30. "The car looks so nice," she said. "What did you do, clean it up for me?"

"I cleaned up the inside a little," he said. "It wasn't hard. Vinyl cleans up nice. There were some stains here and there but they're all gone now. It smells good too, don't you think? I used a little disinfectant."

"It smells great," she said, "just like springtime. What else did you do today?"

"Oh, not all that much. I sat around and relaxed. I worked on my notes. I sent a message to an old roommate..."

"Oh, that's nice," she said. "I bet he'll be glad to hear from you."

"I'm sure he'll be interested. I tried to make it sort of creative."

"I love when you're thoughtful like that," she said. "I've got to take you to the *Hallmark* store just a couple doors down from *Crouper's*; you wouldn't believe the cards that they have now. You might even be shocked by some of them."

"Oh, I doubt it," he said.

"It's great to have you back, Earlon," she said.

"I know," he said. "It's great to *be* back, but remember what I told you—I've got to finish off some things here first, then we can go away. Just you and me."

"I can't wait," she said.

"Neither can I," he answered.

SIXTEEN

"Why don't we go out tonight and get a pizza or something?" Lorna asked. "There's a new place in La Cañada that's pretty good—all you can eat for $6.99. They have spaghetti too. And ice cream."

"I'm sorry, Honey," Harris said. "That sounds really good, but like I told you before—I've got a couple of things I have to do first."

"OK, she said. "It was just a thought."

"Maybe Thursday night," Harris said, pulling on his socks and slipping his feet into some cordovan wingtips he had lifted from the shelf at *Target*. (It was good that he had had his knife with him; when did they start tying *expensive* shoes together in stores?)

"When will you be back?" Lorna asked.

"Late," he said. "You rest. Don't wait up for me."

"Well, be careful," she said.

"Don't worry, I'm always careful," he said. "I've learned how to do that."

Ten minutes after he left the phone rang. It was Roy Haggerty.

"I can't talk to you, Roy," Lorna said. "Earlon is back and I just can't see you anymore."

"Can't or won't?"

"I can't . . . and I won't. I've got to be faithful to Earlon now."

"Why?" Roy asked.

"Because I'm all he's got and he's counting on me. I can't let him down this time."

"He's a piece of shit," Roy said. "He's bad for you. You shouldn't ever have gotten involved with him in the first place."

"That's not for you to say," she said. "Now please don't call me."

"You didn't mind my visits when he was in jail," Roy said.

"That was different," she said.

"I was fine when you didn't have him. All I was to you was a good lay."

"That's not true; you know it isn't, Roy, and don't talk to me like that," she said.

"The hell it's not," he answered. "If you had any feelings for me you'd throw him out of your apartment and tell him to stay the hell out of your life."

"I got feelings for you, Roy," she said, "but I can't live that way. I've got to choose one of you and right now Earlon needs me the most."

"He needs a goddamned shrink and a padded cell is what he needs," Roy said.

"Don't say that about him," she said, "and please don't call me."

"You can't stop me from trying," he said. "And don't tell me that that little prick will hurt me because I'm not afraid of him."

"You *should* be afraid of him," Lorna said. "He's deep. Real deep. And when he's angry he doesn't hold anything back."

"He's deep all right," Roy said. "He's a fucking psycho is what he is."

Lorna put down the phone, choked for a second, and said slowly, "That's not nice at all to talk about people like that, even if they sometimes have problems."

Harris took the Colorado Boulevard exit from the freeway and drove into Pasadena. He passed some fancy auto dealerships, noticed some stores and restaurants that hadn't been there when he was arrested, and checked the first sheet from the yellow pages which he had torn from Lorna's telephone book. **THEATRICS, INC.** was located two blocks east of the peach stucco Jaguar dealership, between a Danish furniture store and a noisy construction site surrounded by a 6-foot plywood wall with placards announcing the future opening of a 16-screen Laemmle cineplex.

He walked in and saw that the clerk was positioned next to the door to guard against shoplifting. The cash register station was elevated, so that the attendant could see over the tops of the merchandise shelves. There were also two closed-circuit TV monitors built into the checkout desk. "Shit," Harris thought to himself, "nobody trusts anybody anymore; I guess they all must have learned."

He tried his best to look inconspicuous as he made a pass through the first three racks of costumes. They were pricey as all hell; fucking Halloween really drove the costs up. Didn't use to be such a big damned deal. He checked out some rubber Nixon masks and monster masks all covered with blood and warts and then went back to the clothing and accessory racks and found the items he wanted. Then he looked for the makeup section. That stuff was expensive now too. He picked up a tube of glue, a can of gray spray dye, and three tufts of artificial brown hair, and took them all to the register. The clerk, a homely blonde with a red birthmark on her neck, put down the weekly edition of *Variety* she was reading and said, "Will that be all, sir?"

"Yes," he said, touching the rim of his cap and adjusting his sun glasses, "that's it."

"Are you a makeup man?" she asked.

"Sometimes," he said. "It's just a hobby for me. You know . . . at the community theatre and such. Most of the time I work as a lawyer. Down in South Pas."

"Wow, a lawyer. I'm a singer," she said.

"Oh yeah, what do you sing?"

"Hip hop, with some funk," she said.

"That's nice," he said, keeping his face averted as he walked out of the store.

He crumbled the first sheet from Lorna's phone book, put it in the small plastic garbage bag hanging from the glove compartment knob, and picked up the second. The store's name and address were circled in red magic marker. Harris checked the street number and drove down Fair Oaks to an old hardware store that sat at the end of a strip mall, adjoining a barber shop. He turned sharply when he entered and went directly to the rear of the store. The clerk was eating a late dinner out of a cardboard tray and talking to one of the customers. It smelled like Chinese vegetables with a lot of heavy sauce and garlic. The smell filled the store. Whatever it was, he was really into it, because he was shoveling it in and not paying any attention to Harris when he entered. The dumbass.

Harris located the rear exit door and saw the neatly-stacked bags of shredded bark, ornamental gravel and top soil laying on the pavement beyond it. He walked slowly through the store, like a recreational shopper, just passing time. He walked past the hand tool and bulk nail section, looking at a number of items and occasionally lifting one for closer inspection. When he found the items he wanted, he checked on the clerk. The moment he turned away, Harris slipped them inside his jacket and zipped it loosely. Then he went through the motions of further shopping, looked at his watch, walked out the back door, checked out the bags of bark as if he was a serious customer, looked at his watch and then returned to his car.

He crumbled the second sheet of paper, put it in the plastic bag, checked his watch, and pulled out of the parking lot. "Show time," he said.

SEVENTEEN

Harris got out of the line of Fair Oaks traffic headed for South Pas, drove over to Raymond, and parked in a lot adjacent to an out-of-business restaurant called the **New Mexico**. A large **FOR LEASE** sign was stapled to the front door; on the porch were two green trash containers with cardboard boxes and aluminum cans spilling over the tops. Harris turned off the ignition, moved back the driver's seat, turned on the courtesy light, adjusted the mirror, and got out the makeup.

He pulled pieces of brown fiber from the tightly wound tuft, fluffed and then shaped it, and set it on the seat beside him. He daubed a thin coat of theatrical glue across the top of his lip and then carefully fashioned the false moustache from the shaped pieces of artificial hair and put it in place, using more material than he would need so that he could tweak it more easily. He opened the glove compartment, took out the scissors he had taken from Lorna's bathroom cupboard, and trimmed the edges neatly. Then he fluffed it, pushed some of the edges against the glue, and trimmed it a second time. He checked it from various angles and then picked up the can of gray dye. Protecting his eyes with a piece of cardboard, he sprayed his temples lightly, checked the results in the mirror, and finally opened his shirt and gave a shot to the hair on his upper chest, making sure that there was no telltale dye on his skin.

He clipped the steel tape measure he had stolen from the hardware store to his belt, put on his cap and glasses, slid a pencil under the arm of his glasses on his right temple, and drove to Santa Ynez Way in Arcadia. The neighborhood was near Santa Anita and the county Arboretum, a pricey piece of California earth with a liberal sprinkling of BMW's, Cadillacs, and Mercedes to accent the landscape.

He remembered something he had read in a tattered prison magazine once—the Arboretum had been used for many of the opening shots on *Fantasy Island*. De plane! De plane! Whatever happened to that little fucker, Harris wondered. He was *good*. The only good thing in the show. Probably had trouble getting chicks though. But who knows? In Hollywood anything's possible. In Arcadia too.

"It's an art, acting," Harris said to himself. "Really and truly it is and I plan to do a damned good job of it. Put my heart in it. It's no fun otherwise. Anyway," he said, catching one more glance in the mirror, "I sure as hell look the part."

Harris parked a half-block from her house, took an official-looking notepad from the glove compartment, folded over the top few pages, and made his way down the street. He knocked at her door and made some aimless jottings on the pad to assure her he was all business. He heard the slide on the peep hole and he made another mark on the pad, tapped it with the pencil point, and slid the stub back under his glasses and into his cap.

The door opened slowly. She peered at him through the narrow crack.

"Yes?" she said.

"Pacific Bell, ma'am," he said. "I need to check your lines."

"Isn't it a little late for that?" she asked.

"Yes, ma'am, it is, but we respond as soon as we hear about a possible problem. Folks want their phones to work, morning and night…"

"But I didn't report a problem."

"I realize that, ma'am, but several of your neighbors did and I need to check each line in the grid to find the point of origin of the problem."

She opened the door. There was no chain lock. Too trusting, he thought to himself. What the hell was she thinking? Somebody like her . . . she ought to know better.

"Here," he said, "let me show you my identification. We always do that first, ma'am."

He took out his wallet, started to open it, and then dropped it on the black slate floor in her foyer.

"Darn," he said, bending over to pick it up. He reached for the wallet with his left hand and suddenly threw all of his weight forward, slamming his right fist into the pit of her stomach. Gasping and shaking, she fell against a three-foot, decorative marble pillar, knocking it over and shattering the glass vase that had been displayed on it. "Whoopsie," Harris said, and kicked the door closed with his foot.

He put his wallet back in his pants and buttoned the pocket. Then he slowly approached her, bent down, grabbed her hair, jerked back her head, and moved his face toward hers, trying to smell her fear. "Hello, Judge," he said. "So nice to see you again."

Her body was still shaking and she could barely catch her breath. Suddenly she started to vomit across the slate floor and the edge of carpeting that marked the entrance to her living room.

"Go ahead," he said. "Let it all out. It's good for you. They used to hit me like that all the time. To get my attention, they said. It works, doesn't it? You take a good punch and suddenly you can't think of anything else. You can't breathe and all you feel is the purest form of pain. Whenever I puked I felt better. They didn't like that though. Especially if I puked on them. Then they'd hit me again. Sometimes they'd just hit me anyway."

Her arms were wrapped around her stomach and a stream of saliva hung from her lower lip. She was breathing in gasps and her eyes were alive with fear. He put his fingers to her throat and jerked her head up, searching her eyes for emotion.

"I usually felt better after an hour or so," he said, "unless of course something was broken. If I got to the infirmary soon enough it was better, but you couldn't always get there. Most of the time you just had to take it. And whenever they felt like it they just started hitting you again. Over and over, until they got tired or bored. I'm not boring *you*, am I? I mean, we've got things to do and we can't just sit here jabbering, but I did want to have a word or two and get reacquainted before we left."

Her eyes were red and moist as she jerked away from him. He grabbed her throat again, harder this time, and twisted her head sharply. "When I talk to you, you look at me and you listen. Understand?"

She nodded.

"You want another shot? I'm willing if you are. It's kind of intimate, isn't it? I show you some of my emotion and then you show me some of yours. That's what makes pain so special. Did you ever think about it that way? My guide talks about that all the time."

"N-n-n-o," she said. "Do-o-nt. Ple-e-ase do-o-nt."

"Whatever you say. I thought maybe you would enjoy it. It seems kind of lonely here. Not much human contact. Pain is better than feeling nothing . . . sometimes it's good. What do you say?"

"N-o-o."

"OK, suit yourself. You're probably thinking about other things . . . wondering why I'm here . . . wondering what it is that we're going to do. Am I right?" he said.

She didn't answer. Her body was still shaking and she was trying to compose herself.

"Don't worry," he said, putting his arm around her neck and pulling her close to him. "It's going to be fun. We're going to a place where you'll feel right at home."

EIGHTEEN

"Hey, Homes, what's for breakfast?" Hector said. One of the uniforms held his gun on the suspect while Hector and Tom went through the rest of his apartment. Their guns were drawn.

"I smell something, but it's not breakfast," Tom said, after they cleared the last room. "It's more like feet . . . feet that haven't been washed in a month or two."

"That or maybe laundry," Hector said, "laundry that hasn't been washed in the last decade."

When they returned to the living room the other uniformed officer had cuffed the suspect and put him on a wooden, kitchen chair.

"So where's your playmate, Rico?" Hector asked. "You know, the one that helps you boost cars—what's his name? You know—the guy with the pimples—Ramon?"

The man didn't respond.

"Your choice, Homes. You can take the fall by yourself or you can help us and do yourself some good. The chop shop is closed. Out of business. Forever. And the mechanics there . . . well, they're all in little interrogation rooms, singing like pretty yellow birds. And I'm not talking garden-variety canaries, Rico. I'm talking birds that could sing grand opera. It's like the three tenors all over again except that one of them sounded a little bit like a soprano to me. Anyway, think about it—multiple grand theft auto beefs . . . that's a heavy bounce, Rico. Oh, I forgot, you already know how much time you can draw for boosting cars. Do you think your former cellmates are going to throw a welcome home party for you?"

"Don't waste your breath, asshole. I'm not rolling over on anybody."

"OK," Hector said. "Then it'll be like that old Burger King commercial. *Have it your way. Have it your **way!**"

"I want to talk to a lawyer," he said.

"No problem," Hector said. "We'll take a little drive down to the station and you can call one. I'd make it a good one if I were you, because we've got enough evidence to send you so far up the river that even Lewis and Clark won't be able to find you."

"Who the fuck are they?" Rico asked.

"The guys on your parole board," Hector said.

"Next stop: Tustin," Hector said, as the two uniforms drove off with the first perp. "I know Ramon; he's the jumpy one; Rico was the boss. Most of the time Ramon was little more than a spotter. Rico worked the slim jim and did the hotwire. It's funny, even the most hardened criminal . . . there's a soft center; they always need a partner. Maybe they're just lonely."

"Or just plain stupid," Tom said. "Sometimes they need somebody to remind them how to get back to the freeway."

"Right," Hector said, smiling. "Like those guys that tried to rob the bank in Costa Mesa last month. Their driver is out on the street, sipping a Starbucks and waiting for them. Except that he forgot and turned off the engine. The other four came running out with their take—which was less than $2200—and the driver couldn't get the car started. All five of them started running down the street . . . three were apprehended immediately; one twisted his ankle and the driver got away. The only problem was that he had been using his own car. The guys on the scene called in his plate number and there were two plainclothes guys waiting in the shadows on his porch when he ran up his steps."

Tom smiled and said, "The fact that they're so stupid . . . it's our comparative advantage. It's like a gift that keeps on giving."

Ten minutes later they pulled up to a rundown apartment building in Tustin. "That's Ramon's car," Hector said, pointing at an ageing Explorer in the carport. "That means he's got to be home. Ramon's too lazy to walk anywhere."

Tom knocked on the door. There was no peephole.

"Who is it?" a male voice said.

"Police," Tom said. Immediately he heard movement . . . a door slamming, heels clicking on a hardwood floor, a wooden object (actually the 2x4 that had been wedged in the slider track) . . .

The slider opened and a set of legs, feet, and untied shoes came over the second floor railing. When the rest of his body hit the weeds and grit below, Hector spun him around, put him on the ground with his face in the dirt, and cuffed him.

"Good morning, Ramon," he said. "Going for a jog? No, wait . . . a job interview."

"Who the fuck are you?" he said.

"Don't you recognize me?" Hector said. "You're breaking my heart, Homes. I'm Ed McMahon. Don't you remember subscribing to all those magazines? I'm here with your prize, an all-expense paid vacation to . . . well, we don't know yet . . . Folsom . . . Pelican Bay . . . someplace special."

"I want to talk to a lawyer."

"My brother-in-law's a lawyer," Hector said. "I don't think you can afford him though. You didn't steal enough cars for that."

"I didn't steal any fucking cars at all," Ramon said.

"You didn't? That's funny. I just talked to Rico and he said you stole all of them. He said you'd probably try to frame *him*, but that he'd gone straight. Said you were the mastermind, the big chimichanga. Or was it the big enchilada? Anyway, it was big. Rico is planning to walk. No cavity searches and nasty-assed cellmates for him this time."

"That son-of-a-bitch. *He* stole the cars. I haven't seen him in weeks."

"Really?" Hector said. The word was dripping with skepticism.

"Yes, really."

"Well in that case I'll tell you what we're going to do, Ramon. We'll give you a few hours to think about all of this and then I'll bring in a stenographer and we'll take your statement. You think about what you're going to tell us. Think about it very carefully. And if you lie . . . well, let's not even think about what's going to happen to you if you lie."

They dropped off the second perp at the station. "Give Ramon a couple of hours," Hector said, "and he'll be ready to help us convict his mother. What do you say, Lieutenant? We're on a roll. How about one more stop?"

"Let's do it," Tom said.

Thirty minutes later they were in an office complex in Costa Mesa. The lettering on the door said **ROSEN INDUSTRIES**. Tom went in first. The woman at the desk removed the iPod buds from her ears. "Yes?" she said.

"Al Rosen," Tom said.

"Do you have an appointment?" she asked.

Tom opened his leather folder and showed her his shield.

"I'll see if he's available," she said, picking up her phone. Tom nodded to Hector and looked to his left. There was only one door behind her.

"He said to take a seat and he'll see you in a few minutes."

"Thanks," Tom said, and walked past her, opening the door.

"I told you to wait," she said, as Hector smiled at her.

"What the fuck?" Rosen said. He was sloppy fat, with male-pattern baldness, an open, sweat-stained collar, and a rank cigar.

"Put that out," Tom said. "You're violating an ordinance, a very important ordinance, and from the smell of that thing I wouldn't say it was worth breaking the law over."

"What do you want?" Rosen said, dragging the cigar across the bottom of a copper ashtray. Hector was tempted to make a comparison with the way in which his sister's dog scooted his butt on her oriental carpet, but instead remained quiet and listened.

"We're here to talk about *Rosen Industries*," Tom said. "Actually one of the industries in particular."

"Which one's that?"

"*Coastal Parts and Supplies.*"

"Yeah?"

"It's a fencing operation."

"Bullshit. Who told you that?"

"Lots of people," Tom said. "And, you know, I tend to be very skeptical about these kinds of things. Car thieves . . . chop shop guys . . . we're not talking about individuals with the highest ethical standards, Al. And when they get caught they start making all kinds of accusations. You know what these kind of people are generally trying to do, Al?"

"You tell me."

"They're trying to divert the attention of law enforcement from their own sins."

"Yeah, right."

"And sometimes they lie."

"Heaven forbid," Rosen said.

"Yes, but not this time, Al. You see, while Officer Campo and I have been talking to these various and sundry lawbreakers, another team has been visiting *Coastal Parts and Supplies*. It's kind of a dump, Al. I mean . . . nice name and all . . . the name *almost* instills confidence . . . but when my guys got there they said it looked like someplace that any self-respecting mice and spiders would have abandoned. Anyway, they also found some parts there . . . and wouldn't you just know it? . . . one of them had a serial number on it. No, check that, Al. A whole lot of them had serial numbers on them. Want to see the list? It's pretty long, Al, but it makes for nice reading. How can I break this to you, Al? *Coastal Parts and Supplies* is closed. And *Rosen Industries*? Finished. It's kaputski, Al. And the President and CEO? Well, put it this way—what do the fortune tellers always say? *He's* about to take a trip. Oh yes, and that trip . . . it's one-way."

"I want to talk to my lawyer."

"Great idea, Al," Tom said. "Your lawyer can explain to you exactly what it means to be a receiver of stolen goods, stolen goods with serial numbers, Al. And guess what—one of the owners of the stolen goods . . . he's a lawyer too, Al. I can just hear him on the stand and hear his deposition in the back of my head. He'll know exactly what to say. It'll get *your* attention, I'm sure. And the jury's."

As they took him out in cuffs, the receptionist stood up, looked sheepish, and said, "Do you mind if I take the rest of the afternoon off, Mr. Rosen?"

"I think this is what they call an *early win*," Hector said. "A nice neat package—the whole operation wrapped up like a birthday present for the Chief. You got the street guys, the middle guys, and the fat bald guy with the cigar."

"The whole chimichanga," Tom said.

"And you know the Mayor will be dancing over this, Lieutenant. Keep the turistas happy, keep them from being separated from their vehicles, keep them coming to Laguna. Like bees . . . rubbing their little legs together, keeping all of that golden pollen in our neighborhood. Street crime's a bitch for business, but a rep for safety and security greases every skid."

"It's not quite like shutting down Murder Incorporated," Tom said, "but when the Chief and the Mayor are having lunch and the Mayor's soup isn't quite hot enough or maybe he's getting a phone call about a sewage problem . . . whatever . . . whatever it is that gives mayors headaches . . . the Chief can lean over and say, 'Well, your honor, there *is* a little bit of *good* news . . . . And that lawyer who lost his car, the guy who was calling for blood . . . he might just write a nice little love note to all concerned, including the gentlemen and ladies of the press.'"

"Unfortunately it's not always this easy," Hector said.

"Carl's snitch made the deal," Tom said. "Carl's got to receive the bulk of the credit. He had everything ready—put it on a silver platter for us."

"Nice way to go out," Hector said. "By the time you work your way through his pile of folders there might be a whole string of attaboys for him."

"Nothing would please me more," Tom said.

"How about some lunch, Lieutenant?" Hector said. "All that talk of chimichangas and enchiladas is making me hungry."

"My treat," Tom said. "Let's check and see if the uniforms are available. This has been a big day for them. A lot more fun than directing traffic or rousting guys for throwing candy wrappers on the beach. And they did a good job."

The whole group walked into a small place recommended by Hector. "This is the real thing," he said. "Strictly authentic. That sign over there above the counter...?"

"Yes?" Tom said.

"Loosely translated it says *We don't use no stinking microwave.*"

"Works for me," Tom said.

"Once you've had this," Hector said, "there's no going back to *Taco Bell.*"

They passed on the fried ice cream, but each had two cups of strong black coffee. Their waitress, Maria, poured the last cup and walked over to the TV next to the bar. She turned up the volume. It was Hector's sister, Estella, with a special report.

NINETEEN

"Good afternoon," she said, "this is an ABC Newsbreak, I'm Estella Rodriguez. A bizarre homicide this morning in Pasadena. Evelyn Garretson, 58, most recently appellate court judge for the ninth circuit, was found strangled to death in the courtyard garden of the Pasadena City Hall. Pasadena and LAPD officers are cooperating in the investigation. Here with a live report from the scene is Darryl Lawson."

The reporter was moving from foot to foot, holding on to his ear piece and fiddling with it nervously as he waited for his cue. Suddenly his eyes lit up and he turned to the camera.

"Good afternoon, Estella. The Police know very little at this time but the murder appears to be the work of someone with an extremely twisted sense of humor. Early this morning a member of the grounds crew found Judge Garretson here…"

He took a few steps to his left and pointed to a wooded area just behind him.

"I'm standing in the courtyard of Pasadena's City Hall, a local landmark. Judge Garretson was found tied between the trunks of the two fan palms you see behind me. She was fully clothed and dressed in a black judge's gown with a silk-scarf blindfold covering her eyes. Her arms were suspended in the air, parallel to the ground. A small metal scale was lashed to her left hand and a plastic sword attached to her right."

"Did you say a *scale*, Darryl?"

"Yes, Estella. The kind of scale you see in old grocery or hardware stores. This was a smaller version."

"Like the traditional statues of Justice."

"Yes, along with the traditional sword in her right hand."

"Go on, Darryl."

"There was also a wooden panel positioned at the judge's feet. The police assume that the murderer placed it there. There were two words written on it in red spray paint."

The camera jump-cut to a still photograph. The blur of a figure passing in front of the panel was visible, as were the bent legs and feet of the victim. The sign read:

JUSTICE NOW

"Darryl, you said that Judge Garretson's arms were tied to the trees?"

"Yes, Estella, with common clothesline. It was stretched very tight, probably to keep her body from slumping."

"So it was almost like a crucifixion."

"Yes, but we don't have too many specifics yet. It could be that the murderer tied her that way so that she would be standing—the way the statue of Justice generally appears. The police told me that the results of the autopsy would take at least twenty-four hours, but I was told that they were reasonably certain that the cause of death was asphyxiation. There were bruises on Judge Garretson's throat, but her neck did not appear to be broken. Except for a large bruise on her abdomen, there were no other suspicious marks on the body."

"On her *abdomen*. Was she struck with an object or did the murderer strike her with his fist?"

"Again, we'll know more after the autopsy, Estella. I don't have any more specifics on the blow at this time. The bruising was reported by one of the officers on the scene. It's not clear that the individual who killed her also struck her, though the policeman said that the bruise appeared to be fresh. He was doing a cursory examination, looking for bullet or stab wounds. We'll know more later."

"When did the murder occur, Darryl?"

"It's too early to say at this point, Estella. Given the condition of the body the officers on the scene considered it likely that the murder happened last night. Police speculate that Judge Garretson was brought here late yesterday evening and murdered sometime between midnight and the early morning hours. We're still waiting for further details."

"Thank you, Darryl," Estella said, shaking her head slightly in disbelief. "Back after this…"

"A murdered judge…" Tom said. "That'll make for a long list of possible suspects."

"Do you know anything about her, Lieutenant?" Hector asked.

"No, not really. The name rang a slight bell, but nothing beyond that. Maybe she was a tough sentencer."

"Not anymore," Hector said.

"Say, Officer Campo…" one of the uniforms said. The man's name was Jim Gallagher.

"Yes?" Hector responded.

"I heard somebody say that that was your sister . . . just then . . . on the news."

"Yes, Estella is my sister. Rodriguez is her married name."

"She's really good."

"Thanks," Hector said.

"Well," Tom said, "I've got a stack of folders on my desk that I'd better get back to. As you can see, Justice is under attack."

"Always," Hector responded.

"Look at it this way," Tom said, "at least there's one thing in life that you can always count on."

TWENTY

When they got back to the station Bill Engle was holding forth. He had been in touch with friends at both the Pasadena PD and the LAPD.

"So let me run it down for you," he said, angling the point of his microwaved leftover pizza slice at the roof of his mouth and flipping a falling anchovy back into the center. "We've got a dead judge hanging out with a toy sword and a pair of scales at Pasadena City Hall, a list of possible suspects as long as Seabiscuit's dingdong, the press in a full-tilt feeding frenzy, the staff of the L.A. Mayor's office jumping up and down, holding their breath and squeezing their peepees, the FBI AD standing in the wings waiting for his call and squat for leads."

"How about physical evidence?" Chris Dietrich asked. Bill hesitated a moment while he chewed his pizza.

"In a space that draws tourists and winos, Chief? Across the grounds there you'll find more random bits of human hair than on the barber shop floor at Parris Island. When you get into all of the various nooks and crannies there'll be pollen from every state in the union and from countries the State Department and the National freaking Geographic have never heard of. My cousin Ralph lives in an apartment right nearby, just below the Rose Bowl parade route. That place is a tourist magnet, Chief. Since the repairs after the damage of the City of Industry quake and the recent retrofit to prepare for the next big one, the number of daily visitors has tripled. That's not just gawkers from the flyovers; that's seismologists from all over the world. We got…"

"How about blood?" Chris asked.

"Nope, no blood, Chief, but they found some nice seagull poop on the ground behind the trees where he tied her."

"How about semen?" Tom asked.

"No, Lieutenant, sorry. The clothes were all clean. They're trying to trace the black robe. They know that it wasn't the judge's. Apparently she had a regular and a backup and they're both still hanging on the clothes rack in her office; the Pasadena PD checked. This was something cheap, probably from a college rental service or some costume shop. Hard to tell. The label was torn off and what must have been a laundry mark was cut out with a scissors."

"Then the perp wasn't completely stupid," Chris said. "Too bad."

"There was nothing under her nails except for some soap residue. The only hairs on her clothing were her own. I figure she didn't know it was coming, since there's no evidence that she tried to resist. Maybe he told her he was just going to tie her up or something and then after she was immobilized he strangled her. The back of her shoes were stained and dusty. She was probably squirming and kicking in an effort to get loose after he tied her between the trees. No chance of that. He really had her trussed up tight."

"What about footprints near the body?" Hector asked.

"Sorry, Hector," Bill answered, "that's where the locals take their bag lunches and the tourists search for a good camera angle to shoot the dome. There are footprints up the ying yang, but they're all on top of one another. It looks like the path to the wailing wall on a high holy day. Also some scrape marks, probably from the side of his shoe, clearing away any marks that he might have left."

"How about prints on the scale and the sword?" Tom asked.

"No, Lieutenant. Each of them was wiped clean. And no manufacturer's marks; each of them was a cheapo version. In short, they got nothing . . . nothing except for a smart perp. You were right, Chief. They're not dealing with anybody stupid on this one. He got the judge in without attracting attention, somehow persuaded her to stand still and not cry out, killed her, and then got back out of the area without being seen or heard. And remember . . . we're not talking about some park in East L.A. or some remote area out in one of the canyons. We're talking about a round-the-clock photo op site."

"What about the bruise on her stomach?" Tom asked.

"They think he just punched her," Bill said. "Nothing fancy. Just . . . *bam* . . . now you can't breathe or talk."

"Gratuitous, you think?" Tom asked.

"Maybe," Bill responded. "Hard to say."

"Maybe that's why she didn't resist," Tom said. "She was surprised and immediately incapacitated."

Bill nodded approvingly.

"Any residue of vomit in the area?" Chris asked.

"Not in the immediate vicinity, Chief. As you can imagine, they clean that place constantly. My pal at the Pasadena PD said that they found a pool of it clinging to a hedge about fifty feet away but it was filled with the remains of some gummi bears and Mexican carry out. Somehow I have trouble thinking about that as her last meal, especially the gummi bears. Tough old girl though. It was a hell of a blow and nothing broke when she was hit. He could have hit her back at her house. There's no remaining evidence, but my Pasadena guy said that her foyer was slathered with Lysol. (That was in Arcadia . . . where she lived.) But then again, maybe she was a neatnik . . . either way there's no evidence that they can use now."

"The scale was the real thing, right?" Tom asked.

"Yes, Lieutenant," Bill said, "in the sense that it was functional. It wasn't so much like the fancy scales that you see Justice carrying, but it was a real scale. The sword on the other hand..."

"What about it, Bill?" Chris asked.

"It was a toy—the kind of thing that kids playing *Romans and Barbarians* would like. It probably came with a plastic sheath originally, because there were little scuff marks along the edges, but if there *was* a sheath it had been discarded. It reminded me of a sword that my son's freshman roommate used to have. Whenever he was stressed out he would jerk it out of its sheath—which he always called its *scabbard*—and say, 'I'll take the adventure!' This one wasn't very adventurous, Chief. It looked like something from an after-Christmas sale bin. And this part wasn't reported to the press: it was super-glued to the judge's hand and fingers."

"Maybe he was mocking her," Tom said, "implying that she was reluctant or unable to dispense real justice, because the sword and scale had to be attached to her against her will."

"That's possible," Bill said. "Maybe a little too subtle though, but then, who knows? I'll say this, if he was trying to make her look *ridiculous*, he definitely succeeded."

"Tell me about her as a judge, Bill," Tom asked.

"That's what I asked my LAPD guy. Back in the day, before she joined the appellate court . . . apparently she was nothing out of the ordinary. Straight-laced. No bullshit. Generally pretty fair. She had a heavy docket, made the normal number of enemies, but didn't hit hard just for the fun of it. They're checking fresh parolees in the area, known acquaintances of people she sentenced or whose appeals she nixed . . . old threats, personal mail, landline and cell traffic . . . all the usual."

"What are they figuring for a motive?" Tom asked, "some kind of payback?"

"Yes," Bill said, "but so far they haven't come up with anything specific. They checked around in her personal life a little. No serious litigation. No fights with neighbors. She and her husband divorced over eight years ago. One child, a boy at Dartmouth. B+ average; anchors the relay team. Everybody on reasonably good terms. No man in her life as far as they could tell.

"Mostly just the work," Bill added. "I guess she raised yellow and pink roses and read French history books, but that's about it. They figure it has to be somebody who knew her. Probably knew her very well. It's not random violence when you bring all that crap with you. And the only people who knew her who were likely to want to kill her were people she sentenced."

"But you said she was always pretty fair," Tom said.

"Yes," Bill said. "I guess she could be a pain in the ass sometimes. She brought the lawyers up short whenever they needed it and she lectured the defendants a little more than most judges, but everybody figured she was just overcompensating a little. When she first hit the bench there weren't too many women trying major criminal cases. The lawyers tested her immediately. When one of them started to cross the line she told him to halt . . . *nicely*. When he crossed it a second time she gave him a ten minute tongue lashing, with the cameras rolling. Most of them didn't generally try for a third time."

"Couldn't blame her for that," Chris said.

"Tough babe," Bill said. "One other thing, Chief. I forgot to tell you . . . when the perp killed her..."

"Yes?" Chris said.

"Her bladder and bowels held. She didn't give him the satisfaction."

"I wonder if his will," Chris responded.

TWENTY-ONE

Harris felt something brush against his cheek and awoke with a jerk, swinging his hands wildly. "What the hell was that?" he said, bolting from Lorna's living room couch.

"You scared him, Earlon. You scared him," Lorna said.

"Scared who?

"Graciela's cat. *Loco*. He comes up here to visit sometimes and I give him a dish of milk and whatever leftovers I have around. He was asleep next to you on the couch. He just wanted to give you a kiss."

"I don't kiss any goddamned cats," he said. "I don't want them licking their asses and then licking my mouth. Tell that woman to keep her cat at home, let him lick *her* goddamned mouth."

"You two looked so cute there," Lorna said. "He was right up against you, laying against your side next to your arm."

Harris brushed off the couch with his hand. "I thought you were allergic to cats, Lorna. Why the hell would you want him here, leaving his hair and dandruff all over the damned place?"

"I'm not allergic to Loco, Earlon. He's sweet. He likes to visit me."

"Well, keep him off of *me*," Harris said. "I don't like to go to sleep, wondering who or what is going to wake me up."

"OK, Earlon, I understand," Lorna said. "I *do* have to talk to you about something else though." She stopped in the doorway between the kitchen and living room and stood there, wiping her damp hands on a soiled dish towel.

"What's that?"

"Where were you Monday night, Earlon?"

"This last Monday?"

"Yes."

"Who wants to know?" he asked.

"A man came by this morning when you were out. He told me that he was a policeman. I asked to see his badge and he showed it to me. He told me it was important, Earlon."

"What did you tell him, Lorna?"

"I told him you were here with me that night. I told him we had dinner, we watched television, and then we went to bed."

"Did he ask you anything else?"

"He asked how you felt now that you were out of prison—what you were doing, whether you had a job or not."

"What did you tell him, Lorna?"

"I thought to myself that that really wasn't any of his business, that he should talk to your parole officer if he wanted to know. But I didn't say that to him, Earlon. I told him that you felt great. That we were happy. That you were helping me. I told him how you cleaned my car and everything. I told him you were looking through the paper for jobs and that you were gonna do real well."

"Did he ask you anything else?"

"No. He just wrote down a few notes and left."

"You did the right thing, Lorna. That was wonderful, just perfect."

"Earlon?"

"Yes?"

"Where *were* you Monday night?"

"I was working, baby."

"Working? For who?"

"For me. I'll tell you all about it when the time is right."

"Earlon, I don't like this. It makes me scared," she said.

"Don't be," he said. "Everything is working out just as I planned that it would. We're right on schedule. I have a few jobs to do here and then we're going to start a new life somewhere. Just the two of us. You and me. Away from here all together."

"When, Earlon?"

"Soon, darlin'," he said, "very soon."

TWENTY-TWO

Hector had good news. One of the chop shop mechanics had rolled over on another pair of car thieves. "Amateurs, Lieutenant, but that doesn't mean that they can't successfully boost an occasional vehicle or do a lot of damage to some other ones trying."

"Kids?" Tom asked.

"Yes, and there's a serious upside."

"What's that?"

"We don't have to comb the streets looking for them. We just drive to their high school and take them out of shop class."

"I didn't know they still had shop class," Tom said.

"No, I just said that, but they probably *should*," Hector said. "Guys like this . . . they could be learning a trade rather than sleeping in the back of the room and dreaming about stealing Beemers and Camrys."

"Go get them, Hector."

"There's more good news, Lieutenant."

"I'm always ready for more, Hector."

"The same guy who put us onto the junior thieves..."

"Yes?"

"He also gave us the name of another black market parts dealer. They preferred to do business with Al Rosen because he paid top dollar, but in a pinch they'd go to this other guy—Jimmy Tessario."

"Go get him too," Tom said.

"Will do," Hector said. "I'm enjoying this."

Tom finished his cup of coffee and got a second. He was working one of the child molestation cases. The suspect's name was Kupher, pronounced *Koofer*. Bill Kupher. He had lawyered up immediately after his wife had pressed charges. The court had issued a temporary restraining order, keeping him away from his daughter, Ellen, but the lawyer was making a lot of noise, issuing multiple denials on behalf of his client and threatening legal action against practically everyone in Orange County.

What the lawyer and his client did *not* know was that the crime lab had come back with the results of a DNA test and the tests on a recent rape kit. Kupher was smart enough to use a condom but stupid enough to forget that he could leave hairs and epithelial tissue behind. In this case, he had left both. The tissue under Ellen's nails might not clinch the case, because the lawyer would plead that they were simply roughhousing or that she was clinging to dear old dad for protection, but the pubic hairs would be far more difficult to explain, particularly in the location where they had been found. The hair from his brush—some complete with bulbs—had been supplied by his wife Melissa; it provided the evidence for the DNA comparison.

With the arrest warrant in hand Tom finished his second cup of coffee, checked his service weapon, and walked out of the station to his cruiser. Twelve minutes later he was standing outside Kupher's office door.

"I'm sorry, but Mr. Kupher is with a client," his secretary said. The edge of fear in her voice suggested that she had been intimidated by him in the past.

"I won't be a minute," Tom said, and opened the door.

Kupher started to object when Tom badged him and informed him that he was under arrest for rape and sexual battery.

"I want to talk to my lawyer," he said. "This is outrageous."

At that point the client seemed to visibly shrink as he headed for the door.

"You have the right to remain silent…" Tom responded.

As he returned to the station Tom checked his watch. It was 11:47; he was scheduled to have dinner with Sarah and he still had a second arrest to make and a growing mound of forms to complete. He put Kupher in Bill Engle's hands and returned to his office. As he was walking down the hall he heard Engle say, "Ever been fingerprinted before, Sonny?"

Sarah had opted for something simple. "There's no need for candle light and cloth napkins," she said. "We'll both be tired and ready to take off our shoes and have a drink."

"Get out of our wet coats and into a dry martini?" Tom asked.

"Sounds perfect," she had said.

They met at his boat. He brought the food and she brought the wine.

"Two bottles?" Tom said. "That was very thoughtful."

"And not a minute too soon," Sarah added. "I brought Chardonnay and Chardonnay."

"I'll have Chardonnay," Tom said. "I would have anyway."

"I remembered you liked it," she said.

"Were they part of your recent trip to Temecula?"

"No, I got these at the wine store. They come highly recommended by Robert Parker. He probably won't be joining us though."

"Didn't invite him," Tom said. "I just wanted to see you."

"That's good," she said. "Do you mind if I take off my shoes?"

"Of course not."

"The white uniform doesn't freak you out, I hope."

"Not at all," he said. "The support hose don't really seem to be *you*, but I can get used to them."

"I can't," she said, slipping out of them as well.

"I got some sandwich stuff," he said, "and some salads of various kinds."

"How about something chocolate?"

"Fresh fruit," he said.

"Really?" she said, disappointed.

"No, I'm kidding. I got some brownies and some of those oversized chocolate chip cookies."

"My man," she said.

"I still have a good memory," he said.

"That's good," she said, unscrewing the cap from the first bottle. "Don't be frightened," she said. "It's still supposed to be very good. The metal cap is more reliable than cork. Slowly but surely the bottlers are moving toward it. Some people are still resisting. It's a cultural thing. We'll all eventually get over it."

"It's delicious," he said, tasting it.

"See?" she said. "I thought you'd like it." She leaned forward and kissed him. "I've missed you," she said.

"I've missed you too," he said. "A lot."

"Your boat looks different."

"It's just been cleaned up and polished," he said. "The cushions on the bench seats are new."

"No, it's something else," she said.

"The microwave in the galley is new."

"Maybe that's it. The old one was black plastic; this one's stainless steel. It looks good. You know, it's been awhile since I sat here with you."

"You always liked these domestic evenings."

"Yes," she said, "feeling the water under the boat . . . even when it's docked."

"I sleep better on the boat than I do in the house," he said. "I'm not sure why. It may be the motion of the water in the marina. I used to think it was the fresh air. Maybe it's both."

"I'll have to give it a try," she said.

"You're welcome any time," he answered.

TWENTY-THREE

His Bunker Hill office awash in files, faxes, printed emails, landline call slips, scribbled post-it notes, and foot-high piles of blue-backed legal cap, Marshall Stern dropped his attaché case on his couch, muttered something to himself about his day, and opened his credenza. The first option within reach was a half-empty bottle of Dewar's. He shoved it aside, found the twelve year-old single malt behind it, and poured four ounces into a short, square, crystal glass.

The phone rang and he let it ring. The answering machine kicked in. "You have reached the law offices of Chandler, Dayton, and Stern. Leave a message after the beep and we will return your call as quickly as possible." There was a long pause before the tone. It was his wife, Marilyn. "Marshall? Are you still there? If so, call me before you leave."

He clicked off the machine and grabbed the handset but not in time to catch her. When he dialed their number the line was busy. He tried a second time; it was still busy. She was catching up, working her way down a list, making a series of calls. "Screw it," he said, flipping through the messages on his desk while he sipped his scotch. He looked at his watch, thought the time was off, and tried to check it against the time on the pyramidal clock on his desk. A gift from his mother, he could never figure out how to read it. He picked up the phone and called for the time. "At the tone the time will be seven, ten . . . and thirty seconds." The battery in his watch *was* dead. "Great," he said in frustration, and went back to the credenza to replenish his drink.

The executive level of the parking podium—complete with purple signage—had nearly emptied by the time that Stern got off the elevator and made it to his BMW. He opened the door, put his brief case behind the driver's seat, slid into the driver's seat and unlocked the Club on the steering wheel. He tossed it into the back seat and heard it bounce off the corner of his brief case. Loosening his tie with his left hand, he ran his right hand over his leather cd pouch, thought a second but then decided to go with the radio instead and extended his finger toward the ignition button. Settling into his private world he sighed and thought about the drive home.

"Not just yet, Marsh."

The voice had so startled him that he was half ready to pee down his pants leg and half ready to come out of his car cursing and swinging. Then he felt the point of the knife enter the side of his neck.

"I wouldn't move that quickly if I were you, Marsh," the man said, "not unless you want to ooze blood all over that expensive upholstery and that pretty lawyer's suit. How much does something like that run now, Marsh? Three grand? I just traded off a suit I could've let you have a whole lot cheaper."

"Who are you?" Stern asked. "What the hell do you want?" The sweat was beading on his forehead and starting to circle around his lips. He wanted to turn but he felt the point pinking the side of his throat.

"You haven't changed at all; you're still a slow learner, aren't you Marsh?" the man said.

He took out a dirty kleenex, wiped away the drops of blood, and showed Stern the red stain. "That's real blood, Marsh," the man said, "and you know what they say—there's plenty more where that came from."

Stern turned his eyes and moved his head slightly. He could see the moustache and the dark glasses. "Do I know you?" he asked.

"Why, by now with all the cases that *you* try you must know just about everybody," the man said. "How about if you and I go for a little ride and talk about it? First, give me that key thing. I don't want you to get any stupid ideas while I walk around to the other side of your car."

"What is it you want?" Stern asked, removing the fob from his pocket and reluctantly handing it to him.

"Why Marsh, your hair's wet. You're sweating. You shouldn't be sweating, Marsh. It's cool out. It's actually seventy-one degrees. That's nearly perfect in most peoples' opinion. I just heard it on the radio. Hard to find out anything with that shitty stuff they call music now, but I was patient, Marsh. I waited and I waited and finally they announced it. Supposed to be nice tomorrow too. Maybe even all week. That's important, you know, Marsh—*patience*. I've got a lot of it. I didn't always, but I do now. It helps you, you know that? You've got to have patience. You can't get by without patience, Marsh."

"Who are you?" Stern asked, the fear and rage palpable again.

"Now Marsh, *you're* not being patient," the man said. "I thought we'd take a little drive, you know . . . talk . . . enjoy the scenery. Especially on a nice day like this. But you know what?"

"What?" Stern said curtly.

"You can't drive, Marsh. I smell liquor on you. And that's terrible. Here you are, an officer of the court, an upholder of the law, and you were about to drive drunk. Where's your sense of responsibility, Marsh? You could cause somebody to die. That would be terrible, wouldn't it?"

Stern didn't answer.

"Well, wouldn't it?" the man said, putting the knife point behind Stern's ear and twisting it slightly.

"Yes."

"You know, Marsh, if you can't hear very well with those ears I could cut them off for you," the man said, slowly drawing the knife blade through the channel between Stern's head and ear, tracing a thin red line. I'd do it real slow. First the left, then the right. Or I could do the right first and then the left. Your choice. You'd look kind of funny, but if they're not working now, who needs them? What do you say, Marsh?"

Stern sat silent, his legs beginning to shake involuntarily.

"No response? I guess I'll go ahead then…"

"No, don't. Don't do it. Don't cut me."

"Whatever you say, Marsh. I told you it was your choice. Now how about that ride?"

"O-K-K," he said, forcing the sounds through his lips.

"Much better, Marsh. Very good. Unfortunately, we still have a problem."

"What k-kind of problem?" he asked, putting his hands on his knees and trying to steady them.

"I don't *trust* you, Marsh. You're drunk and you might do something stupid while I'm trying to drive, so I'm going to have to tie you up. And Marsh, if you try to yell at somebody in another car—you know, to try to get their attention—I've still got my knife. And I think I can outrun most other cars with this one, so I'll have time to get away and pull into some very private place and punish you for disobeying me. Only I won't go for those ears, Marsh. I've got a much better idea. I'll go for the lips. Did you ever see anybody with their lips cut off, Marsh?"

"No," he said, the sweat pooling and running in a single track along his left temple.

"I have."

Tears formed in Stern's eyes. The man saw them instantly. "Don't you get the joke, Marsh?"

Stern didn't answer.

"*Earth to Marsh*," the man said, squeezing the edge of Stern's ear hard between his thumb and index finger and giving it a slight twist and pull.

"Wh-what joke?"

"If I cut off your lips you couldn't be a *mouthpiece* anymore. Don't you think that's funny?"

"N-n-o," Stern said.

"Well how are we going to have any fun if you don't have a sense of humor?"

"I d-don't know," Stern said.

"Then just be *patient*," the man said, "and you'll find out."

TWENTY-FOUR

As they passed the Western Avenue interchange, heading toward the coast on the Santa Monica freeway, Harris realized that Stern still didn't know who he was. He turned on the radio and got a Rice-a-Roni commercial. He started hitting buttons and picked up a rap music station. "What *is* that shit?" he asked.

"It's rap music," Stern answered.

"I know what they *call it*, asshole. You think I'm stupid? I want to know *what* it is."

"I don't know," Stern said, turning his head to free his neck from the damp sweat and blood on his collar.

Harris inadvertently hit the search button and the radio started cycling across the band. Confused, he started hitting the button repeatedly, trying to get the digital numbers to stop changing. Eventually he caught the oldies station, playing "Eye in the Sky" from Alan Parsons. He jerked back his hand, worried that he might change it again accidentally.

"Now *that* is music," he said.

Stern just nodded.

"They call it the Alan Parsons Project. Did you know that once upon a time Parsons was the sound engineer for Pink Floyd?"

"No."

"You *didn't*?"

Stern thought the man was wrong about that but he was too frightened to contradict him. When he didn't answer right away Harris turned to him. He was driving sixty miles an hour in heavy traffic.

"No, I didn't," he said.

"Well he was. A real genius. I don't know why they don't play more of the good stuff. They never play Styx or Kansas or ELO. I heard the Cars the other day. They didn't sound the same. Do you like the Cars?"

"I'm not sure I know who they are," Stern said.

"Shit," Harris said, disgusted. "How about REO?"

"ELO?"

"Not ELO. REO. REO Speedwagon."

"I sort of remember them."

"Shit," Harris said, mumbling something else under his breath.

The song ended and the deejay played a cut from *Cheap Trick, Live at Budokan.*

"All *right*," Harris said. "Do you know that that is the greatest live album of all time after *The Who, Live at Leeds?*"

"No, I didn't know that," Stern said.

"You really didn't?"

"No, I didn't."

"How in the hell could you afford a car with a radio like this and not know a single fucking thing about music?"

Stern didn't answer.

Harris shook his head in disbelief. "How do I make this louder?"

"Use that button on the left there," Stern said, lifting his tied hands and pointing vaguely.

Harris turned it up sharply and almost punctured Stern's eardrums. The dash was vibrating and the drivers of other cars were staring at Harris and shaking their heads.

"All *right*," Harris said. "What the hell are all those little metal things for?"

"They're the tuning devices for something called a graphic equalizer."

"I *like* it," Harris said, sliding the tuners and changing the sound. "In fact, Marsh, I *love* it. You did good . . . buying this car. Even if it cost you an arm and a leg." ('And maybe an ear or two?' Harris said, under his breath.) "Enjoying our little drive?"

"Yes," Stern lied, wondering desperately why he had been selected by some sadistic god to be tied up, helpless, and sitting beside this lunatic instead of home with his wife and his dinner and his scotch . . . especially his scotch.

When they came to the end of the Santa Monica freeway, Harris headed north on the Pacific Coast Highway.

"Are you going to tell me who you are?" Stern asked.

"You know what your *problem* is, Marsh? I can tell you. You've got way too many clients. Don't you know you're in a service occupation? You should remember people. That's an important part of your job. You're there to help the people who hire you, not just parade around in your expensive suits and collect your six-figure fees."

"*You* were one of my clients? When? What were you accused of?"

"Hard to remember, huh Marsh? Hey, look at the beach. The ocean looks all silvery with the sky still lit up. I think this is my favorite time of day and my very favorite beach. I really admire those guys . . . They work so hard to keep it clean. They've got those big machines out there with the stuff that looks like metal fencing attached . . . you know, to drag the sand. They try to keep the beach clear of trash and junk, Marsh. I think that's very nice, don't you agree?"

"Y-yes."

"People don't want to go to the beach and see dog shit and used rubbers all over the place. It's nice to clean it like that. Of course sometimes they run over drunks or people who fall asleep and don't see them coming. Chews 'em up; it's not pretty, Marsh. A lot of times they don't recover. That's a pity . . . but hell, it's not the city's fault, is it?"

"I d-don't know," Stern said.

"You don't know? You *really* don't? Why not? Aren't you supposed to be a lawyer, Marsh? If you don't know about liability and shit, what the hell good are you? What do you think your clients are paying you for, Marsh?"

"The case law's not real straightforward."

"The . . . case . . . law's . . . not . . . real . . . *straightforward?*"

"N-n-o."

"That's no big surprise, is it, Marsh? That's the *whole fucking point.* That way you lawyers can defend either side. Charge them both, right Marsh? And if you lose, it's not as if you were stupid or something. It's just that the case law's not . . . what did you call it?"

"Straightforward."

"Right. Well, Marsh, I've got some very good news for you. You don't have to worry about that sort of thing with me. Not even a little bit. I'm *very* straightforward. I know just what I have to do and I *do* it. I pride myself on that."

"Where are we g-going?"

"Jesus Christ. We're driving north on the Pacific Coast Highway, Marsh. How long have you lived in southern California? You ought to at least know *that.*"

"No, I m-mean, what's our destination?"

"You're worried that you're being kidnapped, aren't you, Marsh?"

Stern didn't answer.

"You're worried that I'm going to take you someplace and get out my knife and do things that will be very unpleasant, things that will make you scream, aren't you, Marsh?"

Again he was silent.

"Well don't worry," Harris said. "It's like I told you. This is just a little outing. It's just for you and me and it won't take all that long. I thought we'd just go get a little exercise. You know—take a little jog, stretch our legs a little. Act like real Californians, huh? What do they say, Marsh—No Pain, No Gain? I like that; don't you? It's not my favorite, though. I've got my own saying. I think it's better. Look here..."

Harris took a piece of paper from his shirt pocket and put it on Stern's leg. His voice deepened and his tone turned ugly and dictatorial. "Read it, Marsh. Read it out loud so we can both hear it."

Stern read it slowly.

Let us ask once more: in what sense could pain constitute repayment of a debt? In the sense that to make someone suffer was a supreme pleasure.

"Isn't that good?"

"I don't know."

"You don't *know*? That's Loyal, Marsh."

"What d-do you mean? Who is Loyal?"

"Shit, Marsh, you don't know who Loyal is? How can you be so fucking ignorant and still get clients? You've got a car like this and an expensive suit and you don't know who Loyal is? How do you survive in this world, Marsh?"

"Is that what you want to d-do, make people suffer? That won't solve anything. What are you really d-doing here? What d-do you want from me?"

"Can't you read either, Marsh? Look. This is about the repayment of a debt. Read the statement. Read Loyal. Read what he tells you."

Harris was silent until he turned off the highway and onto Topanga Canyon Boulevard. "Check it out, Marsh. They call it a boulevard but it sure as hell doesn't look like a boulevard, does it?"

"N-no."

"It's like a mountain road back into history. Ten miles too. All mountains and ravines, and crevices. Beautiful. See deer here all the time. Owls too. Not many cars though. I can't figure out why when it's so beautiful. Nice shortcut to the Valley too."

Harris drove for three miles, passed a garden store that was closed, drove another four miles and then turned left up into a stand of Ponderosa Pine that turned the twilight to near darkness.

"Look at this, Marsh. Privacy, huh? This is where my vehicle's parked. I think you're going to feel right at home with it. After we have our jog

I'll leave you here with it. I need to borrow your car for a little while, but don't worry, you can have mine. Look, it's right up there."

Harris drove a few hundred feet and stopped behind a white truck with stripes and lettering that Stern couldn't quite make out. "Look, Marsh," Harris said, clicking on the bright lights.

"It's an ambulance," Stern said, the tremble in his voice growing with each word.

"It sure is. Nice one too. You know why the words are printed backwards on the front of it?"

"S-so the cars in front can read it in their rear-vision mirrors."

"Well god-damn. Score one for Marsh. He finally got a question right. I'm proud of you, Marsh. You're not as ignorant as I thought you were. Maybe there's still some hope for you. Come on now. It's time to exercise."

"Now the rules are real simple," Harris said. "I don't want you to just run away on me, so I'm going to have to wrap a piece of rope around your neck and attach it to the back of the ambulance. Then I'm going to untie your legs. That will feel good. They're probably getting a little numb on you by now and you're going to need them. You can jump up and down a little and loosen them up. The warm-up is very important, Marsh. *Every* fitness expert will tell you that. Then when you're all ready I'll get in the car and drive and you'll jog. Actually you might have to run a little too. Now I want you to be real careful. The road is old and it has a lot of ruts and rocks. If you should happen to fall you'd be dragged for awhile until I noticed what had happened, because I can't look in the rear-vision mirror all the time; I have to watch where I'm going. You can understand *that*. I'm a careful driver, Marsh, not a person who would drive drunk, like *somebody* we know. Now, like I said, you be careful or you might trip and fall and get all scraped up. It'd be like those drunks in the sand that get caught up in the metalwork and get dragged up and down the beach. We don't want that now, do we?"

Stern didn't answer. His body was starting to shake.

"Do we?"

"N-n-no."

"Of course we don't. Now, if your heart's in real good shape this will be nice exercise for you. I sure hope it is, don't you Marsh?"

"Y-y-yes."

"Well let's get started then. I'll keep my window open so we can talk while you jog. Just so you know, the road's only two and a half miles long, but I'm afraid it's all uphill."

Stern fell twice in the first quarter mile. His clothes were torn and his face was bloodied and pocked with dirt and gravel. The second time his face struck an exposed scrub pine root; as he struggled to his feet he tore the skin from his hands and wrists. He yelled out, begging Harris to stop and instead Harris gunned the ambulance, jerking him to the ground. He leaned out the window and told him if he never learned anything else in his life he should learn not to beg. "It always ends up being harder when you beg," Harris said. "Your clients all had to learn that lesson; it's the first lesson they learned, Marsh. Trust me on this. *I* learned it." He read something to Stern from his Loyal notes but Stern couldn't hear or understand it. His heart was pounding and his breath was gone. He reached out to the ambulance's bumper and used it to help get to his feet, just as Harris said, "OK, here we go." Stern lasted another 200 yards, stumbling and hurtling, and trying desperately to keep from falling. "How you doing back there, Marsh?" Harris yelled, just as he accelerated and Stern fell to the ground, his left arm and chest exploding in pain as his face hit the dirt and he was dragged—unconscious—another twenty yards. Harris got out, checked his pulse, and then removed the rope from his hands and neck. He took one of Stern's business cards from his wallet, stretched out Stern's right arm toward the back of the ambulance, and put the business card between his thumb and index finger. Then he walked back down the road, got in Stern's BMW, and pulled back onto

Topanga Canyon Boulevard. His station was playing Queen's "Bohemian Rhapsody." He adjusted the graphic equalizer.

"I love *that*," he said, turning the volume up another notch and hitting the accelerator.

TWENTY-FIVE

"Hell of a week for the law," Bill Engle said. "First the *Justice Now* display in Pasadena, then we lose two cops on a playground in Anaheim, trying to play referee in a Crips/Bloods steel-cage match; now some hikers find a lawyer with a broken ticker, stretched out behind a stolen ambulance on a deserted road in Topanga Canyon."

"What have they got on that so far?" Chris asked. "I heard a brief report on it on the morning news."

"It really is an ugly one, Chief. The victim had rope burns on both his neck and wrists. It looks like the perp forced him to keep running up this steep, rocky hill behind the vehicle. There were tread marks with footprints in between. They match the tires on the ambulance and the shoes on the vic. If the guy fell, he was dragged—sometimes a long way. They found blood smears and some tissue at three different points; it wasn't pretty at all. Eventually the vic got lucky and his heart gave out. At that point the perp untied him and stretched his body out behind the ambulance. Then, to be cute he put the poor bastard's business card in his hand—you know, like he was trying to catch the body wagon to offer his services but couldn't quite make it there in time."

"Wonderful," Chris said. "Anything solid—anything at all that they could work with?"

"Not much yet, Chief," Bill said. "And talk about adding insult to injury—after killing the guy it looks like the son-of-a-bitch took his car and drove it over the mountain for a joy ride."

"Where'd they find it?"

"Sherman Oaks. On a vacant lot on Ventura—where the *Hungry Tiger* restaurant used to be."

"There was a building there . . . they did custom car upholstery, I think. I haven't been around there for a long time."

"Right, Chief. They tore that down. About six months ago, I think."

"Any physical evidence?"

"Some dirt on the driver's side floor of the car matching the dirt on the road in the canyon where the body was found. No big surprise there. The only real lead they could come up with was a couple of strands of artificial hair."

"You mean like from a wig or something?"

"Probably not. Too short for that and too curly. They're thinking maybe theatrical makeup—a phony goatee or moustache. Maybe one of those soul patch thingies."

"So they figure the lawyer knew the guy but for some reason or other the guy didn't want to be recognized."

"Right," Engle said. "He may also have been throwing a curve to confuse any possible witnesses. He and the victim had to know each other, Chief. Who else would go to all that trouble if it wasn't something personal?"

"Somebody who *really* hated lawyers," one of the uniforms said.

"Maybe," Engle said, skeptically, "but I doubt it. There's another odd wrinkle too."

"What's that, Bill?" Chris asked.

"The lawyer had 320 bucks in his pocket and the killer never touched it. He also parked the guy's Beemer and just walked away. It was a 740i, Chief. That car is at the top of every local car thief's wet dream list, so money didn't figure in this at all. But get this—the one thing he *did* try to take was the guy's car radio, which he couldn't get out of the dash."

"The *radio*?"

"Yeah. The car lists for something like 92K and the guy goes for the radio. He should take home the gold loving cup for Dumbass of the Year."

"Keep me posted, Bill," Chris said. "I want to know about anything that develops on this case and anything that could possibly be related to it—*anything*. We're not that far away, after all. If the perp suddenly develops an urge to drive south I want to be ready for him."

"You got it, Chief," Bill said.

Chris opened his desk drawer and took out the lunch he had brought in the day before. The tuna was way past its prime and he tossed it in the trash. He set the bag of chips on top of his desk and rooted around in the bag for a piece of fruit. He found an apple, but the moment he bit into it his phone rang. It was the desk sergeant.

"What is it, Norb?" he asked.

"A strange one, Chief," the sergeant said.

"Why strange?"

"They got a call at the LAPD. Somebody there said they should bounce it to you, which they did."

"Yes?"

"I've got the guy on the line. He said he's trying to reach Detective Frank Brierly, Chief; I thought you might want to take it."

"OK, Norb," Chris said.

The sergeant bounced the call.

"This is Chief Dietrich speaking," he said. "How can I help you?"

"I'm trying to reach Detective Frank Brierly," the voice said.

"Are you a friend?" Chris asked.

"Yes, I am," the man said, "an old friend. My name's Jim Sloane."

"I'm sorry to have to tell you this, Mr. Sloane," Chris said, "but Frank Brierly died seven years ago."

"Oh no," the man said. He sounded confused and distraught.

"We were partners," Chris said. "Back when I was with the LAPD. No one misses him more than I do."

"Can I ask how he died?" the man said.

"It was a shootout," Chris said. "Drug-related. Unfortunately, nothing out of the ordinary. We lost Frank, a patrolman, and a bystander—a seven year-old boy."

"Thanks for telling me, Chief Dietrich," the man said and then suddenly hung up. Chris got up, walked out to the kitchenette, wiped a coffee stain from the Formica counter and poured himself a fresh cup. When he passed by, the desk sergeant thanked him for handling the call.

"Jesus, Chief, we haven't gotten a call about your old partner for years. And that was from some military guy who'd been stationed in Korea during the time when the Detective went down."

"It's very strange, Norb," Chris said. "*Very* strange. And the guy didn't say that much. He asked how Frank died; I told him and that was that."

"He hung up?"

"Yes. He just hung up."

TWENTY-SIX

Tom came into the office at 7:15 the next morning and found a note on his desk to see Chris. He held off on his first cup of coffee and went directly to Dietrich's office.

"What can I do for you, Chief?"

"Sit down, Tom," Chris said. "It's sort of a private matter."

"Yes…?"

"I got a call from the mayor; he wants us to look into something. Something that requires discretion, he said. He described it and I told him I'd send you, that you were my best man for something like this and that you could definitely be discreet."

"What is it, Chief?"

"Well, the thing is . . . the mayor owns some property in Burbank. He leases it to a distributor who operates under the name of *West Coast Novelty and Toy*. When the lessee—a guy by the name of Charles Powers—signed the lease he used his own name, not the corporate name, which the mayor hadn't yet heard; he told the mayor that he would be using the property to distribute *retail items*. The mayor probably should have asked some more questions at that point. The thing is, he didn't. When he started getting his rent checks they were under the corporate name rather than the personal name of the lessee. Now he's got some concerns…"

"He's thinking this Powers guy may be distributing something illegal?"

"Not so much illegal as embarrassing—sex toys, maybe. Something he wouldn't want to be associated with in the case of a scandal or problem."

"I can understand how he feels," Tom said. "The O.C. is pretty conservative. They wouldn't elect somebody who hangs out with Larry Flynt's readers as the mayor of one of their most upscale communities."

"The operation is probably harmless," Chris said, "but the mayor would feel a whole lot more comfortable if somebody would check them out. I know this isn't the sort of thing you signed on for when you got your lieutenant's shield, but it's something you could handle quietly and well."

"And the mayor doesn't want anyone from L.A. law enforcement to go in..."

"No. It's like . . . if you can't take No for an answer, don't ask. He doesn't want the lessee spooked on the one hand and he doesn't want any possible leaks to the local press."

"So he doesn't want me flashing my shield."

"No. He wants us to check them out without revealing that we're part of law enforcement."

"I don't think that's illegal," Tom said.

"No, it's not," Chris said. "It's just a little . . . let's say . . . out of the ordinary."

"It might actually be fun," Tom said. "Do you have an address, Chief?"

"Yes, I do, Tom. Here . . . and thanks."

Tom cleared some paper work, grabbed a cup of coffee, and checked Mapquest and Google Earth. The rental building was near what the Chambers of Commerce in search of an advertising trifecta call the Burbank-Glendale-Pasadena Airport. It was a 10,000 square foot box bolted to a concrete slab and surrounded by carbon-copy structures in identical shades of Navy-surplus gray. The man he was looking for, Charles Powers, had a minimalist website; he listed himself as the company president and chief executive officer.

Tom swung by his house, checked his available wardrobe and

selected a simple shirt, grey poplin work jacket and black cotton slacks. He rooted around in his kitchen drawer and found a collection of keys, which he hung from his right front belt loop. Then he got on the **5** and headed north. The traffic was dense but moving. He covered the 60+ miles in an hour and thirty-five minutes. Not bad for that time of the morning. He checked the address, slalomed between the metal boxes in the industrial park and found the number on the post-it note that Chris had given him. He parked his unmarked car away from clear lines of sight and knocked on the black metal door. It contained nothing but a lock and a peep hole.

When the door opened he was greeted with a simple "Yeah?" from a guy in a soiled purple tee shirt that read: **You Show Me Yours and I'll Show You Mine**. He didn't smell very good.

"I'm here to see Charlie Powers," Tom said.

"He know you?" the man asked, reaching under the edge of his tee shirt with his right hand and picking at something on his belly.

"Yes."

"He know you're coming?" Now he was picking at the other side with his left hand.

"Do I look like somebody who would drive 67 miles to Burbank and 67 miles back from it without checking first?" Tom responded.

"This way…" he said.

They walked past some splintered skids piled high with cardboard cartons. The boxes were marked with numbers but the contents weren't identified. Tom scanned the rooms and open areas that he could see but didn't notice anything out of the ordinary. Everything appeared to be clean and in good order.

"He's back there," the guy said, picking at his seat now with his right hand and pointing with his left. Tom could see a glass-enclosed office on the north wall of the building. Powers was on the phone as Tom approached the door. He was pacing. Powers caught Tom's eye and gestured to him to come in.

"Sit down," he said, holding his hand over the phone. "I'll be done here in a second or two."

Tom said thanks and sat down in a green plastic chair with a pitted chrome frame. The office was neat and well organized but Charlie hadn't invested any of *West Coast Novelty and Toy's* hard-earned money in frills. He had an *HP* computer with a blistered *RadioShack* service sticker on the side and an adding machine with a long steel handle that could have drawn a crowd of curiosity seekers at the **Smithsonian**. His stained, cardboard coffee cup looked as if it was long overdue for the recyling bin. Powers was holding a ballpoint between his thumb and index finger and tapping impatiently as he spoke.

"Listen Rollie," he said, "I'm trying to be sympathetic and I *do* understand your problems, but I've got a large operation to run here and a family that's addicted to food. Yes . . . I realize that. The simple fact is that if New York is unable to deliver, I'll just have to say my good-byes and take my business elsewhere. It's real clear, Rollie. I've got to have product and it's got to be right. Half the stuff you sent last Tuesday is on its way back . . . yeah . . . right . . . no, it's all wrong, Rollie . . . yeah, I understand . . . read the contract, Rollie. OK, listen. I'll give you an example. Take the men's briefs. I ordered twenty gross of the simulated leopard skin and I specified the sizes I wanted. One of the guys in your factory goofed up and printed *small, medium,* and *large* on the labels. Rollie, nobody who shops for $2.95 leopard skin shorts will buy *small*. I asked for *he-man, real-man,* and *super-man* and I specified that the waist sizes should be listed under the titles in small print . . . no, I'm not taking them at a discount, Rollie. Your printer screwed up, so he's got to make it right. And I want them in seventy-two hours, Rollie. Now . . . the fake virility pills. I ordered eighty gross in four flavors: cherry, strawberry, chocolate, and piña colada. I got sixty gross of blueberry and twenty gross of butterscotch. You like blueberry candy, Rollie? They're on their way back to New York . . . what? . . . no, the X-ray specs are fine . . . yeah, I think the whoopee cushions are OK too. I've got to check them a second time, but I think they're OK. You can't be too careful with those things, Rollie. If it's too hot they'll melt and if there isn't enough powder inside, the fill flaps stick together and you have a devil of a time blowing them up . . . yeah, I think these survived . . . no, I *didn't* get the *Twister* games. Where in the world are they? You still owe me two hundred units, Rollie. We talked about this last month, remember?" He put his hand over the phone again and said, "I'm sorry…"

Tom nodded sympathetically.

"Forget all that Batman stuff, Rollie; the market's glutted. I still need the Nixon masks though, but hold the rubber masks of Margaret Thatcher. My customers don't have the slightest clue who she is . . . what? . . . oh, right . . . yeah, the little highball jock straps . . . we can always use those . . . and the dribble glasses and the pens with the swimsuit models . . . I can't keep those in stock. OK? Do we understand one another? Fine . . . thanks . . . I know you're doing your best. You just have to see it from my side. No product, no business. No business for me, less business for you. Right…"

He hung up and turned to Tom. "It's always something, isn't it?"

"You can say that again," Tom answered. "I'm Jerry Dillard."

"Charlie Powers. Have we met?"

"No, actually, we haven't. I was given your name by a friend. I've just got a quick question."

He looked a little suspicious. "Yes?"

"You see, I'm looking to rent some space and this guy Malkin—I guess he's actually the mayor of some beach community in Orange County—has a building in Victorville. For years I've been renting from this Arab in Long Beach, who suddenly starts jerking me around on the lease renewal. I talked to Malkin's rental agent, told him I wanted out of my present place, but that I would absolutely not sit still for any bullshit. He told me Malkin is strictly straight arrow and then he gave me your name, told me that you've worked with him, and that you'd give me an honest answer. So that's why I'm here. What kind of a landlord is this guy?"

"Tops," Powers said, relieved at being asked an easy question. "Absolutely. A deal is a deal with hizzoner. I never abuse the property and he never hassles me. Hell, he's even tried to help me out. I was getting royally screwed on the insurance I carry on my inventory here. This ripoff artist said we were high risk and that our premiums were gonna double. Hell, this place is tighter than a toad's ass. I mentioned it to the mayor and he recommended I call a pal of his at *State Farm*. I thought it was very nice of him. I called the guy, he called the regional manager and, to make a long story short, they came up with a very fair price. I think the broker is one of the mayor's supporters or something, a guy named Wrightson. You know politicians; they know everybody. Anyway we shook hands on the deal and I'm a happy camper."

"Thanks a lot," Tom said. "I appreciate your taking the time to talk to me. This was very helpful."

"Not a problem."

As Tom walked to the door, he said, "So you mostly distribute party items, that kind of thing..."

"Lava lamps," he said, smiling. "They're *huge* again. That's my biggest seller. I move a lot of Halloween masks too, except . . . it's funny . . . in L.A. they sell all year round."

"They shook the nuts from the trees and they all rolled to the west coast," Tom said.

"Hey, it puts food on my table," Powers said. "Anyway, like I said, you won't go wrong with the mayor. He's all right."

Tom thanked Powers again for taking the time to talk to him, drove a block and a half to a *Texaco* station that also rented *U-Haul* trucks, bought a large Pepsi, savored the sunshine for a minute or two and called Chris. "Not to worry, Chief," he said. "The company's legit."

"What do they sell, Tom?" he asked.

"Well, it's not like they're selling bibles or Corning ware, Chief, but they're selling actual toys and novelties—the kind you can buy in any mall—plastic ice cubes with flies, lava lamps, trick dice, leopard skin underwear, Magic 8 Balls . . . that kind of stuff."

"I had one of those Magic 8 Balls," Chris said. "When I was 10 my friends and I could amuse ourselves for hours with that thing."

"They're still selling, Chief."

"How about the lessee?"

"I don't see any problems. It's not like he's a diamond or wine merchant, but he's an honest businessman and his operation's solid. Everything was clean; he's taking good care of the mayor's property. He also had a lot of nice things to say about him. He said he helped put him in contact with an insurance broker who gave him a fair deal. He's got nothing but praise for the mayor."

"I'll pass that along. You know politicians, Tom. Campaign contributions and fulsome praise are their mother's milk."

"Right. I doubt that the guy who's leasing his property votes in Laguna, but I'm sure that the mayor'll be happy to learn that he's loved."

"Thanks for handling this one, Tom."

"No problem, Chief. I almost felt as if I was playing hooky. It's nice to see what honest people spend their day doing."

Chris laughed. "I'll see you when you get here. Meanwhile I'll call the mayor and make his day."

Tom got back in his car and headed toward the Golden State. He reached in his glove compartment, pulled out his iPod touch, found *Steely Dan's* "Countdown to Ecstasy," and turned on "My Old School". 'This isn't bad at all,' he thought to himself. 'Nobody shooting at me. A nice drive in the sun. Keeping the politicians in our corner but not breaking any laws in the process. Not bad. Not bad at all.'

TWENTY-SEVEN

Bill Engle came into Chris's office with a stack of notes and forms. He handled the miscellaneous sizes for miscellaneous purposes the way a skilled mechanic handles a micrometer or a torque wrench. He still gave off the sense of early-morning eagerness, despite the fact that he was in his late 40's and had deeper lines under his eyes than the sergeant's stripes he wore on his sleeves. He put the stacked-and-sorted forms in an efficient configuration on the table next to Chris's desk and put the notes in his in-box. "Nothing pressing, Chief. How about a refill on your coffee? I'm getting some."

"Thanks, Bill," Chris said. When Engle returned he said, "Fresh too. How often can you say that?"

Chris smiled.

"I've also got an update on the dead judge in Pasadena and the dead lawyer in Topanga Canyon."

"Good," Chris said.

"I wish I had more. You already knew about Judge Garretson. We talked about her and her reputation."

"Right," Chris said.

"The name of the murdered lawyer was Marshall Stern. Eight years in private practice, the last four very successful. Partnership in a prominent firm, house in Westwood, mid six figure take-home, plus the juicy Christmas split—the standard, sweet deal. Before that he was working in the public defender's office."

"I saw him around a few times," Chris said, "but I didn't have much to do with him when he was part of the public defender's crew. Frank was senior to me and when we had to go to court they usually tapped him to testify."

"Right. Anyway, the Pasadena PD and LAPD are working on the theory that the cases are related, so they tried to check his list of clients against the judge's list of defendants and the state's list of recent parolees. The numbers are a real problem. Judge Garretson tried thousands of cases and Marshall Stern was involved in a serious proportion of them. Some days in court they must have looked like a pair of subway workers, operating a turnstile, he hurrying them in and she hurrying them out, he pleading them down and she clearing the aisles for the next day's set. He used to seek out more than his share of cases too, especially the ones he found interesting. Most public defenders try to pare back their caseload so they can spend more time on less clients and raise their batting average. Not Stern. He was always ready for more, especially the bizarre stuff—the kind of perps and crimes the papers like. He used to say that the public defender's office was like an inner-city emergency room on a Saturday night and he was like a senior resident trying to learn *everything* he could as *fast* as he could."

"Before he practiced on real patients—the ones with the complicated business dealings and bulging check books," Chris added.

"Exactly. Now the question is—how are they going to work through all this? After the judge was killed they did a quick and dirty spot check of very recent parolees from California institutions who are now living in the metropolitan area. They came up with a list of names of people whom she had sentenced. Each of them (including those who had been represented at one time or another by Marshall Stern) had an alibi for the time of her death."

"But that list is much too short," Chris said.

"That's what I'm getting at Chief," Engle said. "They could easily be looking for a repeater. He might have been tried a half-dozen times before different judges and taken a half-dozen falls for different crimes.

He might whack another judge a week from now and two more lawyers next month. Maybe he isn't a recent parolee; maybe he's been spending his last months or years planning his revenge party. Maybe he's been in prison out of state and is just getting around to paying them a visit or maybe he's still in jail and has hired somebody to do the jobs for him, while he sits with a rock-solid alibi. The only systematic way to go about this is to work from a list that includes (for now) all of the people Judge Garretson tried and all of the people Marshall Stern defended. The last possibility—a guy still in jail—might be a likely one, since the murders look like they were done by a wingnut; on the other hand the whole point could be to get them to focus on the M.O. rather than on the identity of the actual perp. They could do this piecemeal, of course, and hope that they'll get lucky, but I don't like the odds there. The M.O.'s are too weird and the guy seems to be very smart, at least as far as escaping from the scenes and leaving minimal evidence behind goes. What I'm saying is I think there's a good likelihood that they're being jerked around and that they've got to proceed logically and systematically and resist the temptation to start running in all directions."

"How many of the recent parolees that they checked after the judge's death were also defended by Stern?"

"A little over a dozen," Engle said, "but when they say *recent* they mean in the last 180 days."

"And you said that they all had alibis?"

"Yes, but they haven't checked yet to see if they had alibis for the time of the lawyer's death too."

"They should," Chris said. "If that doesn't turn anything, they should start sifting through the files of her defendants and his clients. If it was me I'd start with people who *have* been paroled and have been out, say, twelve months. Look for possibles. Find out if any of them mouthed off, making threats. See who had the opportunity. You don't have to worry about motive. They've all got that."

"And if that didn't work you'd go back another six months on the parolees. Whatever it took."

"Exactly," Chris said, "and you can't figure that because somebody claims to have an alibi that he actually *does*. You've got to really press them and you've got to press the people who are alibiing them."

"Right," Engle said. "Anyway, Chief, if and when I hear anything more I'll let you know."

"Thanks, Bill," Chris said, returning to his paper work. He thought about his days in the LAPD. The *crazy times* he called them. Exhilarating. Interesting. Never dull. But always crazy.

Tom arrived forty-five minutes later. "I talked to the mayor," Chris said. "He's bouncing off the walls with joy. I think he realized that he screwed up big time in not checking on the business that was being conducted on *his* property. Now it's like he's gotten a Get-Out-Of-Jail-Free card. No harm. No foul. Plus the guy who's renting from him loves him."

"Makes for a nice Wednesday," Tom said.

"He said he'd send us some Angels tickets," Chris said. "He realized that it was a little off-the-books and he wanted us to know how much he appreciated it."

"That's nice," Tom said. "The Angels are looking pretty good this year, at least so far."

"My father would say 'Enjoy it while you can.'"

"So would mine," Tom said.

"By the way, great job on the vehicle theft cases. I don't think this will close down all of the car operations in Orange County, but you put a serious dent in the problem."

"Carl's leads were terrific and Hector helped a lot," Tom said. "He's got an excellent sixth sense for that kind of crime. One or two wrong steps in his own life and he could have been doing that sort of thing himself. He's got a great feel for it."

"I agree," Chris said.

"The uniforms had fun too. They don't usually have that much excitement in a month."

"It's not all bad for them though…" Chris said. "When you're checking on the litterers down on the beach you think, hell, I was made to crack big-time cases, not brace kids and little old ladies, but when you actually deal with the ugly stuff . . . deal with it constantly, the way that Frank Brierly and I did . . . well, you get your fill pretty quickly.

"Those cases in Pasadena and Topanga Canyon . . . we saw blood like that all the time. I can't say that the killers were always that loopy and creative, but they were certainly that violent. When you regularly see the results of a shotgun or magnum at close range and smell decomp as often as you smell perfume . . . the litter at the beach is suddenly a lot more inviting.

"Anyway . . . I didn't mean to run on like that. Thanks again, Tom, and give Hector another attaboy. I'll call Carl and tell him how much we appreciate his work. By the way, the various O.C. departments are thinking about putting together another anti-gang task force; that could be right up Hector's alley. In the meantime I've got a quickie for him."

TWENTY-EIGHT

"I don't really like that, Earlon," Lorna said. "I know it's important to you, but to me it's just . . . it's just creepy."

"But it makes the sex so much better," Harris said. "When are you going to understand that?"

"It doesn't make it better for me, Earlon, and I wish that you cared a little more about me and not so much about yourself."

"It's not like I asked *you* to read, Lorna. We've been all through that."

"When you're loving somebody you should be thinking about them, Earlon, not reading some sayings from your guide."

"Don't you understand that it helps me?" he said. "Don't you understand that it makes me feel more . . . real? It's almost like electricity going through me. You haven't been complaining about the sex, Lorna. You've got to admit it's been good."

"The sex isn't as important as being close to you, Earlon, and when you're reading it's as if there's somebody else there with us. Somebody I don't know and don't understand. It scares me, Earlon, and you shouldn't want somebody that you care about to be scared."

"I think you make too much of it," he said. "Different strokes for different folks, Lorna. We're not all the same. Some of us like to do things that other people don't understand. It's not that big of a deal; at least it shouldn't be to you."

"But Earlon, I see you sitting there sometimes, reading those notes, making comments with your pencil or scratching things out . . . it's like you're totally absorbed. It's like he has some kind of a spell on you. It doesn't seem healthy. It doesn't seem healthy at all."

"That's because you're not a spiritual person, Lorna. You sit in that store all day, selling wooden forks and spoons and all that other kitchen shit . . . don't you understand that wanting and buying that stuff is all just . . . materialistic? You've got to lift up your thoughts, think about something bigger and more important. That makes *you* more important too, don't you see that?"

"You call yourself spiritual, Earlon? Why? Because you read those notes? When was the last time you even went inside a church?"

"Church doesn't have anything to do with spiritual," he said. "That's all just a scam. It's a racket, a way to get your money. You think if Jesus was here right now He'd be going to church? I'll tell you what He'd be doing; He'd be getting out that whip of His and driving those money changers out into the street. He wouldn't be in no damned church."

"Well, He wouldn't be reading that stuff about making people suffer and taking pleasure in it, settling debts by causing pain. He wouldn't be reading *that*, Earlon."

"Give me your damned car keys," Harris said, getting out of bed and getting dressed. "I'm not gonna sit around here and listen to that kind of shit."

"They're on the dresser. And don't bother coming back if you're going to act like that and talk to me like that," she said.

"I just may not," he said. "You can go back to your damned Roy. I bet he's very spiritual. Probably says a couple prayers every time he gets you to spread your legs for him."

"Earlon, that's terrible to say something like that."

"Is it? It's the goddamned truth and you know it. That's all he ever wanted from you. I try to introduce you to something more important and what do I get for it?"

She was about to respond when he grabbed his jacket off the couch, opened the door and stormed out, slamming it behind him.

Hector was working his way through the club. The woman who had filed the complaint with the LBPD—Carla Mirada—was returning to her table from the bar, balancing drinks for herself and her girlfriends. She had stopped short of accusing the man of sexual battery but she had said that he was "in her face" and that he had "crossed the line," talking to her in an offensive way and not leaving when she had asked him to.

His name was Rudy Montalban; he referred to himself as the Rude Man. For the previous three nights he had bothered Carla and her friends. They put up with it at first, but after the third time Carla filed the complaint. She had been told that the LBPD would check it out.

Montalban was short, but thick and fit. Hector had a mug shot of him, taken when he was arrested for disorderly conduct—a bar confrontation that had stopped just short of serious violence. He had spent the night in jail and was issued a warning from the judge that the punishment would increase significantly the next time he was seen in court.

"A real jerk," Officer Bill Napier said. "It was all I could do to keep from taking out my nightstick and going to work on his mouth. He thinks he's God's gift to women and when they look at him as if he smells like spoiled yogurt he gets abusive."

Hector hadn't seen him yet. Earlier he had discreetly identified himself to Carla when she was on her way to the ladies' room. Now he was moving through the crowd, nursing his second ginger ale. Fifteen minutes later, Montalban entered the bar.

He downed two shots of Cuervo Gold and walked away from the bar carrying a third. The glass was filled to the top and he was carrying it carefully. Surveying the room, he saw Carla with her friends at a distant table and began to make his way toward them. Hector saw him and checked the mug shot. Montalban had added a goatee and soul patch since the picture was taken. Hector followed him.

"So," Montalban said, "which of you ladies wants to take me home tonight?"

He didn't notice Hector standing behind him.

"It'd be the best any of you have ever had," Montalban said, "and I bet you've had plenty and liked it all." Then he felt the hand on his shoulder.

"Who the fuck are you?" he said.

"I'm a friend of the ladies," Hector said. "I don't think they should have to listen to talk like that. Trust me, sonny, they're not interested."

"*Sonny*? Maybe you'd be interested in losing some teeth and having your head shoved up your ass."

"No, I don't think I would," Hector said, "but I'd be happy to step outside and discuss it."

Montalban looked at him apprehensively. "Well then, what the fuck are we doing standing around here? Let's go outside. Watch my drink," he said to the women.

As Montalban opened the door Hector saw him reach in his pocket for a knife or sap.

"Don't take that hand out of your pocket with anything in it but lint," Hector said, "not if you want to be able to use it again for the next few months."

Montalban pulled out a gravity knife and flicked it open. "Yeah? You gonna give me fucking orders, greaseass?"

"I believe I warned you," Hector said.

"You warned me. Now come and try to take it from me," Montalban said. "This time *I'm* warning *you*; you're about to take it up the ass."

Hector took a step and turned abruptly, just as Montalban lunged. Before he could reposition himself Hector had driven his boot into Montalban's right knee. He winced in pain and stumbled, but then he lunged again, awkwardly, his anger superseding any reason or common sense. Again, Hector turned aside, this time grabbing his right wrist and snapping it, as the knife fell against the concrete sidewalk leading to the parking lot.

Before Montalban could close his mouth or eyes Hector had snapped his fingers as well and was working on his thumb. Montalban cried out in pain as he fell to the ground.

"Is that how the Rude Man sounds when he has to deal with a man instead of a group of women?"

"Fuck y-you," he said, rolling over onto the grass and grasping his right hand with his left.

"Listen sonny," Hector said, putting his foot against his throat, "I'm going to make this very simple, so simple that even the Rude Man will be able to understand it. If I or any of my friends ever see you mouthing off to those women—or any other women—again, they're going to be looking for whatever parts of you are left over in at least twenty different garbage cans. I'm not talking about a simple wrist or finger snap; I'm talking about a full carve-up. Understand?"

There was vomit coming from his mouth as his body started to convulse.

"I can't hear you, Rude Man."

Montalban nodded.

"I'll take that as a yes; now crawl away and keep reminding yourself that you're never coming back here again."

Montalban got up on his knees and reached for his knife with his left hand. Hector put his foot on his left hand and started to exert pressure. "Want to try for two?" he asked.

Montalban's body slumped as Hector took the knife, broke the blade against the cement and threw the pieces into the trash container at the edge of the parking lot.

Tom picked up his cell phone and called Sarah. "Hi," he said. "How's your day going so far?"

"Not too bad. It's good to hear your voice."

"Thanks. I wanted to hear your's too."

"Better *just* to hear my voice," she said. "I've been in the ER for nearly six hours. I was glad to have my cap and mask on. That way no one could see my face or my stringy hair."

"I've seen that face and hair," Tom said, "and they always look good to me."

"You're sweet," she said. "And not afraid of blood the way most people are."

He smiled. "I guess we both have the same occupational hazards."

"It's good to have something in common," she said.

"I've got to work late tonight," he said, "unfortunately. How about dinner tomorrow?"

"Can't," she said. "I've got to attend an afternoon and evening conference. Something to do with sutures…"

"Sounds romantic," he said.

"Right," she said, "but I could do it the next night. I could even eat at a civilized time—like before 8:30."

"Then we're on," Tom said. "Think about what you'd like to eat and give me a call. I'll be looking forward to it."

"Will do. And so will I," she said.

TWENTY-NINE

With Sarah unavailable until the next night, Tom finished a day that had started at 6:45 and drove to the family home in the Laguna Hills. His dad now spent all of his time on his own boat and seldom visited him there. He said he felt closer to his wife when he was on the boat, a boat he had named for her. "She was always happy when she was there," he said, "and she was never sick." Tom had grown up in the home in the Hills and lived there until he left for college at UCI; he still felt both of his parents' presence there.

The cupboard wasn't quite bare, but it was seriously challenged. There were a couple of frozen segments of lasagna in the freezer and plenty of beer in the refrigerator. Tom opened a can of Founders All Day IPA (a treat—recently on sale at the Irvine *Sam's Club*) and poked around in the cheese drawer. There was a chunk of sharp cheddar. Tom put it on a plate along with a paring knife and a handful of crackers, and turned on the TV.

His father's former pride and joy, a 65" Sony projection TV that he bought before the flat-screen era, still worked well. It also filled the better part of the opposite wall. Wayne had dubbed it his 'big boy'.

Tom slipped off his shoes, put the cheese and crackers and the bottle of ale on the coffee table, and sat down on his father's prized leather couch, a maroon, three-cushioned affair on which Wayne Deaton had logged a lot of hours of rest in the past. Tom caught the opening edge of a special report from ABC's L.A. affiliate, leaned back and took a drink. Marie White, their primetime news anchor, was armed with her microphone on a live remote, interviewing a plainclothes officer at a crime scene. He was standing patiently, waiting to field her questions. A lab tech and his team were standing in the background; he was shifting from foot to foot, rooting around in his jacket pockets. They were waiting on his orders. There seemed to be at least a dozen officers on the scene and an even larger number of reporters firing flash cameras and waving microphones.

"I wonder where they all are," Tom said, to no one in particular. "That's a lot of people at a single scene." He put down his glass and scooted forward in his seat but heard a knock at the door and had to get up.

It was Paco, the landscaper, ostensibly bringing Tom some ripe avocados from one of the trees on a piece of rental property which he maintained for a leasing company, but actually waiting to pick up the $50 that Tom gave him each month to keep a special eye on his dad's house, particularly when Tom was on his boat for extended periods of time. While Tom hurried him through their monthly ritual, the television screen gleamed against the darkening windows, playing to an empty room.

"This is Marie White. I am standing live, in front of the *Four-Star Wine and Liquor* store on Reservoir Street in Silver Lake. With me is Lieutenant Bill Bondeson of the LAPD. Lieutenant, can you describe what you found here this afternoon."

The camera came in for a tight shot of the lieutenant's face.

"Yes. We received a call at approximately 6:15 today concerning actions at the store which the caller considered suspicious."

"And what were those actions, Lieutenant?"

"The caller informed us that the proprietor of the store was giving away merchandise to customers."

"*Free* merchandise—liquor, wine, snack foods, cigarettes—that sort of thing?"

"Yes. Customers came in to shop and the proprietor was forcing free goods on them."

"What did you do?"

"We asked the caller if the merchandise could be part of some special promotion or whether it could be a thank-you for regular customers as part of some anniversary or other celebration. The caller informed us that that was not the case, that the gifts were substantial and that there was no particular reason for them."

As the lieutenant finished his sentence Tom said good-bye to Paco and hurried back to the living room. He rolled the volume wheel up on the remote and sat down. The reporter was still asking questions.

"What did you find when you investigated further?"

"A police cruiser was dispatched at 6:20 and arrived at 6:32. The officers found the body of the proprietor, a male caucasian, age approximately 60 years. The individual was the victim of a gunshot wound, apparently self-inflicted."

"Why do you say *apparently*, Lieutenant?"

"The weapon, a .22 caliber revolver, was in his hand when we arrived."

"But there was something else that cast doubt on whether or not this was, in fact, a suicide?"

"I can't comment on that at this point," Bondeson said.

"Could you tell us the man's name, Lieutenant?"

"I'm sorry," he said. "The victim's name is being held, pending notification of next of kin."

"One passer-by informed us that the body was nude when it was found. Can you confirm or deny that, Lieutenant?"

"I'm sorry; I can't comment on that at this time."

("Wonderful," Tom said. "Where in the world are they?")

"What leads are you pursuing, Lieutenant?"

"All I can say at this time is that the situation is under active investigation and that we are using all means at our disposal to ascertain what happened here this afternoon."

"Thank you, Lieutenant Bondeson," Marie said. "This is Marie White on Reservoir Street in Silver Lake. Back to you at the studio."

The camera pulled back, revealing the full background: *Four-Star's* tin sign above the front window and an array of cardboard point-of-purchase displays with liquor and beer logos and hand-lettered price cards just beyond the window and door.

"Holy God," Tom said, "no, no…" He raced for the phone on the side table at the far end of the couch and knocked over the picture frame that sat in the center of it. He let it lay on the floor. It was a picture of Sarah, dressed in a swimsuit with giant palms and the snow-topped San Jacintos forming the background as shimmering sunlight reflected off the pool at her feet. She was smiling up at him through a line of broken glass. He grabbed the phone and punched in Sarah's cell phone number but the call rolled over to a recorded message. He rapped his knuckles against the table in frustration. "This is Tom," he said. "The moment you get this message contact me or someone at the station immediately. Do not go to your apartment. I am very serious; do *not* go to your apartment. I'll explain as soon as I can talk to you." He clicked off and called Saddleback. He reached the head nurse after two call bounces.

"Janice Redmond," the voice said.

"I'm trying to reach Sarah Ritter," Tom said. "This is Lieutenant Tom Deaton, with the Laguna Beach PD. Sarah is a personal friend."

"Sarah's at a conference today; can I take a message?"

"Do you know where the conference is?"

"It's in La Jolla, I believe, but I don't have the location. I can give you her cell phone number."

"Thanks, I already have that," Tom said. "Please check on the conference site. We have to get to her as quickly as possible. Her life is in danger. If you reach her tell her to stay away from her apartment and to stay away from Saddleback. Tell her to call me promptly. That's *Tom Deaton*. She has my cell number. She can also call Chris Dietrich, the Chief of the LBPD. If you're nervous about any of this, check with the duty sergeant of the LBPD. His name is Bill Engle. He'll confirm who I am and that I'm a friend of Sarah's."

He called Sarah's apartment number, left a similar message, clicked off, and punched in Chris's cell number, tapping his fingers nervously on the coffee table as the phone rang. Chris picked it up on the third ring.

"Dietrich," he said.

"Chief, it's Tom."

"I just tried to call you on your landline, Tom, but it was busy. I missed you at the office; you had probably already left. I was just about to try your cell."

"I'm trying to reach Sarah," Tom said.

"I've got Hector on that," Chris said. "Don't worry. He'll find her. There aren't that many places in La Jolla that are set up to run a health science conference. She's probably somewhere at UCSD."

"Right. I tried the head nurse at Saddleback; she didn't know."

"I don't know if Hector tried them. We started with the H.R. office there. They said she was on an official absence, to attend a professional meeting. All she had to put on the form was the subject of the meeting and the city location."

"Did you see the news, Chief? It was just on."

"No," Chris said. "I'm on the 5; I got a call from an LAPD lieutenant."

"Bill Bondeson?"

"Yes."

"He's still at the crime scene," Tom said. "He's now probably supervising the door-to-door and interrogating key witnesses. ABC just had a special report a couple minutes ago."

"I should be there in a little less than an hour," Chris said. "You stay in Laguna and protect Sarah. I'll check with Bill and see what they've learned so far. And Tom…"

"Yes."

"Remember—as dangerous as murderers are, they're also all stupid in their own way. We'll get him."

"Right, Chief."

"I'll call Hector as soon as I get off the phone with you and bring him up to date on the details. I'll tell him to call you immediately."

"Sounds good, Chief. Thanks."

"Protect Sarah, Tom. That's the first order of business. As soon as we get her sequestered we can go after this guy."

"Will do, Chief," Tom said, and clicked off. He muted the television, holding for Hector's call and any new reports from the murder scene. Suddenly his appetite was gone and he could feel his heart pumping insistently.

THIRTY

The traffic lightened as Chris hit Hector's number on his speed dial.

"Hi, Chief," Hector answered. "I reached Sarah Ritter. The San Diego guys have already picked her up. They were very helpful, particularly a detective named Rick Samuels. I'm on my way there now. I'll take her to a safe house and have a policewoman stay with her. I'll leave a message with Bill Engle as to who and where. After that I'll pick up a van and park nearby, just in case anybody suspicious turns up."

"Perfect, Hector. Thanks. Would you please call Tom Deaton on his cell and tell him what you just told me. I'm sure he'll want to talk to Sarah as soon as he can."

"Will do, Chief."

Lieutenant Bill Bondeson was standing beside a cruiser in the four-space blacktop lot in the rear of the liquor store. The doors were covered with black and yellow crime-scene tape. When Bondeson saw Chris Dietrich approaching he walked over to him and turned him aside, away from the other policemen.

"Thanks for coming up," he said.

"No problem," Chris said. "Good to see you again, Bill."

"Were you able to reach the nurse?"

"Yes. She's on her way to a safe house."

"Good," Bondeson said. "Let's go grab some coffee. I can fill you in on what we have so far. Just hold on a sec while I ask Neil if he wants to join us."

A few seconds later Bondeson returned with Neil Phillips, his lab tech. The three of them left and found a Cajun chicken carry-out two blocks away, picked up three black coffees, and drank them in the car. The only language they heard in the restaurant and parking lot was Spanish. Neil had a tin of cocktail franks in his pocket but both Bill and Chris passed.

"I know they're a little bit nasty," Neil said, "but they're protein and they can survive forever. I heard this woman once on this talk show—on cable," he said. "She was telling about how to let a man know when the love affair's over. She said that what you do is you serve him cocktail wieners but you don't scrape the gelatin off of them. Then he knows he's history. Can you believe that?" he said, pulling off the lid and downing one of them. "The gelatin is the best part. The poor owner . . . he used to sell them by the box. That son-of-a-bitch made him give his whole stock away as well as die on an empty stomach."

"What actually happened, Bill?" Chris asked. "What have you learned since we first talked?"

"It's weird as hell, Chris, but it's also very clear-cut," Bondeson said. "We've got six rock-solid witnesses. Each of them had come in to buy something and when they tried to check out, Nate forced them to take along some freebies. I'm talking about serious stuff, not a bag of peanuts or a pack of gum. He gave one guy a case of Stoli pepper vodka and another a case of $86 a bottle champagne. It must have been going on all day because there's hardly anything left in the store. Most of his walk-ins probably thought he was drunk or crazy and just took whatever he offered them and got the hell out of there before he could change his mind, but the half dozen who came forward and agreed to talk to us were all old customers. They knew Nate and they knew that something was wrong. We've got each of their names and addresses and can verify that they were long-time customers using their credit card receipts. Each of them told the exact same story. They said that there was another guy in the store while they were there. He was standing in the corner behind

Nate, laughing and clowning and cheering Nate on, telling the customers to get it while they could."

"What did he look like?" Chris asked.

"Nondescript. Medium height and medium weight. He had a nylon jacket and plain baseball cap. Nothing fancy. We pressed them and each of them said that they really couldn't see all that much. He was back behind the counter, partially hidden by the rack of corkscrews and bar supplies. He had on sunglasses and the hat was pulled down over his forehead. Several people commented that he was wearing a thick moustache."

"Hair color?"

"One guy said he looked sort of gray at the temples but nobody else really remembered anything," Bill said. "The best description we could get of the moustache was that it was darker than the hair at the edges of the baseball cap.

"So he was standing there, making fun of the store owner," Chris said.

"Right," Bill answered.

"I just don't understand this," Neil said. "Who would force a vic to give his stock away to people off the street; why not just take it from him directly? Whoever did this was risking a grand larceny beef without receiving any of the fruits of the crime. One of the witnesses—a guy who came in later, not one of the six who called us initially—said that the guy in the glasses and ballcap made the store owner dance—that he was sweating and then crying and that the more he sweated and cried, the more the guy in the glasses laughed. He told him he should have been happy—that God loves a cheerful giver and that his generosity should make him so damned cheerful that he couldn't help but dance."

"Did the guy have a gun on him?" Chris asked.

"Nobody saw a gun," Bill said, "but I can't imagine Nate giving away all of his stock without a powerful reason to do so. I'll tell you this for sure and certain, Nate Lasser could really strangle the eagle. He foiled at least seven attempted holdups and carried enough stitches from knife wounds to look like a discarded practice dummy from *Surgery 101*. Nate didn't give away *anything*. So the creep tries to find a clever way to get back at him. He turns him into Santa Claus. Makes him give away everything in his store."

"Including his clothes," Neil said.

"Including his life," Chris added.

"There is *some* good news," Bill said.

"What's that?" Chris asked.

"We found some artificial hair back where the guy was sitting. It was on the floor under a wooden chair; it must have fallen off when he was jerking Nate around. It's brown and it looks exactly like the material we found at the earlier crime scene . . . with the lawyer. One of Neil's guys is checking it out now."

"That'll be important when we get to court," Chris said.

"*If* we get to court," Bill added.

THIRTY-ONE

"I should have put it all together sooner," Chris said. "I don't know what's wrong with me. Too much paperwork . . . too many phone calls…"

"Why do you say that?" Bill asked.

"Because three days ago I took an over-the-transom call from a guy. The call had been bounced from the LAPD. He wanted to talk to Frank Brierly."

"Wait a sec, Chief," Neil said. "Back up a little. I understand that we've got a killer who's real proud of his sense of humor, but I don't understand what a dead officer would have to do with any of this."

"You were still in the Bay Area when it all went down," Bill said. "This all happened years ago. Tell him, Chris."

Chris took a long drink of his coffee.

"The whole thing was a comedy of errors from the beginning," he said. "This young punk is driving through Silver Lake, looking for a convenience store or liquor store and he sees one, stops, and attempts to hold up Nate Lasser. He's trying to make one good score so he and his girl friend can get married and ride off into the sunset together. At least that's what he testified later. Anyway, Nate pulls a pistol on him. Tells him he'll blow him all over the street, that nobody screws around with Nate Lasser. The kid's been waving a hunting knife at him but he suddenly ducks as Nate pulls out his revolver and starts shooting. The guy instantly realizes that Nate means business and he scrambles for the door, but the door opens out rather than in and the guy is pulling at the handle like a madman while Nate is firing away.

"The problem is that Nate can't see worth a damn at a distance because he's too cheap to buy new bifocals. He got a pair of $17.99 reading glasses at the drug store several years earlier but they didn't correct for distance. Otherwise the guy would have been dead after the first couple shots. Anyway, the guy's so flustered and scared at this point that he figures that the only way out of the liquor store is through the display window, so he starts throwing bottles at Nate, trying to distract him. Nate empties his revolver and before he can reload the guy takes a running leap, crashes through the window, and lands on his face on the street. By now he's raving mad and still scared half-to-death, waiting for the bullet with his name engraved on it, but at least he's alive.

"He scrambles to his car and starts heading toward the place where his live-in works, some camera store in Highland Park. By the time he gets there he's bleeding all over himself from the glass cuts. She's afraid he's going to bleed to death, so she drives him to the emergency room at County General. Now it's a Saturday night and there's lots of blood everywhere—nothing out of the ordinary—but the resident and the interns are all doing triage, so the nurse on duty is told to pick the glass shards out of the guy's face and arms and legs. Which she does, but as she's doing that she suddenly discovers another wound. It seems that along with all the glass cuts the guy also caught a slug from Nate's revolver—in the right cheek of his butt. From the physical evidence it looks as if it was probably a carom shot off the door hinge, because the wound is not that deep and when the lab boys finally tote up all of the spent rounds from Nate's revolver there's one slug still missing and no more holes in the plaster or door frame.

"The nurse realizes there's a problem, tells the guy that another patient needs some attention for a minute or two, and leaves momentarily to tell the head nurse to call the cops. *Procedure*, whenever there's a gunshot wound. Then the nurse comes back, cleans the wounds, and finishes patching him up. The cops arrive and they promptly cart him downtown. Nate i.d.'s him and he's suddenly living in a small room with an iron-bar door and a toilet that doubles as a sink.

"A couple months later he's ready to go to trial. The public defender takes him aside for a few minutes before they go into the court room, tells him he's looking at a heavy bounce, talks him into pleading guilty to a couple of lesser but still serious offenses, and in they go. The judge hears the plea and punches his ticket to San Quentin. The whole proceeding takes less than ten minutes, after which he goes away for ten years and change."

"And now he's paying them all back, one at a time," Neil said.

"Right," Bill answered. "He's working backwards. First he got the judge (Evelyn Garretson), then the public defender (Marshall Stern), who handled his case. He wanted to get the arresting officer but he was too late. Some other punk got there first and already killed him."

"Frank Brierly," Neil said.

"My former partner," Chris added.

"That leaves the nurse who found the bullet," Neil said. "Do you remember her name?"

"She was fresh out of nursing school," Chris said. "She graduated at the top of her class at Pasadena City College. Soon after that she moved to Orange County. She lives in Laguna now. That's why Bill called me right away. Her name is Sarah Ritter."

THIRTY-TWO

Bill drove back, pulled up in front of *Four Star Wine and Liquor* and tripped the door locks on his cruiser. The crowd had dissipated but the barricades were still in place. Chris and Neil got out and stood on the sidewalk as Bill walked around toward them. "This one tears it for him," Bill said. "Anybody could have wanted the judge or the lawyer dead. They each handled thousands of cases. But Nate Lasser only shot one guy. Most of the time when skells tried to rip Nate off, they'd have knives. Nate'd get out his baseball bat and invite them to try him, give them a fighting chance. Sometimes they'd cut him, sometimes not; most of the time they'd walk away—no harm no foul. As he got older he got tired of that and bought a revolver. This is the only time that a robbery at *Four Star* actually resulted in a gunshot wound and a long visit to the Q. There's no doubt now about the killer. And there's no doubt about the fact that now he *has* to know that *we* know. He's standing out there just as naked as Nate Lasser, knowing we'll come after him."

"He should have spaced them out . . . should have given himself much more time," Neil said. "This was too quick, too tight. He's made it too easy for us to connect the dots. That's the difference between an amateur and a pro."

"You're talking logic and sanity," Bill said. "That's not what we're dealing with here. We've got a psychopath hot for revenge. His head's ready to explode and he's completely forgotten about *control*. He's been waiting for over ten years to do this, thinking about it every minute of every day, thinking about them—the people who put him there—planning how he'd do it, how he'd set up every step and then finish each and every one of them off, how he'd balance the books, pay them back for every slight, every indignity, every bit of pain he'd ever suffered. He couldn't wait to see the shock in their eyes when they realized what was happening, the looks on their faces just before they died. This is a movie he's been watching, scene-by-scene, in the back of his mind. He just couldn't wait any longer to put it on the big screen."

"Not necessarily," Chris said.

"What do you mean?" Bill asked.

"The timing's not really the problem. He *could* have killed them all right away. The problem is that he refused to make the deaths look accidental. This isn't Peoria, Bill; this is L.A. The casualties are stacked higher than the palm trees and on any Saturday night the hospital emergency rooms are more crowded than a Tokyo subway in a Monday morning rush hour. And lawyers and judges are no big deal. We're waist-deep in lawyers and judges. It's not like he just croaked Andy Hardy's old man and spoiled the whole Fourth of July parade and church festival fish fry. Around here . . . we see well-dressed corpses every day. No, he wanted it to happen just *this* way. He had to have his moment, no matter what it might eventually cost.

"Think about the choices he had. He could have spread the bodies all over the beach and basin and Valley. Cooked up some car accidents, some drownings, a fire . . . whatever. A real pro . . . hell, he'd just put a set of .22's in their brainpans and let them rattle around until they stopped, take them out to the desert, dig a hole in the sand and bury them. A psychopath pro . . . he'd shoot them in the knees and then bury them alive. Either way, instead of three big-headline murders you'd have—eventually—some unconnected missing person cases. By the time the dots were connected he'd be in Pago Pago with his girlfriend, sipping mai tais. But he just *couldn't* do it that way. He had to reach for the stars, go for the big gesture. All very cute. Mr. Clever. He wanted to see that film at 11:00. Each death had to be a little play or video, something grim and ironic. And each one had to fit his view of the victim—the judge who thinks she represents justice but doesn't; the lawyer who's now wearing $3000 suits and $175 ties and won't face the fact that he'll always be an ambulance chaser; the tough store owner who charges ghetto prices, pockets every loose penny, and thinks he'll get by with it forever. In the past they all controlled him in some way. Not now. He's shown *them*. He's been the director for a change and now they're nothing more than bit players in his revenge movie."

"And none of them made it through the first reel," Neil said.

"OK," Bill said, "but that still means that the nurse is next and he's planning to do something soon. He knows that he can't kill Frank Brierly and he knows that he can't wait around forever now that he's committed himself. Either he goes for Sarah Ritter right away or he splits."

"He won't split," Chris said. "That's not the way his movie ends. He has to get *her*. She's the grand finale."

THIRTY-THREE

Neil checked with Terry Salter and the other members of his lab crew as Bill walked Chris back to his car. "I think you're absolutely right, Bill; we have to try at both ends," Chris said. "Sarah's perfectly safe right now. First thing in the morning we'll put a police officer in green scrubs and a surgical mask and have her wear both Sarah's name tag and a size-6 flak jacket. In the meantime you get your warrant and send the S.W.A.T. team welcome wagon to our little friend's apartment on the off chance that he might be there and might want to come out and play."

"Sounds like a plan," Bill said.

"I've got a favor to ask," Chris said.

"Sure, name it."

"I've got a lieutenant who I think would like to go in with the S.W.A.T. team. His name is Tom Deaton; he's a friend of Sarah's."

"He can ride with me," Bill said.

"I'll call him," Chris said.

"By the way," Bill said, "I called Headquarters before you arrived; I'm having Harris' prison record fax'd from San Quentin. I thought we might learn something from it that we don't already know. What time is it now?"

"Nine fifteen," Chris said.

"We'll hit the apartment at 2:00, give him some time with the sandman. Take away whatever edge we can. Normally I'd go right in, but this guy's smart and if he's there he may have something ready for us. I posted unmarked cars outside his apartment the moment we made the connection with the other killings. If he's inside he's not going anywhere."

"Unfortunately that's a big *if*," Chris said. "Anyway, I'll call Tom now and tell him to get on the road."

"Right, I'll call and alert the team."

Each of them completed their separate calls and put away their cell phones.

"Have you got the court record on him?" Chris asked.

"I'm not sure it's there yet, but I had Jimmy Edwards call for it," Bill said.

"How'd you locate his apartment?" Chris asked, making small talk.

"We got the address from his parole officer."

"Nearby?"

"San Fernando," Bill said.

"That won't take long. How many are you going in with?"

"Eight. Not counting me and your lieutenant," Bill said. "Meanwhile, we've got several hours to kill. Why don't we go pick up the records and then grab a sandwich?"

The pedestrian traffic on Wilshire was light as they turned into the curb across from a bar owned by an ex-marine named Lou Carlson. A woman in a brown overcoat with a growling mongrel was sitting outside, at the end of a bus stop bench, watching them with a single opened eye. She was drinking sloe gin from a pint bottle and picking at the inside of her ear with her little finger. She didn't say anything as they walked past her. The dog, who had been sitting beside her, occupying the middle of the bench, was now up on his front paws and growling louder. No one was rushing to take the seat on the dog's right.

"You know what I always liked about this place besides the food and beer?" Chris asked.

"The ambiance?" Bill answered.

"That's pretty hard to beat," Chris said, "but that's not what I specifically had in mind. No, what I like most of all is the fact that the place is called *Lou Carlson's Bar*. No pretensions. No upscale name. It's nothing more than a bar. And it's Lou Carlson's bar. And Lou owns and runs it. Not the ABCXYZ Corporation or Capital Ventures or Williams and Williams Inc. And it's not a *subsidiary* of anything. It's just a bar."

"You should be in the Midwest, Chris," Bill said. "They still have the major corporations but every now and then you see something family-owned and a familiar face behind the counter. My brother Matt lives in a small town outside of Kansas City. It's still like that, mostly."

"It's not that I hate the corporations; sometimes they give you quality control at least. I just like to be able to deal directly with people, people who are personally invested in what they're doing. It seems like every time we have a problem we're immediately talking to lawyers and gofers. I like to be able to tell an owner that he did a good job or that it was *his* kitchen that gave me food poisoning. Then I want him to have a chance to respond. I'm tired of dealing with wage-slave functionaries. The company gives them the corporate manual, tells them which button to push to get a medium coke, how long to cook the fries and when to turn the burgers, how many teeth to show when they smile, and to be sure to remember to remind the customers about the special discount on the filet-o-fish. You know what really frosts me?"

"What's that?"

"When somebody makes you a cold sandwich and the MBA's have determined how many pieces of meat and how many pieces of cheese you're going to get. They put those little sheets of wax paper between the slices. If you want anything beyond the 2.125 ounces, you have to pay extra. I like a guy who just starts stacking the stuff and asks you when you want him to stop. I'm happy to pay, Bill. Just spare me all the regimentation and impersonality and nickel-and-dime approach to every last part of life."

"Then I think we came to the right place, Chris," Bill said, as they walked into the bar. "What do you feel like?"

"Let's ask Lou what he'd recommend," Chris answered.

They had to work their way between three aging bikers and a guy with a sweaty red bandanna and striped gray overalls.

"How the hell are you, Lou?" Bill said. "What's good tonight?"

"It's all good," Lou said. "Chris. Long time no see. Where the hell have you been?"

"Laguna, Lou."

"He's trying to keep Orange County safe and I'm trying to keep the streets outside your door safe," Bill said.

"Well where's your goddamned howitzer then?" Lou asked.

Bill smiled. "Seriously, Lou. What do you recommend?"

"The beef's good. A little rare maybe, but it's been cooking in the juice for an hour and a half now. The ham is great. Smithfield. A little salty, but I like it that way. It makes the customers order more beer. I got fresh seeded rye and also some kaiser rolls. Both OK. Skip the cole slaw. It hasn't killed anybody yet but it just doesn't taste right to me."

"Ham for me," Bill said. "On rye. With some mustard and maybe a slice of cheese."

"Swiss?" Lou asked.

"Sure."

"Ham sounds good," Chris said. "On a roll. Just a couple dabs of mustard, but hold the cheese and put some olives on the side."

"There's olives and pickles on the tables," Lou said. "New touch. Help yourself. Any peppers?"

They passed on the peppers. "Beer?" Lou asked.

"Mexican," Bill said.

"And for me," Chris said. "What's the freshest?"

"Who knows?" Lou answered. "I get them from a supplier in East L.A. He won't tell me how long he's had the stuff. I bitch a lot but he just shrugs. Try the *Carta Blanca*. I had one a few minutes ago and it went down pretty well."

"Sounds good," Chris said.

They sat at a corner table, away from the bar noise, sipping their beer and waiting for their sandwiches. "Here it is," Bill said, putting an accordion folder with two manila envelopes on the table. Jimmy said there isn't a whole hell of a lot there; I haven't had the chance to take a look for myself."

Chris opened the file from San Quentin and started to read aloud.

"**HARRIS, EARLON G.** Number 06538549. Born 6 April 1984, Platteville, Wisconsin. Certificate of completion of eighth grade; no record of further education. Intelligence quotient estimated at 145."

"Jesus," Bill said. "Just what we need—a genius psychopath."

"Arrested 4 August 2004 on the grounds of Hillcrest Country Club, West Los Angeles, after altercation with Mrs. Florence Fenden, 260 Sawyer Crescent Drive. Complainant's dog attacked Harris after he urinated in her swimming pool. Harris lost index finger of left hand, two toes on right foot, and left testicle."

"Wonderful," Bill said. "That's probably part of the reason why he's so damned mean."

Chris continued.

"Miscellaneous arrests for shoplifting, driving while intoxicated, and assault and battery, the last charge dropped when victim refused to appear in court to testify. Arrested in 2010 for attempted robbery, assault, destruction of property, possession of a concealed weapon, and some change. Nice boy," Chris said.

"And he did *ten* years for that in this day and age?" Bill said.

"Yes, well, Judge Garretson would take no shit before its time and, of course, he wasn't being represented by Perry Mason. I figure Stern was late for lunch and he jumped at the first deal the D.A. offered. Harris didn't know any better and he couldn't afford a private lawyer to advise him. He was just a kid. He's learned a lot since then."

"And that experience along with all the other stuff in his head just keeps festering," Bill said.

"There's also a note that he had trouble with each of three different cellmates. The last one gave him a nickname. Called him *Snack*."

"Sounds about right," Bill said. "Take his clothes off and walk him into a prison shower and he'd look like something that'd been nibbled on by something large and hungry."

"I doubt that he liked it very much," Chris said, his finger running down the page in the file. "There's a handwritten note here to the effect that Harris may have arranged to have his last cellmate assaulted after he left, but so far they haven't been able to prove it. Wanted to have his ears cut off."

"Cute. Was the guy successful?"

"Apparently not."

"By now that boy must be carrying enough material for a very heavy grudge," Bill said.

"He's a little lighter now," Chris said. "At least three bodies worth."

"What time is it?" Bill asked.

"Eleven-ten."

"Just under three hours till game time," Bill said.

"Wait a second, here's something else," Chris said, pulling out a loose sheet of yellow paper.

"That's probably the social worker's report," Bill said.

"It says that the whole family moved to California in the mid eighties. His father runs a foundry in Bellflower and his mother takes care of his brother. That's a full-time job; the brother's severely retarded."

"Jimmy Edwards called the family," Bill said. "Harris doesn't have anything to do with them. Hasn't for years. They said they loved him and that in the past they had tried to help him, but that it just wouldn't work. They couldn't connect with him."

"So he's not abused or deprived or anything like that."

"Oh no," Bill said. "Jimmy said the parents sounded like a pair of saints. When he talked to the mother she was bragging about Harris' brother, praising him for being able to feed himself so well. She was going on and on, talking about him as if he was Einstein. He's thirty-two, Chris."

"The bad one got all the brains and the parents got all the heartaches."

"Right," Bill said. "All the brains in the world. And what use does the son-of-a-bitch make of them?"

Chris shook his head and picked at his sandwich. "All he can do is think up weird ways to dole out pain and leave behind a trail of blood and puke and nightmares."

"Maybe we'll have the opportunity to sit down and have a little chat with him about his career," Chris said. "Talk about where he went wrong and where he's headed from here."

"Count on it," Bill answered.

THIRTY-FOUR

Except for the occasional sounds of feral cats hunting for a date or a late dinner, the streets around Lorna's apartment were silent. The single street light reflecting off the metal railing of her building's balcony was fading rapidly and after shorting momentarily it popped and died, leaving the street with nothing but clouded moonlight. Bondeson approached the lead stake-out car on foot. The driver's name was Elaine Diener.

"Anything so far, Elaine?" he asked.

"All quiet, Lieutenant," she said. "They turned in around 12:30."

"They?"

"Yes."

"You actually saw a man in there with her?"

"I couldn't from this angle, Lieutenant, but Gerry Robinson saw one."

"And the man hasn't come out since?"

"Nobody's come out, Lieutenant. We've got both the front and back covered and a man keeping an eye on her car."

"Her name is Pillett?" Bill asked.

"Yes, sir. Lorna Pillett. She works at a kitchen utensil place in Tujunga. That's her car, across the street there. She got home about 7:30—in a cab."

"And Harris was here, waiting for her."

"Yes, sir. We got here twenty minutes after you called. No one's gone in or out except for the Pillett woman, so Harris had to have been here when we got here. Of course, we don't know what time he arrived."

"Thanks," Bill said. "Get ready. We're going in in five minutes."

"Watch that door," Bill whispered to the officer with the ramming bar. "It looks like an interior door. Not solid wood . . . just a filled piece of junk. You hit it in the center and the bar will go right through. Hit it just above the knob, right at the side of the deadbolt."

He stood back, caught the eye of each member of the team, and then said to the officer with the bar, "Go."

The door shattered instantly and they hit the living room in a second. When they looked down the hallway the bedroom door was closed, but before they could set up on either side to go in, it suddenly swung open. A man stood in the doorway in his shorts and undershirt, his finger on the trigger of a 12-gauge shotgun.

"Freeze, Harris, or you're dead where you stand," Bill said.

Lorna cried out from the bedroom. "Don't shoot. Please don't anybody shoot."

There were four shotguns and Bill's Glock aimed at his heart.

"I'm not Harris, goddamnit," the man said, handing his shotgun to the nearest officer. "What in the fuck do you think you're doing here?"

"Who might you be?" Bill asked, lifting his undershirt to check for anything that might be concealed in his boxer shorts.

"His name's Roy," Lorna said, coming out of the darkness and tying the sash on a pink robe that barely reached her thighs. "He's my friend. He's here to help me. To protect me."

"My name's Haggerty," the man said. "I still want to know what you're doing here busting up Lorna's door and pointing all those goddamned guns at me. Why aren't you out catching that crazy son-of-a-bitch, Harris?"

When Lorna came into the hallway light Tom saw the bandaged cut above her left eye and the bruises on her cheeks. "Who did that to you, Miss Pillett—Harris?"

She nodded yes.

Bill sent the members of the S.W.A.T. team back to their vehicles. "Take his shotgun along with you," he said. "We'll be down in a few minutes."

"Hey, you can't take private property like that," Haggerty said.

"Put a lid on it," Bill said. "Why don't you go put your pants on while we talk to Miss Pillett."

Haggerty said something under his breath and went back into the bedroom.

Elaine Diener asked Lorna if she could do anything for her but she said no.

Bondeson asked her when she had seen Harris last.

"I saw him this morning, sir."

"And that's when he hit you?" Tom asked.

"Yes, sir."

"What happened?"

"He said we had to leave, that we had to leave right away. He told me that I wouldn't have time to pack anything and that I shouldn't plan on getting anything later. I told him I couldn't do that, that I had to work. I told him that this was my whole life here in my apartment. I couldn't just leave things."

"Did he say where you would be going?"

"No. Just away." She pulled a wrinkled kleenex out of her robe pocket and blew her nose. "I didn't plan for it to be like *this*," she said.

"What do you mean?" Bill asked.

"Earlon said all along that we'd go away. He had some business to take care of first and then we'd leave. We'd start a whole new life. But he didn't say anything about just rushing off. I was scared. I didn't understand."

"And then he hit you?"

"Yes. Over and over. He was yelling at me and calling me horrible names. When I got away from him and made it into the bathroom and locked the door, he left."

"But he didn't take your car."

"He couldn't, officer. It's not running. The battery went out yesterday."

"So he left this morning. Did he say where he was going or what he was going to do?" Tom asked.

"No, he never tells me about anything like that," Lorna said.

"And you called Haggerty?"

"Yes. Like I said, I was scared. I didn't know what Earlon would do. Roy came right over, helped patch up my eye, and then drove me to work. My boss was really mad. Said I couldn't help the customers looking like that. He put me back in the stockroom. Told me not to come out, not even for lunch. Said he'd send somebody out to handle sales and that I should make myself useful and clean up."

"Sounds like a real humanitarian," Tom said to Elaine Diener.

"Did Harris say anything about coming back?" Bill asked.

"No," Lorna answered, "but he has to. That's why Roy stayed here, with his shotgun. He was waiting for him."

"Why does Harris have to come back?" Tom asked.

"Because all of his notes are here. He could never just run away and leave *them*."

"His *notes?*"

"Yes, they're right there," Lorna said. "In his case."

THIRTY-FIVE

"By the way, Miss Pillett, you were recently visited by a police officer who asked you about Earlon Harris," Bill said.

"Yes, sir. The Mexican man."

"Detective Chavez."

"Yes."

"He asked whether or not Harris was with you on the evening of the 12th and you said that he was here, with you, all night. Is that correct?"

"No," she said, covering her eyes with her left hand.

"No—what, Miss Pillett?" Bill asked.

"No, it wasn't correct, Lieutenant. I lied to the detective. I know that I shouldn't have. I'm so sorry."

"Harris was *not* with you on the night of the 12th."

"No, sir," she said. "I don't know where he was or what he did, but he wasn't here. I should have told the detective the truth. I was just trying to protect Earlon."

"Do you know what time he came back on the night of the 12th?"

"No, I don't, Lieutenant. I slept right through it, I guess."

"You didn't see anything on the news or in the paper that made you suspicious?"

"I don't get the paper, Lieutenant, and the news is usually off by the time I get home from work. Mr. Crouper always wants me to stay late so that I can help him close up."

"The judge who sentenced Earlon Harris was murdered on the night of the 12th," Bill said. "Since then, the lawyer who defended him and the liquor store owner whose store he tried to rob eleven years ago were both found murdered."

"Oh my God," she said, her eyes red with tears and shock. "I didn't know. You've got to believe me when I tell you that, Lieutenant. I really *didn't* know."

"Calm down, Miss Pillett," Bill said. "Now tell me about these notes of Harris'."

"They're right there, Lieutenant," she said, pointing to a vinyl attaché case next to the base of a black metal floor lamp in the corner of the living room. "When he first came back here he kept them in his yellow and black plastic bag with his other things, but about a week ago he found my father's brief case in the cupboard and he put them in there. When he left this morning he took the plastic bag but he was so angry and upset with me that he forgot the notes. I know he'll be back for them, Lieutenant. They're really important to him. He'll blame me for his forgetting them."

Bill opened up the case and put the papers on the coffee table. Haggerty came out, walked into the kitchen, opened the refrigerator, looked around inside, closed the door, and walked back toward the bedroom.

"Can I help you, Roy?" Lorna asked.

"No, forget it," he said.

"These are notes written in Harris' handwriting; is that correct?" Bondeson asked.

"Yes, Lieutenant," Lorna answered.

Tom noticed that she seemed upset when Bill flipped through them. "What's the matter, Miss Pillett?" he asked. "Are you all right?"

"I'm OK, sir," she said. "It's just that . . . I don't like those notes."

"Why not?" Tom asked.

"They're not nice," she said. "They're not . . . they're just not nice."

"Then you've read them," Bill said.

"Earlon made me read them. He made me read them to him," she said.

"Read them *to him?*" Bill asked.

"Yes."

"Why?"

"I don't know. They turned him on or something."

"Pardon the question, Miss Pillett," Bill said, "but I have to ask."

"Go ahead," she said. "I don't mind. It's time I started telling you the truth."

"Are you saying that it was some kind of sexual thing with him—that your reading these notes to him somehow aroused him?"

"Yes, Lieutenant."

It took Bill nearly thirty minutes to read through Harris' notes. "Who or what is Loyal?" he said to Lorna.

"I don't have any idea," she said. "I think he's Earlon's hero or something. Earlon has a prison tattoo on his left arm that says **Loyal Forever**. He said once that Loyal was his *guide*."

"Tom…"

"Loyal . . . first name or last?"

"I don't know," Bill said. "All that Harris writes is the single name."

"It doesn't ring any bells," Tom said. "Here, let me take a look."

Tom read carefully through the first of the wrinkled sheets and then read one passage aloud:

> **Only a horizon ringed about with myths**
> **can unify a culture. The forces of imagination**
> **and of Apollonian dream are saved only by myth**
> **from indiscriminate rambling. The images of myth**
> **must be the demonic guardians, ubiquitous but**
> **unnoticed, presiding over the growth of the child's**
> **mind and interpreting to the mature man his life**
> **and struggles.**

"Sounds like somebody who's into comic books," Bill said. "Super-heroes, stuff like that. Maybe Loyal's a comic book writer."

"That's not anybody called Loyal," Tom said. "That's Nietzsche."

"Nietzsche?" Bill said. "You mean we're trying to track a homicidal psychopath with a grade school education and a 145 IQ whose hero is Nietzsche?"

"That's right," Tom said. "That's exactly what we're tracking."

"What in the world would you call that?" Bill asked.

"A nightmare to last a lifetime," Tom answered.

THIRTY-SIX

"This all makes so much more sense now," Tom said. He and Bill were sitting in an all-night Hollywood diner, drinking black coffee, eating stale cheese danish, and watching a bored street cleaner grind wet grit into the high gutters of the boulevard. "No wonder he wanted to get Lorna out of there. He knew that the moment the store owner died the whistles would blow and the cruisers would roll. But he just couldn't wait to murder him. In some ways he's out of control, in others he's hyper-controlled. The Nietzsche notes explain a lot too. Harris is following him to the letter."

"How so?" Bill asked.

"OK, in the first place, Harris has to fancy himself as some kind of an artist, because Nietzsche *loves* artists. Harris doesn't have a choice, not if he wants to follow the master. He probably believes that by planning and structuring all of these murders as if they're some kind of art works he can live up to the ideals of his idol. Nietzsche was very big on shape and form—always preferring them to chaos—and he wasn't all that particular on the materials that were used. A sculptor chiseling the shape of a face or a warlord redrawing the borders on a map—either one would get his seal of approval. So if that's what will make 'Loyal'—whoever or whatever he is—happy, that's what little Earlon is going to do.

"Of course, life to him is little more than violent revenge, but that's OK—he makes points with his master by doing revenge like some kind of sculptor or painter . . . creating images, scenes . . . what the *artistes* in the SoHo lofts would probably call *tableaux*. But he's not quite doing it the way that they would. He always adds his own little nasty touches. The murders are his masterpieces; he's turning the city into a gallery for his one-man show. He's writing the story of his last big fall and he's writing it in his victims' blood.

"He's got Nietzsche's old will-to-power number going pretty strong too. Harris' victims all dominated him in some way or other and now he's the one who's suddenly dominating them. He's finally in charge and he's loving every minute of it, but not like some cheap thug, knocking his victims on the head with a 2x4 or hitting them in the face with a piece of iron pipe. No, he's doing it with style.

"You see, Nietzsche is writing Harris' script and to Nietzsche the whole world is divided into what one of my old college teachers at UCI used to call *energy* and *order*. The two tend to counterbalance one another. There's an impulse to raise hell and an impulse to create and shape. The energy part is wild and irrational. Testosterone-overload time. Harris loves that part. It gets him juiced; that's why he made his girlfriend read his notes to him. But he also knows he has to balance it with order and form. Nietzsche requires the creative part . . . like I said, he actually prefers it. So Harris has to give us both: the works of art to please 'Loyal', but works of art that bear his personal stamp—the products of a mind short-circuiting in all directions and ready to explode.

"It's a head trip and a crotch trip simultaneously. It's like he's one step out of the cave, killing animals with his hands and thumping women on the head and dragging them behind him. Mr. Id, slobbering at the mouth and throbbing in his loincloth. But then there's the other side too. Suddenly he's also painting great pictures. The difference is that *he* paints *his* pictures with his victims' blood. And that doesn't matter to him because it doesn't really matter to Nietzsche or 'Loyal'. The important thing is the picture, not the material.

"Harris doesn't give a damn about his victims' pain. It's just raw material for the picture he's painting or the film that he's shooting. Nobody else's story matters. Only his. He's controlling everything. The fact that his victims suffer and die is nothing more to him than an incidental part of the plot. He probably wonders why they're standing there crying and bleeding when they should be applauding him and inviting him up on stage to receive his Oscar and enjoy the glow of the spotlights.

"There's no empathy at all. To him it's almost make-believe violence. He doesn't feel it. He just watches it and enjoys it. The important thing to him is that he's recasting the world in his own terms, giving us his personal epic, whether we want the damned thing or not. In that regard he's a conventional psychopath."

"He's starring in it, directing it, and finally getting to play the hero," Bill said.

"Oh yes, he's the hero all right," Tom said. "And he's getting the chance to recreate himself in the process, to get rid of all the weakness and failures of the past and substitute a newer, braver Earlon Harris. But he knows his Nietzsche well and he takes his cues properly. You see, Nietzsche's heroes aren't necessarily abstract-type artists, hunkering down and checking out their own navels. The big N figured that some of the bloodiest conquerors were also among the best creators. They shaped their civilizations by bludgeoning and pulverizing whatever was there before they arrived; actually, they *reshaped* them."

"By pounding the crap out of whoever was there first," Bill said.

"Exactly. So now Harris can crush heads and spill blood and still be every inch the artist that his beloved hero 'Loyal' envisioned. And the whole art trip is also a sexual turn-on for him. He gets to see his victims squirm and suffer. He also gets to feel the rush when they see he's in control and is about to hurt them."

"In its way it's fairly complicated," Bill said.

"Yes," Tom said, "when you talk about it abstractly, it definitely is, but when this sort of thing is all said and done the freaks are usually a lot simpler than their lawyers make them out to be. You know what I think we've got here?"

"What's that?" Bill asked.

"I think we've got the village punk who regularly got the crap beat out of him. Then, suddenly, he finds a book that can change his life. Maybe one day he just walks into the prison library, wraps his fingers around its spine, and it glows in his hand. He's like a college sophomore, taking the last thing he read as his life-long guide, only now this whack job is holding Nietzsche in one hand and a four-foot magic sword in the other. It would have been a hell of a lot better for all concerned if he had picked up Norman Vincent Peale instead. Unfortunately, he didn't. Now for the first time in his life he's the one who's taking charge because his cute little how-to book has told him that he *can* take charge. And every time he kills one of his enemies and actually gets away with it he feels even better. He's the little twerp on the beach getting the sand kicked in his face who sends away for the secret instruction book and is suddenly transformed into the All-Powerful Lord of the Universe, complete with sword, shield, secret password and winged helmet."

"But take away the sword," Bill said, and all you have left is a mean little shit behind a shield that's three-times his size."

"Bingo," Tom said. "But remember that he is absolutely *convinced* that he's for real and that he's the master. He can win through sheer will power."

"All he needs is a little Hitler moustache and he's ready to take his act on the road."

"Right. Only he thinks of himself as more like Rodin with his best hammer and chisel, the difference being that he goes for the balls instead of the rough edges around the fig leaf."

"But what's with all this damned *Loyal* business?" Bill asked.

"I don't know," Tom said, "but I know how we can find out easily enough."

At 9:00 Tom called the Philosophy department at UCI. He told them who he was and asked if he could speak to somebody who was an expert on Nietzsche. He hit the speaker button on his cellphone.

"I doubt that anyone's in yet," the secretary said. "Why don't you try around 11:00?"

"We're in the wrong racket," he said to Bill.

At 9:20 Tom reached a man in the Philosophy department at USC named Rupert Treyz, who referred him to somebody in the English department named Chester Pinckney. The English department receptionist gave Tom his home phone number. "I don't think he'll mind if you call him there," she said, after pausing to check the time.

Tom called him, identified himself, told him he was serving as a consultant with the Robbery/Homicide division of the LAPD, and asked him if there was any connection between the name *Loyal* and Nietzsche.

"Any at all," Tom added.

"Well of course," the man said. "Dr. Richard Loyal is a distinguished colleague of mine who studies Nietzsche. Richard is currently editing a series of texts entitled *Critical Interventions*."

"*Interventions?*" Tom asked. "You mean like *military* or *economic* interventions?"

"Well, it would take me a long time to explain," Pinckney said. "Suffice to say that each volume in the series is devoted to the writings of a thinker Richard admires and each consists largely of quotations from the writer in question. Richard believes that a studied acquaintance with these writers will both redirect contemporary discourse and empower readers."

Tom gave Bill a look of dismay.

"Do you happen to have a copy of the Nietzsche volume, Professor Pinckney?" Tom asked.

"Yes," he said. "I believe I have an examination copy here somewhere. I'll have to go into the other room. Just a second . . . ah yes, here it is."

"What does the title page look like, Professor? Is Nietzsche mentioned on it?"

"No, not really," Pinckney said. "There's a list of the pertinent thinkers for the various volumes on a facing page, but nothing on the title page *per se*. Of course, that's not really odd. We consider the commentators much more important than the writers these days."

"So Loyal's name is on the title page."

"Why, yes. I thought I made that clear."

"Yes, you did, professor," Tom said. "I just wanted to be sure. Thanks very much."

"Have I been of help?"

"Yes, you have," he said. "Thanks again."

"Splendid . . . you're quite welcome."

"Just one more thing," Tom said. "Where does Richard Loyal teach?"

"Richard spent most of his career at Minnesota, Wesleyan and Brown, but last year he moved to Duke," Pinckney answered.

"In the English department, not the Philosophy department."

"Yes, of course."

"Thanks again," Tom said, and hung up.

"So?" Bill asked.

"Earlon Harris picked up a collection of Nietzsche's sayings edited by some professor named Richard Loyal. Now he thinks that Nietzsche's ideas are actually Loyal's and that Richard Loyal is God. At least."

"And Earlon is his number one son."

"Converting with his sword," Tom said. "And Sarah's name is now at the top of his extra-special to-do list."

THIRTY-SEVEN

"Oh, Sarah, Sarah, we're going to have so much fun," Harris said, bumping his nearly empty plastic glass of store-brand bourbon onto the floor with his wrist and nearly taking out the bottle with his elbow. He tried to compose himself, blinking and focusing his eyes and curling his fingers into fists. "What a game we're going to play. It will be life and death, Sarah, and things may get a little messy at times, but it'll be worth it, because the life and death games are always the best, don't you think?"

He retrieved the glass, scooped up the droplets at the edge with his fingertip, tasted them, and poured four ounces of fresh bourbon, set the bottle safely out of reach, and eased half of the fluid over his tongue and down his throat.

He was sitting in a darkened room in a dive on Coronado called the *Excelsior Arms*. There was a yellow vinyl chair with slit cushions, a metal-framed bed, a splintered oak desk chair and a long laminate table with a missing drawer. A black and white Sylvania TV sat on a metal cart in the corner. Harris had spread a white handkerchief across the top of the table and he was adjusting the metal, gooseneck table lamp.

"Now," he said, talking out loud to himself, "where is my little bag?" He turned around, thought for a second, lifted his jacket off the bed, and picked up the plastic bag that had been lying beneath it. "Right here," he said. "Oh, Sarah, I think you're really going to be proud of me. I've thought long and hard about this. I'm really giving you my best work yet. And it's going to be so perfect. You'll remember what happened eleven years ago and you'll think — 'My, that Earlon is *so* clever. How *did* he think of this? How did he *find* everything? And wasn't it thoughtful that he made me the last? That's so like him. I know just what Loyal would call it—Pride of Place.'

"No, Sarah, it wasn't just thoughtful. It was *beautiful*. You had to be last, darling, because yours is so complicated. The others were simple, but you're so special that I wanted to do it just *right*, just *right* for you.

"Now, what do we have here . . . oh yes, all my little capsules. Do you know how many of them there are, darling? Twenty-five. Twenty-five of them. And they weren't easy to get. That pharmacist thought I wanted drugs. I told him that just because I had a gun didn't mean that I wanted something as stupid and trite as drugs. He didn't have any imagination, Sarah, but then what do you expect from somebody who just counts pills and types labels all day? And that silly little tray of his . . . it's like a kid's toy. 'One . . . two . . . three' . . . all day long.

"I had to hurt him, Sarah. That's all some people understand, I guess. *Then* he decided to cooperate with me. A little blood here and a little blood there and suddenly I had his attention and he was ready to help. So he filled the first twenty-four with the baby laxative I gave him and then I gave him the poison to put in the twenty-fifth. Of course, I didn't call it poison. I just called it special white powder. And he didn't know what it was. Can you believe that? A pharmacist and he doesn't even know what things are. His hands kept shaking all the while. I'm glad I don't have to count on *him* anymore. He was completely unreliable, but even so, I bet he made a lot of money anyway. Oh well, he's gone now and he won't be doing anyone else any harm.

"And now I have all of my capsules and you and I will be able to play our special game."

Harris spread the capsules on the handkerchief, separating the twenty-fifth from the others by keeping it in its clear plastic bag. He drained the plastic glass, poured another drink, capped the bottle, and lifted the glass toward the window. He turned it in his hand, staring at the light through the multiple, overlapping fingerprints surrounding the amber liquid.

"Now here's what we'll do, Sarah. I'll start by giving you something to make you go night-night and when I wake you up you'll have a big surprise. After I remove all your clothes I'm going to take my best needles and work all of those little capsules under your skin as deep as I can get them. There'll be little bumps all over your face and body. You'll feel funny and look funny. Then I'm going to explain everything that I did, tell you all about the rules of our little game, and give you a scalpel. I don't think we'll be able to find the one you used on me; I'm sure that it's gone now. That's really too bad, because that would have made it *really* perfect, but I know you'll understand that I did my best. Anyway, the main thing will be that you'll have your scalpel but you won't know which one of those capsules has the magic powder in it. So you'll have to hunt all over your body and dig and cut at yourself and get all of them out just as quickly as you possibly can, because the capsules will be dissolving from your body heat and you won't want the one with the magic dust to dissolve before you get to it. No, no, that wouldn't be good at all, because if you got there too late it would be bye-bye Sarah.

"And I just *know* you're going to enjoy it. You found the bullet in me. I don't think anybody else could have done that, Sarah. Well, now it'll be your turn to find the bullet in you. My bullet won't just lay there though. It will explode, Sarah. That magic dust will be floating through your veins and making you go night-night for good. But first it will make you sick. You'll cough and puke and shake; I'm afraid it won't be very nice. *Then* it will make you dead. In fact, if you don't hurry and find the right capsule early in our game it will make you so sick that you'll probably be happy to die. And you know what? I won't be able to tell you which of the capsules is which, but I *can* tell you that it's going to be quite a nice little hunt. And we're going to be looking in some very *private* places. I'm sorry; I forgot to mention that part. And you can't get too hot and sweaty, because that will only make those capsules melt more quickly. And you can't get too nervous, Sarah. You don't want your hand to slip because if you cut too deep and lose too much blood you might pass out and then you won't be able to continue our game and it won't be any fun anymore.

"And you know what I especially like? The fact that you have to have skill and courage as well as *luck*. What a great game. I hate those things that are all chance or all just a matter of age or size or weight. This is a real *game*, Sarah. I can't wait to watch.

"Now you be patient. We'll be ready soon. I'll come pick you up and then we can play. All I have to do now is find a place where we can go—some place that reminds you of that old emergency room where we first met. And of course I have to look out for all of those policemen who are going to try to catch me. They know who I am now. Even *they* are smart enough to figure that out. So I have to change my disguise a little and think of something clever, but it won't be hard. They won't be able to stop me. So you sit tight. I'm coming for you and I'll be there very, very soon."

He lifted the glass higher, toasting his plan. Then he threw back the drink, swallowed, and gently placed the glass down on the desk.

THIRTY-EIGHT

"Tom, I've got to get out of here," Sarah said. "I feel like I'm the one who's been put in prison instead of Harris. Chief Dietrich's given orders to the officers guarding me; they won't let me leave, not even to go to the store for five minutes. Look at this—four blank walls, a chair and a bed. They don't even want me to use my cell phone."

"Wait till they start in with the bologna sandwiches on Wonder Bread," he said.

"Don't make jokes," she said. "I know what you're trying to do and you know I appreciate it, but I can't let my ER team down. Ambulances are arriving every few minutes and there's an inexperienced recent-graduate standing where I'm supposed to be. We've also got people scheduled for surgery and they don't want a strange face looking down at them. Couldn't we work something out?"

"I'm afraid not, Sarah," he said.

"Come on," she said. "Couldn't the chief assign some guards both to my work station and to the ER? Just there, not the apartment. I can return to the safe house at night."

"No," he said. "As soon as we give up absolute control of the situation we put you at risk. And we're not going to do that. This guy wants you and he's ready to do anything he has to to put your body in a cold drawer in the cellar."

"Do you have to be so literal?"

"Yes, I do, Sarah," Tom said. "If Harris is able to get to you and we're unable to protect you, sliding in and out of that drawer will be the most pleasant part of the experience."

"Stop being so melodramatic," she said. "I'm going to work."

"Look Sarah, you know what hospitals are like. The only real difference between them and battlefields is that hospitals have fewer dead bodies and linoleum floors. The patients only think things are under control. No, there are simply too many contingencies to cover. You're not going. That is not negotiable."

"Tom…" she said angrily, working up to a full assault.

"I know what you're going to say," he said.

"No, you don't," she snapped.

"Listen," he said, raising his voice slightly. "This guy could cut out your heart and lungs and spleen with a rusty spoon and smile while he was doing it. He wants to *hurt you*, Sarah. He wants to *humiliate you*; he wants to *violate you*, and then he wants to *kill you*. And he wants to do it in a manner so strange and so ugly that those who eventually find your body will have trouble believing their eyes and even more trouble holding down whatever's on their stomachs."

She listened to him in silence.

"He's too dangerous and he's too intelligent. I agree completely with Chris Dietrich. Our best shot is to try to decoy him. We're putting the stand-in in place and we'll have just enough police presence around her to make him think we're serious. The moment he tries to make a move we'll either drop him on the spot or arrest him and send him straight back to San Quentin."

"What if he doesn't bite?"

"Then we'll have to try something else," Tom said.

"And I'll have to stay here."

"Yes. You'll have to stay here."

She turned away from him in frustration. "OK, just go then," she said. "Just go."

He bent down to kiss her but all she offered him was her cheek. It felt like cold canvas.

The ER waiting room at Saddleback was packed with people riffling through tattered magazines and looking up occasionally to check the time. Meanwhile, Officer Ellen Turner was standing outside the scrub room on the surgery floor talking to Chris. She was as close to a Sarah Ritter lookalike as they could come and they had been forced to pull her back from maternity leave to work on the case. Both Chris and Tom liked the fact that she looked tired—just like an ER/med surg nurse with a full room and a crammed schedule. Sarah's hairdresser had done the cut and style and Sarah herself had (reluctantly) provided the makeup. The height and weight were about right and the tinted contacts made her eyes look green enough to be convincing.

"Look, Ellen," Chris said. "We're going to take this very slowly until you feel up to anything more."

"I told you not to worry, Chief," she said. "I'm ready; I'll be fine."

"I know what you said, but we're doing a few minutes a day and that's all. I've got officers in the waiting room, the ER and in the recovery rooms. You're going to act just like a doctor—you're going to appear, smile, and then promptly disappear before anybody gets a chance to ask more than two questions. If Harris is here he'll have to move fast, because we're not exposing you any more than we have to and we want him to believe that the police protection is absolutely legit."

"I'm telling you, Chief, I feel fine," Ellen said. "You shouldn't worry."

"That's good," Chris said, "because you may need everything you've got. Still, we're not giving him any more than a quick look at you. If he's going to try anything it's going to be strictly on our terms."

They got on the elevator and went down to the rear entrance to the ER. They stood in the hallway, looking through a door with a small glass window. "The volunteer in the candy striper's uniform behind the desk on your right there has a SigSauer P320 on her lap," Chris said. "Her name is Rizzuto and she can get a dozen rounds in the air before anyone can turn and see where they're coming from. The guy back in the far corner reading the old magazine . . . the guy who looks like he hasn't had a good shave in awhile . . . he's also one of ours. His name is Landers. I'm going to go through this door in a second, look at my watch, and disappear as if I have to make a phone call. You come in just behind me, then walk across the room and approach Landers. All of the people in the room are waiting to hear about their relatives who are on the other side of the glass wall. You go tell Landers that everything went fine and that his wife should be in recovery for about forty-five minutes. Ask him if he has any questions. He won't ask any; he'll just tell you thanks. Then I want you to walk back across the room and come back into this hallway. Don't stop. Except for catching Landers with your eye when you first enter the area, I don't want you to look anywhere else. Just go give him that message, pat him on the shoulder, and take off. OK?"

"OK, Chief."

The room was crowded, mostly with women, but there were a number of men, several of them black. Ellen knew that Harris could hire someone to follow her or to seize her, so there was no way she could determine who was safe and who was not. Two of the black men were talking and one was reading an old *Reader's Digest*. A fourth was sitting with a woman who appeared to be his mother. One of the white men was working at a laptop computer and another was reading a Tom Clancy novel. A man who appeared to be Hispanic was holding a baby and keeping its attention with a small plastic rattle.

Ellen followed Chris through the door and looked around the room. She spotted Landers and then walked directly toward him. She passed the man with the baby who waited for her to pass and then whispered to it quietly. "Don't cry," he said. "Your mother's going to be fine. She's not hurt. She's just asleep for awhile. You'll be with her soon."

Ellen finished with Landers, turned, and walked toward the hallway.

When she got to the man with the baby he dropped the child's rattle at her feet. Ellen bent over, instinctively, and picked it up. "Gracias, señora," the man said, took it, and shook it gently in front of the baby's eyes.

Ellen opened the door to the hallway and paused, wondering for a moment why the man hadn't called her *nurse* or *enfermera*. She turned around and saw that he was gone.

Chris approached her. "Everything OK?" he said.

"I'm not sure," she said. "There was a man with a baby . . . he dropped the rattle that he was holding. I picked it up. As I was leaving I turned around and suddenly he was gone."

"In here," he said, hurrying her into an adjoining single-patient room. Bill Engle was behind the door, holding a .38 revolver.

Chris ran through the waiting room and into the hallway on the other side. He took out his weapon but the hallway was empty. He saw the red plastic **EXIT** sign for the stairwell at the far end. He raced down the hall, cocked his weapon, and opened the door. Laying in the trash on the top of a garbage can, clutching a used syringe, was the baby. He was crying, shaking with fear and looking up at Chris as if to ask what was going to happen to him next.

Chris carefully took away the syringe, picked up the baby, patted it gently, and went back into the hall. He stopped a nurse, told her to take care of the baby, and then ran down the stairs. He listened, but heard nothing.

Three flights above, in the bathroom of a heavily-sedated cancer patient, the Hispanic man was already peeling off his moustache and wiping the dark makeup from his face with a clean white bath towel. He took off his jacket, slipped it into the plastic bag he had carried in the interior jacket pocket, and put on a tie. He checked the knot, pulled back his ears to see if he had missed any dark makeup, and picked up his bag. Five minutes later he rode the main elevator to the cafeteria, where he had two cups of coffee and a piece of apple pie with a thick slice of cheddar cheese.

Forty minutes later he left the hospital, walking deliberately in the morning air, the temporary control gone. His face was suddenly frozen in rage. He was talking and gesturing to himself and walking directly toward a young couple on the sidewalk in front of him. When they saw and heard him they moved out of his way. "That wasn't nice, Sarah. That wasn't nice at all. You and I both remember the mole on your right wrist. I'd never forget that. I saw you holding that tool with my blood on it. Saw it right in your hand. How could I ever forget that mole? You think I'm stupid, don't you? You're working with them now and they're trying to trick me. That was cheap, Sarah. It wasn't worthy of you. Did you really think I'd forget? Did you really think you could betray me with some impersonator, some *fake*? Probably some police bitch. I won't forget her doing that to me. I owe that fucking cop too. Giving the orders, bossing everybody around. Why, Sarah? We could have had such fun. I would have given you a chance too. Maybe; . . . now you've made me angry and you and I aren't going to have fun anymore. I'm going to let people know that you tried to trick me. I'm going to let them see what happens when you do that to Earlon. There's going to be pain, Sarah. A lot of it. And it's all going to be your fault."

THIRTY-NINE

"Sarah wants our heads on fence posts," Chris said. "*Then* she wants to throw bricks and broken bottles at them. And I can't really blame her. I can't believe that we let him get away from us that easily."

"He's not stupid, Chief," Tom said. "If you had turned the hospital into a fortress he would have sensed it immediately and not shown his hand at all. What else could you have done—put an infantry division around the building? You can't stop ambulances; you can't close down emergency rooms; you can't suspend scheduled tests and operations; you can't keep people from visiting sick relatives. There were just *enough* officers there to let him think that Ellen was really Sarah and that she was really under police guard. That means that there weren't enough to keep him from escaping."

"Thanks for the thought," Chris said. "I still think we screwed up royally. And the baby . . . the baby could have died. We're lucky that whack job didn't just drop it down the stairwell. We found the mother, by the way—in the trunk of her car in the hospital parking lot. She'll live, but she's got a nasty head wound. We think he hit her with a tire iron."

"Like we've always said," Tom answered, "he's a complete psychopath. He's firmly convinced that the world revolves around him and everybody else's sole purpose in life is to be used by him to feed his ego. I *do* hope that one of us gets the opportunity to wrap our hands around his scrawny little throat for a minute or two. Or maybe three. What are you going to do now?"

"Keep Sarah hidden and incommunicado and advise Bill Bondeson to keep the stakeout on Lorna Pillett's apartment. We tried to pick up some prints from the hospital, but we couldn't get any. You know something—so far we *do not have* a single piece of physical evidence that directly connects Harris to any of the murders. The circumstantial evidence is great, but that's all it is—circumstantial. We don't have a single print, a single human hair, a single, solitary drop of body fluid…"

"And you don't have any witnesses," Tom said, "at least not the kind who can confidently testify to the fact that Earlon Harris is your guy."

"That's right. Ellen Turner saw someone who looked more like Juan Valdez than our precious little Earlon. With his height, weight and body type she could testify that that *might* have been him underneath all the makeup, but that's as far as she could go. That's not a whole hell of a lot of help. And wearing makeup is not against the law. Hell, in some sections of L.A. eighty percent of the men are in makeup and twenty percent of the eighty are wearing skirts or dresses."

"And some nice pumps," Tom added. "Basically, you've got two choices, Chief. You can either catch him in the act or find out where he's living and try to turn some evidence there that will link him to the killings. He didn't leave anything at Lorna's place except for his Loyal notes and you can't convict him on them."

"And they were wiped clean," Chris said.

"The guy is really smart; I've got to give him that," Tom said, "and he's pathologically cautious. He's seething inside but somehow he still manages to maintain control of himself. Wiping the Loyal notes . . . there was really no reason to do that."

"Unless he thinks they're holy and somehow unworthy of being soiled by his fingerprints."

"Not beyond the realm of possibility," Tom said.

"Anyway, it's not very likely that we'll catch him in the act," Chris said. "We haven't been able to so far and now he's really on his guard. His prime target is Sarah and he *won't* be able to find her. I think our best chance is to try to locate *him*. Maybe we can find his makeup kit and match his moustache material to the artificial hair we found. There was some found in the hospital also; I don't think I mentioned that. It's not much but it would be something."

"He really plans things too," Tom said. "He usually steals things for each crime and then leaves them behind. It's not like he's got some pet weapon or recurring M.O. Each crime is unique."

"And how do you take that to court?" Chris said. "Ladies and gentlemen of the jury, we ask you to find Earlon Harris guilty of three counts of murder and we ask you to recommend his death by lethal injection. We don't have jack shit for evidence but I'm sure you'll agree with us that he's got to be guilty because each of these crimes was so wonderfully *unique*. They don't have a thing in common with each other, so they have to have been committed by Mr. Smartass here."

"The *victims* are all connected though," Tom said. "And you've got motive and opportunity galore. And now that Lorna's come clean he can't use her to alibi him for the night of the judge's murder."

"That's true," Chris said, "but I can already hear a defense attorney's summation in the back of my head. What if some third party—the real killer—wanted to *frame* old Earlon? Hell of an easy mark, don't you think? Everybody'd believe *he* could be guilty. Maybe the real killer just wanted to whack the judge and the lawyer; he knew all about Earlon and went after the additional victims to sidetrack us by framing him. You want a list of possibles . . . here it is and it's long.

"Or try this instead—Earlon actually had a partner 10 years ago. They've both kept quiet up until now but since Earlon's been out of prison his partner's refused to share the fruits of their earlier thefts with him. What's worse, he's afraid that Earlon might implicate him as payback, so he's trying to frame the poor forlorn son-of-a-bitch by killing the people from the Nate Lasser job (people who Earlon had long forgiven). Suddenly, Earlon's the pathetic victim, rather than the perp.

"And it wouldn't be hard to buy himself a fresh alibi for the times in question either. How about this—Earlon wasn't off killing his old enemies; he was playing Bounce-the-Beautyrest with his backup girl friend. Naturally he had to lie to Lorna. You see, it's about sex, after all, not murder. So have some mercy—the guy's been in stir for 10 years; he's got needs. He's got more love to spread around than one woman can handle. Ladies and gentlemen of the jury: meet Tiffany. Choose your story, Tom. Make up a few of your own. With no witnesses and no physical evidence, all you need for his defense is to plant the reasonable-doubt seeds and spread on enough fresh manure to make them grow. And you only need to develop enough doubt to satisfy one juror. We're not talking about a slap on the wrist here; we're talking about the big needle. If it turns out that Earlon's *really* innocent you can't bring him back later. That makes judges and juries very, very nervous, especially southern California juries."

"You're right," Tom said.

"By the way, I forgot to tell you something," Chris said. "After we went through those notes of Harris' I called the warden at San Quentin and asked him to put me in touch with the people at the prison library. Not that there was a great chance that we'd find out anything new, but I was just curious. You know . . . sometimes things turn up."

"What did they say?"

"The Loyal book was there; some public-spirited person had donated the whole series."

"It's another piece at least."

"Right. There's more. Anecdotal stuff; tells you about our boy. The chief trusty in charge of the library had just been paroled—a guy named Clements. The local cops chased him down and found out he was back in Oakland, working on the repair of a collapsed section of the freeway."

"Poor bastard—still breaking rocks."

"Yeah. Anyway, he remembered Harris vividly."

"What did he say?" Tom asked.

"Clements had a gofer named Dixon. A little guy, in for robbery.

Sort of frail . . . young . . . the kind they chew up and spit out in a place like that. Clements got him the library job to keep him away from the pick-up-the-soap crowd. Sounded pitiful: borderline retarded . . . sickly . . . jumpy."

"The perfect victim."

"Right," Chris said. "Anyway, Dixon had this mouse which found its way into the library. He started feeding it and eventually it became his pet. He held it and talked to it all the time, even carried it around in his shirt pocket. You see, he was the guy who went from cell to cell with the magazine and paperback cart. Apparently Harris asked him for something one day and Dixon forgot to get it for him. It happens, right? The guy's got an IQ barely in the double digits. Anyway, this really hacked Harris off and Harris is not exactly the sort who's quick to forgive. He was also trying to find a way to impress his new hard-case cellmate, some P.R. called Roderigo Vargas."

"He decided to beat up on Dixon so Vargas would think twice about beating up on him," Tom said.

"Right. Anyway, what he did was go into the library one day when Dixon was out. He found the cardboard box with the air holes where Dixon kept the mouse, took it out, broke its neck, and stuck it in the library card file drawer. Typical Harris. Always had to be cute. He staged it as if the mouse had got its head caught in the drawer. Then he scotch-taped a piece of paper above the mouse's head like a cartoonist's balloon. It said **CRUNCH TIME!**"

"Darling."

"It gets worse," Chris said. "When Dixon found the mouse he started sobbing. Clements had to hold him and try to calm him down. Later, when he went on his rounds with the library cart he stopped at Harris' cell and told him that he shouldn't have killed the mouse. And you got to remember—this guy's barely coherent; he's stuttering and sobbing, hanging on to Harris' cell bars and shaking all over. Harris gets up, walks over toward the bars, tells Dixon never to forget things again when *he* asks for them and then stomps the fingers of Dixon's right hand against the bar, breaking three and completely crushing a fourth."

"Son-of-a-bitch," Tom said. "We've got to get to him somehow and put him out of business."

"But how?" Chris asked.

"Let me think about it a second," Tom said, opening the refrigerator and taking out two bottles of Pacifico. He looked at Chris, tipping one bottle in his direction. Chris nodded yes and Tom opened both of them. He handed the first to Chris.

Chris said thanks. "Anything in there to eat? I don't want to be a bad guest, but I need something to help me concentrate. Nothing fancy; don't go to any trouble."

"No trouble at all," Tom said. He went back to the kitchen, got out a block of Black Diamond cheddar and a box of crackers. He opened a drawer, looked, closed it, and then opened the dishwasher. "Here it is," he said, taking out a paring knife and stabbing it into the center of the block of cheese. He put the food on the living room coffee table and returned to the kitchen to get two more beers. He opened them, returned to the living room, and put them on the side of the table.

"My compliments to the chef," Chris said.

Tom finished his beer in four pulls, put the bottle down, and thought for a moment. "I think I may have an idea," he said.

"That's a *good* thing. We could *use* an idea. Let's hear it," Chris said.

"What if we bring Professor Loyal to sunny southern California?"

FORTY

"We can ask Marie White for help," Bill Bondeson said. "She's Frank White's ex." Frank was an LAPD lieutenant.

"The woman who does the primetime news on the L.A. ABC affiliate," Chris said.

"Right," Bill answered.

"One of my officers has a sister who works for ABC in Orange County," Chris said. "Small world . . . I think it would be better though to use the L.A. station—broader viewing area and it's far more likely that that's the station that Harris would be watching."

"I agree," Bill said. "We'll give her a call."

Marie agreed to do a thirty-minute interview with Richard Loyal and to take call-ins. She also agreed to do her best to persuade the station management to advertise the show as widely as possible prior to air time so that Harris would have a reasonably good chance of knowing that his hero was coming to Los Angeles. The interview would also be conducted during a time frame when the affiliate's studios were not being rented to production companies to tape other programming. "I know it's a lot to ask," Bill had said, "but we want to maximize security and we don't want to have to work around the tourists nervously waiting in line to watch the free taping of *America Says*."

Marie had agreed. "Don't worry," she said. "That's taped at NBC Universal now, but we still don't want you staging any firefights outside of our door when we have guests in the area. Otherwise—as long as the cameras are rolling—it'd probably be OK. We'd be more than happy to grab the exclusive on the triple murder story and keep the cameras running if and when your psycho-boy tries to get into the studio to throw himself at the feet of his idol."

Unfortunately, ABC proved to be far more cooperative than Richard Loyal. Chris called him and explained the situation in detail.

"I can't imagine what you were thinking; I have no intention of becoming a target for some lunatic," Loyal said.

"You needn't worry, Professor Loyal," Chris said. "The studio will be empty except for the interviewer and the crew. There is no live audience. The entire space will be completely sealed. If the suspect *does* come to the studio we will have armed officers posted outside to intercept him. What we really hope to do is elicit a phone call. The studio switchboard will be equipped to indicate the calling number and what we will do is locate the phone he is using and immediately dispatch officers to place him under arrest. You will be perfectly safe."

"One is never *perfectly* safe, Chief Dietrich," he said. "*If* he calls, you will *attempt* to locate and arrest him."

"Granted," Chris answered. "You will be as safe as we can possibly manage."

"I'm not sure that that will be good enough. I would expect to be housed at a safe location and to be taken directly from the studio—under armed escort—to the airport after the interview."

"Of course. Armed officers will meet you at the airport, take you to a secure location, accompany you to the studio, and then take you to your flight, insuring your safety at all times. I'll pick you up myself, with one of my senior men."

"I should also point out that we have not yet spoken of an honorarium," Loyal added.

Chris asked him to hold, put his hand over the phone, and turned to Tom. "Guess what, he wants an honorarium. I'm surprised he hasn't requested a gold medal from the Commissioner and a merit badge or two from the Mayor."

"That may come next," Tom said. "This is really one civic-minded citizen."

Chris took his hand off of the cell phone speaker. "What would your normal honorarium be, Professor?" he asked.

"Since you're not asking for an original, formal address, I would expect a minimum of fifteen hundred dollars. *Plus* full expenses, of course."

"I believe we can manage that," Chris said.

"One other thing, Chief Dietrich, I will *not* carry travel expense debts on my personal credit card. I expect a prepaid ticket overnighted to me and a prepaid hotel room when I arrive. It would be best if I could simply sign for any meals I take at the hotel."

"That should be easy enough," Chris said. "We can have you register and sign under an alias; that will provide further security."

"Good. Also, I fly both American and Delta for frequent flier mileage, but I prefer to use Delta for a trans-continental flight."

"Fine. We use both airlines," Chris said. "We'll give you the available times for each and you can pick the one you prefer."

"I assume we will have a day or two's lead time on this, so that I will have the 24-hour leeway to order a special meal on the flight."

"Absolutely," Chris said. "We want to promote the program well in advance of its airing, so that the suspect will be aware of your presence in Los Angeles."

"Mondays and Fridays are generally not good for me, but I suppose I could make some sort of exception if it were necessary to do so."

"When are your classes, Professor Loyal?"

"Wednesday afternoon."

"We wouldn't want you to have to cancel them," Chris said.

"That's not a particular problem," Loyal said. "I have a senior doctoral student who takes over for me from time to time. I just don't want to cut too deeply into my weekend."

"We'll check with the station, ask them to look at their schedule, and get back to you, Professor. We hope to do this as soon as possible."

"I understand," he said. "Thank you for your help. I'm happy that we've been able to have this opportunity to discuss my expectations. I know that you'll do what you can to meet them."

"We certainly will," Chris said, and hung up.

"How does he sound?" Tom asked.

"Let me put it this way," Chris said. "He sounds like a person who could truly be the perfect hero for Earlon Harris."

FORTY-ONE

Chris and Tom met Richard Loyal's Delta flight when it arrived at LAX. Loyal had expected someone to be there waiting for him, holding up a limo driver's card, but Chris said that the less attention that was drawn to his *presence* the better. Loyal had laughed at the comment at the time but not explained why. Instead of letting him come into the gate area and draw possible attention to himself they planned to meet him on the jetway, just outside the door to the aircraft, take him down the side steps and hurry him toward an unmarked cruiser parked at the edge of the tarmac.

When they saw him they were both immediately struck by his physical appearance. Tom was at Chris's side but caught a glimpse of his expression from the corner of his left eye. Harris' superhero looked like an older, grayer, more pointy-noised, miniaturized version of the Durham D.A., Mike Nifong. He was no taller than 5'3" or 5'4" and no more than an ounce or two over 115 pounds, with a very large head and exceptionally thin neck. He wore English walking shoes with thick crepe soles, pressed wool slacks, a brown tweed jacket, blue Oxford cloth shirt, and yellow bow tie. His voice was a shrill treble and it was clear from the manner of its use that he enjoyed hearing its every sound. His head twitched and his face continually darted in different directions, as if he wanted to sting someone.

He had a bar-fly's nose, with broken blood vessels starting at the tip and spreading over his nostrils to the edges of his cheeks. He looked like

Spiderman wearing a crinkled mask. His collar was tight and he suffered from an additional tic that made him strain his neck as if he was trying to release his chin from some invisible form of bondage.

"Welcome to Los Angeles, Professor," Chris said. "I'm Chief Dietrich. This is Lieutenant Tom Deaton. He is a senior officer, working with me on this case."

"Do you think that you should both be *here*, rather than out trying to arrest that madman?" the professor asked. Obviously there weren't going to be any social pleasantries.

"Lieutenant Deaton has an additional role; he is representing an individual who has been threatened by our suspect," Chris said. "He is a personal friend of that individual."

"You say he *represents* him?"

"Her, actually," Chris said.

"Whatever," he snapped. "You mean that Lieutenant Deaton enjoys power-of-attorney?"

"No," Chris said, "I meant that she is particularly concerned because of the suspect's threats and he is looking out for her interests."

"*Represents* is an interesting word, don't you think?" Loyal asked. "It's as if he's a *representation* of her, which is quite impossible, unless, of course, *she* resembles *him*." Loyal laughed. "Or perhaps since she has presented herself and then gone he is *re*-presenting her. But not, of course, as a *representation*. Unless, as I said, they look alike."

"I think he represents her in the sense that he is *present* for her," Chris said. "He's standing up for her. We both are."

"That's wonderful," Loyal said, laughing again. "Surely you must be aware of the fact that *presence* is an illusion, Chief. There is no such thing as *presence*. You may *believe* or *imagine* that something is real, but that hardly makes it so." He was still chuckling, amused that Chris and Tom had apparently not yet learned something that the whole world had agreed upon for years.

"Our imaginary car is right here, Professor," Chris said, as Tom repressed a smile or a further comment. "Where would you prefer to sit—in the imaginary back seat or the imaginary passenger seat?"

Loyal got in the back seat without comment and rode in silence for the first twenty minutes.

The traffic on the Santa Monica was jammed from the Crenshaw interchange to the Harbor freeway. As Chris crept forward a few yards at a time Loyal slumped in his seat, folded his arms, and sighed. Once on the northbound freeway it took them twenty-five minutes to get their sullen passenger to the Hilton hotel in Pasadena.

"You're close to everyone here, Professor," Chris said, "and not too far from ABC. We're working in consort with Lieutenant Bill Bondeson of the LAPD. He lives in Pasadena and the Pasadena PD is providing their own help and cooperation. You're registered in the name of Dr. Charles Robinson. Take your meals through room service and sign for them using the Robinson name. The Department will take care of all of the expenses. Here, I've written down all of the contact information for you on this sheet."

"Do you have my honorarium check?" he asked.

"Not yet. Department policy requires prior performance of the duties for which you are to be paid. I'll give you the check right after the broadcast."

Loyal sighed again. "If I understand you, Chief Dietrich, you expect me to stay in my room, like a schoolboy being punished for some petty infraction. Is that correct?"

"Your presence . . . your *appearance* in Los Angeles has been heavily publicized, Professor. We have a suspect who we believe has committed at least three violent murders and possibly a fourth—an individual who happens to be very interested in you. We would like to keep you safe while you are within this city. This location is a little off the beaten track and that should increase your personal safety. Any cooperation which *you* could offer would be very much appreciated."

"I *always* take a morning walk before breakfast," Loyal said.

"Would you like a police escort?" Chris asked.

"No, I would *not*, Chief Dietrich, but I *do* wish to walk and I assume that you will feel the need to provide me with such an escort."

"I have just the man," Chris said. "He could even join you for breakfast afterwards."

"And what is the man's name?" Loyal asked.

"Sergeant William Engle," Chris answered.

FORTY-TWO

"What a total, complete, and consummate jerk," Tom said.

"Yes, he is that," Chris said. "I hope Bill brings along something special to breakfast tomorrow—a nice tin of oily sardines or maybe a bag of pork rinds and a can of warm cream soda."

"I almost wish we could turn him over to Harris," Tom said. "It'd be interesting to see how he'd decide to kill him once he figured out that Loyal was not, in fact, God, or at least the Emperor of this particular galaxy."

"I know how I'd do it," Chris said.

"How?" Tom asked.

"I'd make him work for a living for awhile instead of just making cute observations. I can see him as . . . yes, a roofer. A couple of weeks with the sun and the tar would probably prove fatal."

"You'd better warn the TV interviewer," Tom said. "You don't want her saying something to him on the air that might ruin her career."

"Not Marie White," Chris said. "She'll just smile politely until they say 'we're on'; *then* she'll start carving him up a chunk or two at a time."

"I pity the fool," Tom said, in his best Mr. T. inflection.

"And you should," Chris said, "if he tries to pull that kind of crap with Marie he will be one disappointed customer. She's a live one. She had this radical southern preacher on once. He got very huffy with her when she challenged something he said and he countered by telling her that she should be ashamed of herself. Then he said—on the air—that she had grown too comfortable with all of her money and acclaim and that it was widely felt in the 'community' that she wasn't doing enough for her people."

"Oh yes, I remember that," Tom said. "They had a piece about it on Fox. She braced him off-camera and called him an Alabama porch jockey in front of his entourage."

"That's Marie," Chris said, smiling.

"What time do you have to get his highness to the studio tomorrow?"

"Two-thirty for a four o'clock broadcast," Chris said, "but I think I'll get him there at two o'clock. Their makeup department may have to send out for an extra couple of pounds of powder to cover up that freeway map on his nose."

"How are they going to keep that neck inside his collar?" Tom asked. "Good lord, I looked at him once or twice in the visor mirror when you were driving us to Pasadena and I got exhausted just watching him. He's burning at least two hundred and fifty calories an hour with that one tic alone. And you just know—he's going to stab somebody with that witch's nose."

"I'll warn Marie not to get too close," Chris said.

"What do you rate the chances that Harris will call in?" Tom asked.

"Not great," Chris said, "but at this point what else have we got? I think it's at least worth a shot."

"And it doesn't cost you that much—just the illusion of being in the *presence* of little Richie Loyal for a day and a half."

"He noticed the lack of *presence* of his check though, didn't he?"

"Oh lord yes," Tom said. "The only kinds of things that aren't illusions to people like him are the things that *they* want to believe in."

"If Harris comes after him with his little bag of tricks I have a feeling he'll seem real enough," Chris said.

"He better not disappoint Harris," Tom said. "He thinks Loyal's his messiah. If *that* idol falls off its pedestal, Harris will be stomping on it like a flamenco dancer and peeing on it like a 16 year-old after his first six pack of 3.2 beer."

FORTY-THREE

Chris and Tom were sitting behind Marie's switchboard operator, who was sitting behind both a call-in screen and a 48" studio monitor. "Bill's got cars all over the city," Chris said. "They're ready to move the moment Harris calls. Assuming, of course, that he *does* call."

"How did the morning constitutional go?" Tom asked.

"Do you know what that little twerp did?"

"I'm afraid to even guess," Tom said.

"It probably won't come as much of a surprise," Chris answered. "Bill got over there at 7:15, knocked on his door, and Loyal came out in his hotel bathrobe. Bill said that the bottom of it was practically dragging along the floor. Loyal told him he thought he'd skip the walk that day, since he had had such an arduous trip the day before."

Chris was still shaking his head in disbelief.

"Well, he *did*, Chief," Tom said. "I don't know why you're being so hard on the poor guy. He had to warm an airline seat for five and a half *hours* yesterday; that's *very* hard work. And that's not counting the hand and arm motions in all that eating and drinking they probably made him do. Then he had to sit quietly in the back of the car and endure the 45-minute ride to Pasadena from the airport. If that all wasn't enough, he also had to carry his garment bag at least—what would you say—thirty feet? And I haven't even mentioned the calories burned by those tics."

"Dipshit. Well, at least we got him here now. I told Marie that he could be thorny and she told me not to worry."

"I'm pretty sure she can take care of herself," Tom said, as the first bank of studio lights came up. "Here we go..."

Marie came out of her dressing room, removed her makeup towel, sat down in the upholstered chair on the set, and clipped her microphone to her blouse. Loyal came out a few seconds later, guided by a production assistant, and sat down opposite her. The bright overheads came on and the cameramen positioned themselves. Loyal blinked his eyes nervously and looked up briefly at the studio lights, which appeared to irritate him.

"Look, his feet barely reach the floor," Chris said.

"Watch the monitor," Tom said, as the cameraman moved in closer. "He's going to cut him off at the knees. Doesn't that sound like something *you'd* like to do?"

"You bet your life," Chris said.

Before Marie could brief him on the format, Loyal spoke.

"I want to outline my ground rules before we start," he said.

"Yes, Professor Loyal?" she responded.

"I will not answer any questions about my personal life. In particular I will not answer any questions concerning the terms of my appointment at Duke. Also, I will not be badgered. Once I have spoken I do not expect to be subjected to a series of follow-up questions. I also think we should do everything that we can to keep the interview lively and interesting. If you want me to simply speak without being questioned I will be happy to do so. Do *you* have any questions?"

"Oh, a few," Marie said. "Let's let them be surprises. We'll have more spontaneity that way."

"Ten seconds," her producer said.

"What do you mean, surprises?" Loyal asked.

"Sh-h-h-h, Professor. Sit up. And smile," she added. "We're about to be on television."

"And four, three, two and one..." the producer said.

"Good afternoon. I'm Marie White and this is *Newsmakers*. Thank you for joining us for what we believe will be an interesting discussion. Our call-in number is now appearing at the bottom of your screen; we encourage you to phone us with your questions. We're happy to have with us today Professor Richard Loyal. Dr. Loyal is Professor of English at Duke University. He studied at Amherst College and at Yale and is an expert on the relationships between literature and philosophy. Professor Loyal will be taking questions from our audience at home in just a few moments, but first I would like to ask him a question. Professor Loyal, what do you think is the major concern facing higher education today?"

"I believe (and I've written extensively about this)," Loyal responded, "that the major issue which the educational community *must* engage is the impact of what I have termed the postmodern intervention."

"Could you elaborate on that?"

"Of course. Postmodern thought has increasingly made its importance felt within the humanities and human sciences. Now it is imperative that that thought permeate the entire university curriculum."

"Perhaps you could clarify something for me, Professor…"

"Certainly."

"You used the term *postmodern.*"

"Yes."

"I believe the dictionary defines *modern* as referring to the *present* period in history. How can one have a school of thought that exists after the present time? What I'm saying is that if it already exists it should be *modern*, not *postmodern.*"

"Ms. White, *modern* does not refer to the contemporary but to what we term the period of high modernity, the period—give or take—between the two world wars."

"But that was over eighty years ago, professor."

"Yes, of course it was."

"Then that would make the period of the fifties and sixties *postmodern…*"

"No, not exactly…"

"And the present time would be post-postmodern."

"You've misunderstood me. You see…"

"Excuse me, Professor, but we must take a commercial break. We're talking to Professor Richard Loyal of Duke University. *Newsmakers* will return in a moment."

"That was outrageous," he said. "You just interrupted me."

"I'm sorry, Professor," Marie replied, "but Mr. Procter and Mr. Gamble pay the bills for *Newsmakers* and when they say that it's time for us to let *them* talk we have to do it."

Loyal mumbled something under his breath. "I trust you'll allow me to respond to your point as soon as we get back on the air."

"Sorry," she said. "We've got to get to the phones. Besides, I don't think that was really going anywhere, do you?"

"Well…"

"Five seconds," the producer said.

"And four, three, two and one…"

"Welcome back," she said. "I'm Marie White and you're watching *Newsmakers*. Professor Richard Loyal from Duke University is with us today and we're ready to take your calls. Remember, our number is 556-2900. For those of you calling long distance, our area code is 818. First caller, please. You're on the air."

"Hello…"

"Yes," Marie said.

"Hello…"

"We hear you," Marie said, "please state your question for Professor Loyal."

"Thank you," the voice said. "I'd like to ask Professor Loyal whether or not he thinks the price of a college education today has gotten too high for the average person to afford."

"Nothing is more expensive than ignorance," he said. "If America would invest in education instead of weapons the world would be a saner as well as a safer place."

"Yes, Professor, but you see—all the cuts in the defense industry in southern California have put a lot of people out of work here and it's getting more and more expensive to send our kids to college."

"I understand your dilemma, madam, but I am powerless to change it. I suggest you contact your congressperson and express your concerns to him or her."

"What do you mean, Professor?"

"*Write* to him or her. *Call* him or her."

"Who is the other person, Professor? You said him or her. Our congresswoman is Nancy Slater. There isn't any him."

"I was attempting to use a gender-neutral phrase, madam."

"Well, Congresswoman Slater is not neuter. She's a woman."

"*Neutral*, madam, not *neuter*. I am aware of the fact that the congressperson has not been neutered."

Marie smiled. "I won't follow up on that, Professor," she said. "Thank you caller. Next caller, please…"

It was a woman's voice.

"Professor, my daughter is a sophomore at Cal State-San Marcos. I don't know if you know where that is. Anyway, she's doing real well so far and she's interested in becoming a lawyer, so I was wondering if you could give me some idea as to what law schools are looking for when they receive an application."

"Madam…"

"You see," she said, cutting him off, "she hasn't decided on a major yet and she figured that there might be certain majors that the law schools would say are better than others. What do you think?"

"Madam, I have no idea what law schools consider when they evaluate applications. I suggest you contact them."

"Does your university have a law school? What school did they say you're from?"

"I teach at Duke University, Madam. Yes, we have a law school."

"Is it a good one?"

"It's a fine one, madam."

"But you don't know what they're looking for when you apply to their law school."

"No, madam. I do not."

"Well . . . thank you," she said, and hung up.

"Next caller, please," Marie said.

"Hello, I'd like to ask the professor a question," the voice said. The speaker was a young man; he sounded polite.

"Thank you for calling," Marie responded. "What's your question?"

"I wanted to ask the professor a question about modern literature."

"Go right ahead, young man," Loyal said, scooting forward in his seat in anticipation.

"OK. I was wondering which of Tom Clancy's novels you think is the best. He was out here just before he died, you know, autographing his books and all, and I went and he spoke for awhile first. It was at this bookstore over on Wilshire, down toward town—they call it *mid-*Wilshire, but it's not exactly in the middle. Anyway…"

Marie interrupted him. "About your question, caller…"

"Right. Well, I was wondering . . . you see, Tom Clancy said his favorite of all his books is *Patriot Games*, but I still think *The Hunt for Red October* is the best. *Cardinal's* OK . . . I mean, you can't really understand it without having read the earlier stuff, but I still like *Red October*. I mean, the movie was a real disappointment but, you know, all of us really figured it would be. You just can't do all that stuff in a movie."

"Professor?" Marie said. Loyal had moved back in his seat, his interest gone and his sullen expression increasing.

"I think the caller is a better judge of that man's books than I would be," Loyal said.

"I think we have time for one more call before we break for a message," Marie said. "Caller number four, you're on the air."

"Who is that goddamned fraud sitting next to you?" the voice said.

Tom and Chris both tightened up.

"I beg your pardon, caller," Marie said. "This is Professor Richard Loyal of Duke University."

"That's not Richard Loyal," the man said.

Chris jumped up and looked at the number across the top of the switchboard. The second phone, on Chris's end of the operator's table, was connected directly to the Police Administration Building. Chris picked it up. "Bill," he said. "I think it's him. He's calling from 403-3962 . . . yes, I'll hold."

"Richard Loyal is a great man," the voice said. "He's a genius. Not some beady-eyed little college professor in a faggy-ass bow tie."

Marie gestured off camera to the engineer, shaking her hand from side to side and indicating that the caller shouldn't be cut off, regardless of what he might say.

"Richard Loyal wouldn't sit there taking all that shit and listening to all those stupid goddamned questions."

Loyal started to respond. Marie held up her hand, knowing that she had to keep the caller on the line.

"Sir, we sincerely appreciate your call. Could you tell us more about Professor Loyal's work and how you've come to admire him so much..."

Chris turned to Tom. "It's a fleabag hotel near downtown. They can't identify the specific room. We've got four cars on the way."

"Why should I talk about Loyal?" the voice said. "When you put a goddamned imposter on the air and insult people like that . . . you ought to be goddamned ashamed."

"Sir," Marie said, "if you doubt that this is Professor Loyal, perhaps you could ask him a question and see whether or not he is capable of answering it. I'm certain he would be anxious to respond to you."

"Fuck that," the voice said. "I'm not wasting my time with some goddamned fake." He slammed down the phone. The producer was standing at the side of the stage with her mouth open, while the engineer was shaking his head from side to side. The switchboard operator was smiling like a kid skipping school and Marie was turning to the camera, completely composed.

"It's certainly an interesting world we live in today," she said. "We're sorry if some of you were offended by the last caller's language. Let's take a commercial break. This is *Newsmakers*; we'll be right back."

Chris called to the engineer. "I need three copies of that footage," he said, "and the best sound that you can manage."

"You got it," the engineer said.

Chris and Tom ran into the parking lot and got into Chris's cruiser. "We'll voice-print that puppy. I know it's circumstantial but it's still another piece."

"I'm sure that was Harris," Tom said. "Who else but Harris would be that upset and talk that way about it? The rest of Loyal's fan base (such as it is) probably know what he looks like and the sort of things that he'd be likely to say."

"I agree," Chris said, pulling out of the lot and heading toward the freeway. He hit the siren and the accelerator and tightened his grip on the wheel. "I hope we can get there in time. I want to collar that bastard so bad I can taste it."

"Marie White did well," Tom said, as Chris hit the corner of a pothole and the undercarriage of the cruiser slapped against the street.

"She always does," he said, hitting the accelerator hard.

FORTY-FOUR

"Where are we headed?" Tom asked.

"A dump called the *Excelsior Arms*," Chris answered.

"The one a couple of streets from LaFayette Park?"

"Right. We're almost there."

"Don't you want to put on a pair of roach stabbers before you go in, Chief?"

"I probably should," Chris said, smiling, "but we don't have all that much time." He turned left onto West 6th and hit the accelerator.

The street wasn't barricaded but the entrance to the hotel was blocked by four black-and-whites. Chris double-parked and ran up to the officer at the door. His name was Tuller.

"What have we got, Steve?"

"I don't think very much, sir," he said.

"What room was he in?"

"Room 312. Right next to the stairs."

"Did anybody see him leave?"

"We haven't found anybody yet who did."

They hurried toward the elevator but it was bolted shut. A piece of stained cardboard with writing that looked like the work of a six year-old was attached to the door with yellowed scotch tape. It said ***Out of Order***. "They probably put that sign up the day the place was built," Tom said.

The third-floor hallway consisted of frustrated police officers and an unbroken line of curious residents standing in open doorways. Most of them were holding bottles or cigarettes. Several were still in their underwear. A couple were talking to one another about the excitement; one of them was absentmindedly picking at parts of his face and body. Chris and Tom walked into room 312. Bill Bondeson had gotten there a minute before them.

"The seat at the desk was still warm when the first car arrived," Bill said. "Gorman and Benson. They had to stop at the front desk, wake up the clerk, and help him get his eyes to focus on Harris' picture. By the time they got to the room he was gone. Either he walked out the front door while they were at the desk or he went down the back way while they were coming up. Probably the latter. There's a parking lot in the rear. He either had a car there waiting or he picked up the first one he liked and split."

"He could have left on foot," Chris said. "Is anybody checking the streets?"

"We've got people going door to door and some plainclothes types in both of the parks, but I think he's out of here. In fact I'd bet on it. He's too smart, Chris. He knows we can trace the call and he knows we can search the neighborhood. He's a transient. Why should anybody around here hide him or help him? Hell, if he had any money they'd just hit him over the head and take it. No, his only chance is to clear out quick. Trust me, he's gone."

"What did he leave in the room?"

"Maybe a fingerprint or two. Not much else."

"But the call definitely came from this room."

"Just a second," Bondeson said. He called to Bill Gorman and asked about the call. Gorman walked over, greeted Chris and Tom, and told them that all calls had to go through the hotel switchboard and that the call to the studio definitely came from Harris' room. "Cost him seventy-five cents," Gorman said. "The times of calls are recorded; his is labeled *local*, but the time of his call coincides with the time of the call received at ABC. They didn't even tack on a surcharge. Not that it matters much, since he's not going to come back to clear his tab anyway."

"Hell of a bargain these days," Bondeson said. "Of course, this isn't exactly the *Beverly Wilshire*."

"Circumstantial," Chris said, "but it's another thing to throw on the pile. A fingerprint or two would help also."

"Look at it this way, Chief," Tom said, "even if you don't have the evidence for a lead-pipe cinch conviction, you've got enough to know in your gut that this has to be the boy. Everything hangs together. There are no other possibilities. So we may be running all over the county and state, but we know we're looking for the right guy. And you know what?"

"What's that?"

"I think we're getting close. We may even be due for a break."

"Why do you say that?"

"Because," Tom said, "this guy's not just a crook. He's a true believer. And that's not only a hell of a lot more dangerous, it's also a hell of a lot more risky. He tried to steal the first time around to make a life with Lorna. That was much simpler than any of this. This time he's trying to clear away everything in the past that screwed up his original plan and he's trying to do it with style. The problem is that it's all suddenly impossible—Lorna's no longer interested in him and the two of us are determined to keep getting in his way. Everything he had planned is now falling apart. That's pissing him off monumentally and tipping him toward the edge. Calling the studio was stupid. It's not like him to do that. He just couldn't keep his hands off of that phone. You know what I think? I think he's getting ready to roll the dice on the last bet."

"Then the stakes are going to be high," Chris said.

FORTY-FIVE

Two days passed. Then three . . . and four. Sarah was moved to another safe house, her fifth so far. Always stay a moving target, Chris thought. He increased the surveillance wherever he thought it might yield results. So far there was nothing. Richard Loyal returned to North Carolina with everyone's blessings. The locals there kept an eye out for Harris, in case he decided to pay a visit, but that was a *bona fide* longshot, since Harris had insisted that the professor was a phony. Roy Haggerty was still doing his best to keep Lorna calm and her movements were being checked every few hours by a two-team set of plainclothes officers in unmarked sedans. So far no one had visited Sarah's Laguna apartment except for the mailman and an earnest team of Seventh Day Adventists. No big surprises on any front, but as Bill Engle pointed out, it always pays to cut the cards.

Tom worked other cases, but the Harris case was never far from his mind. He sought continual reassurances that Sarah was indeed safe and visited her every other evening, even though many of their conversations were strained, their renewed romance kicked to the curb by recent events. For a time he immersed himself in paperwork, rearranging hardcopy as well as computerized files, and reorganizing the materials in his office desk and cabinet. He made calls and ran errands, performed some routine maintenance on his boat and checked in with his dad. His life was essentially on hold. Harris had inserted himself into it and Tom knew that he could not comfortably return to it until Harris had either been arrested and returned to prison or stretched out on the medical examiner's table. On Saturday morning Tom and Chris met at the department pistol range, fired a half-dozen magazines of ammunition each, and then drove into Costa Mesa for lunch.

They went to a new place just off the freeway, a few blocks from the mall called *The Gondola*, ordered some olive salad, some veal, fettucine and a bottle of Italian mineral water.

"We're doing everything we can," Chris said. "I don't know what else we can do except wait."

"Don't worry," Tom said. "He's still out there. He's not going anywhere yet because he's still got work to do. Sooner or later he'll surface."

"We've been checking out all the petty thefts and muggings—anything that could get him some quick pocket money."

"He doesn't need that much," Tom said, "not if he's willing to stay at places like the *Excelsior Arms*. Remember, Chief, this guy's been eating prison food for ten years. To him a *Bob's Big Boy* breakfast buffet probably looks like a Roman emperor's coronation feast."

"We've checked the costume shops and makeup stores too," Chris said. "I figure he might have run out of phony hair or something and wanted to change his appearance. We haven't turned anything though. The little son-of-a-bitch is getting more coverage in the mainstream and tabloid press than Brad and Leonardo. Bill Bondeson said that his image has appeared everywhere except on *Entertainment Tonight*. I also checked on his friends in prison to see if he could be using a connection there to find some kind of hidey-hole in L.A. We learned (and this will come as no surprise to you) that Earlon Harris doesn't really have any friends, but we checked on acquaintances and basically anybody who would talk to us. We did find out one thing."

"You did? What's that?" Tom asked, sipping his water and then refilling both his glass and Chris's.

"Remember the note in his file—his last cellmate had been attacked in prison. Probably a contract job—some guy named Chelton. A real dirt bag—murder, extortion, assault, grand larceny, rape . . . you name it, Chelton does it. They thought Harris paid for the job but they couldn't prove it. Anyway, the attack was unsuccessful. A few days later an Angeles Forest ranger out in the San Gabriels found a body straddling some telephone and high tension wires below the main highway. The guy wasn't practicing wire-walking. He was a known associate of a friend of Harris' cellmate. And he was fried to a crisp."

"The cellmate Harris tried to have killed."

"Yes, or at least physically assaulted."

"So maybe the cellmate sent somebody to visit Harris and teach him a lesson, but Harris beat him to the draw."

"Right. We can't prove it, but it's got the Harris touch."

"Harris' idea of a joke. The dead guy is sending a wire or making a phone call to the folks back home."

"Exactly," Chris said. "There were also multiple stab wounds and an extreme makeover of his mouth and what was left of his teeth, probably with a sap or some handy expedient like a sock full of quarters. If it *was* Harris, he was playing with the guy for awhile before he killed him. And he was playing rough."

"At least he's staying in character," Tom said, pausing and thinking for a moment. "By the way, Chief, how do you like this veal?"

"It's pretty good. This is the place you recommended to me a month or so ago, isn't it?"

"Yes."

You want a cup of coffee?"

"Why not two or three? Until we catch a break in the Harris case we don't have much else to do."

The next Monday Tom drove up to L.A. to check in with Bondeson and the members of his lab team. Nothing new on that front, beyond the results of the artificial hair sample comparisons. On the way back he checked in with Hector, who was working one of the molestation cases.

Again nothing new; the suspect was in Boston for the week. He made some other calls and ran some errands. He was still just burning time. On the way home he bought some flowers for Sarah and took them by Chris's town house so that Chris could pass them on to the guard at the safe house before the change of shift. Chris had told Tom to meet him at 5:00 but when Tom arrived Chris was gone. There was no note and there had been no cellphone or landline messages.

Tom returned to his own place, put the flowers in water, and opened his refrigerator to see what he might have to drink that would help his leftover dinner go down a little more easily. As he did the phone rang.

"You know who this is, asshole," the voice said. "Go to the phone booth in the *Ralph's* parking lot on Lake in Pasadena. Just below the freeway, on the east side. You've got an hour and twenty minutes to get there. If you don't make it in time, Dietrich dies. If you try to bring anybody with you tell them to be sure and bring a body bag too."

Tom tried to call Chris at his town house and then at the office but couldn't reach him. He called his cell number. Nothing. He had an hour and seventeen minutes left as he hurried to his car.

The traffic was tight. He had to use his siren and move in and out of the breakdown lane.

As he pulled into the lot with only seconds to spare the phone was ringing. He left the motor running, jumped out, and picked up the receiver.

"I'm only going to say this once, asswipe," the voice said, "so take the shit out of your ears and listen. I've got your old buddy here and I've got some demands. I need you to be my messenger. If you don't show, he dies immediately and I grab somebody else and call you again until you stop playing games and start following my directions. Understood?"

"Understood," Tom said. "Where and when?"

"You know the parking lot on top of Mt. Wilson?"

"The one below the snack bar?"

"Yes."

"I do," Tom said.

"Nine o'clock sharp."

"It closes at five. The gate's already locked and chained."

"Tomorrow morning, asshole, not tonight," the voice said. "One other thing. You come in your car. Alone and unarmed. If I see anything or anybody that looks suspicious—*anything*—I whack little chiefie and we go back to square one. Understood?"

"Understood."

"By the way, he's not looking too good right now. I don't think being held captive is agreeing with him. Maybe the fact that I love-tapped him a couple of times has something to do with it."

Before Tom could respond the phone clicked. He got back in his car, drove behind *Ralph's* and headed south on Mentor, figuring that Harris might have been watching him in the lot. He took out his cell phone but got a screen message that service was currently unavailable; he then crossed Colorado, Green, and Cordova and turned into the shoppers' parking lot behind the string of stores on Lake. He hurried into the Pasadena copy of the London Burlington Arcade, went into the transplanted London phone booth there, dropped his coins, and punched in eleven numbers.

"Hector," he said, "this is Tom. Harris just called; he says that he's got Chris. I need you."

FORTY-SIX

Chris had his doubts about Hector, but no doubts concerning his abilities. Before moving to the O.C. Hector had grown up on the streets, in East L.A. As a result he always carried more weapons than his service automatic; some of them were improvised; all of them were lethal. "You can take Hector out of the mean streets in a mean neighborhood," Chris would say, "but you can't take the streets out of Hector. I'm always afraid that he's going to revert."

Tom reassured him that Hector was disciplined, that he had changed, that he would not cross any lines or skirt any edges.

"It's only a matter of time," Chris would say. "It's a question of survival, Tom. If Hector is threatened, *significantly* threatened, he'll fall back on the ways and means that enabled him to survive in the past."

"That was years ago, Chief. Decades now."

"Just the blink of an eye," Chris said, "when somebody twice your size comes at someone you care about with a razor or an ice pick."

"Look at the upside," Tom said.

"What's that?"

"He's on our side, Chief."

He had said that on several occasions. Now the point came home. They might need Hector and the circumstance could easily be extreme. Tom would also need Hector's discipline, however, because if Harris was aware that Tom had disobeyed his order and brought someone else along he would not hesitate an instant to murder Chris Dietrich. He might even be looking forward to it, since Chris had been responsible for Harris' being set up at Saddleback, where Harris was nearly taken.

Tom was unsure of what Harris might do, but he was confident that Hector would play his own role well. A year and a half earlier they had responded to a domestic violence call. Though such cases are always dangerous since you can easily find yourself caught between two angry, dysfunctional, armed individuals, this one appeared to be one of straightforward wife battering that had escalated. When they arrived they quickly realized that they themselves had been set up.

A gangbanger from Santa Ana was trying to earn his colors by killing a cop. "The best way to get one is to order one," he was told. "You call up and have one sent out." When they arrived at the caller's apartment a woman met them at the door, her left eye bruised and her lip split in two places. There was blood on her chin, neck, and the top of her blouse. When she let them in, the apartment was quiet. She had told them that her boyfriend had left a few minutes before their arrival to pick up some cigarettes.

When they entered, the door slammed behind them and they found themselves facing a teenage Latino with a sawed-off shotgun. "Well, well," he said. "A twofer."

Hector immediately spoke to him in Spanish. His voice was soft, his words measured. When he finished the boy laughed.

"You think you can sell me that bullshit? You sound like that bitch there. I told her I wanted her to call the police and get a cop here. She hesitated. After I popped her a couple of times she reached for the phone. She didn't think I was serious until she started tasting her own blood. Then she knew it was for real."

Hector remained calm as Tom asked the kid to allow the woman to go into the other room. "She doesn't have to see this," he said.

"But she might like it," the kid said. "For a change it won't be her blood."

Tom began to speak again, but before he could complete his initial sentence Hector leaped forward. He was counting on the fact that the kid was hesitant to kill in cold blood and was grateful for the words that enabled him to postpone the action. When Tom started to say something the kid's reaction was to relax, if only for a second, and allow him to complete his thought.

By the time that Tom's first sentence would have been finished Hector had dodged the barrels of the shotgun as he forced it into the air. The weapon discharged and the ceiling was shredded; Hector quickly twisted the weapon, snapping the kid's fingers like dried twigs, and then removed it from his grip, shattering his jaw, nose and cheek with the butt in a single, follow-up motion.

The kid was now covered with blood and crying and convulsing; Hector flipped him over, held him against the floor with his knee, cuffed him, and quietly turned to the woman, saying, "I'm sorry you had to see this, ma'am; are you all right?"

When Tom called him about Chris, Hector asked him where he was.

"In Pasadena," he said.

"I can be there in a little over an hour. What have we got?" Hector asked.

"Hard to say," Tom said. "I can't raise Chris on either his cell or his landline, so at this point I have to assume that Harris is telling the truth. I have to take his word that he's got him and that Chris has probably been injured. Harris also said that he had some demands and that he wanted to use me as his messenger. That means he's going to keep Chris as a hostage until I convey whatever message he has in mind. It sure as hell won't be a Best Wishes greeting card to the citizens of Los Angeles. By now I'm sure he's really seething; he couldn't get to Sarah and when he got his hopes up over seeing his darling Loyal he was tricked (he believes) by an imposter. His brain is always simmering; now it's on a rolling boil."

"And you didn't get to hear Chris's voice."

"No, unfortunately, I didn't."

"You figure he wants to kill you too?" Hector asked.

"Maybe. I'm sure he wants to kill somebody. He's probably found out that I'm Sarah's friend and that Chris is the one who's been hiding her. I figure he wants a piece of both of us and using Chris as bait will bring me to the scene."

"When?"

"At nine o'clock tomorrow morning."

"Where, Lieutenant?"

"At the top of Mt. Wilson."

"That's interesting," Hector said.

"Yes," Tom said. "That's when the gate at the top opens. The place is pretty deserted then, except for the snack bar crew and the people operating the telescopes. Nine o'clock is too late to catch the sunrise and the morning clouds and smog often limit the views of the valleys and basin. Most people wait to go up until later. Otherwise you're looking at a 19 mile drive up a narrow, twisty road to sit on the top of a cold mountain and look out at nothing but mist and fog."

"And because of the road and the time, Harris can keep an eye on the traffic and make certain that you're the only one coming through that gate."

"Right. I can't go in followed by a string of police cruisers. He'd spot that instantly. We don't know where he's keeping Chris. He could sit in the woods next to the parking lot, disappear the moment he sees something suspicious, kill Chris, and then start the process all over again the next morning."

"I've been up there a lot," Hector said. "There are six separate trails leading to the top, varying from about seven miles to almost fourteen. He can't watch them all. Besides, I'm used to making myself scarce in the woods and brush. I was a scout, remember? I could take the old 1864 trail from Sierra Madre. I've been up that one so many times I know every fork and bend. Let's do this, Lieutenant—you drive to the summit and

I'll climb. You talk to the bastard and I'll stay nearby for insurance. I'll bring an assortment of weapons—enough so that I can react to whatever it is he plans to try."

"You've got to be very careful, Hector," Tom said. "He's a psychopath but he's also smart as hell. Chris's life is on the line."

"I'm always careful when I'm angry, Lieutenant," Hector said. "You've seen me angry, haven't you?"

"Once."

"And what happened? Do you remember?"

"You kicked ass and took names but I can't say I recall the taking of too many names. I do remember a crushed jaw, crushed cheek bones, crushed nose, broken fingers, and a lot of blood."

"I don't like it when people come after my friends, Lieutenant," Hector said. "It reminds me too much of my youth . . . and my youth wasn't always very pretty."

FORTY-SEVEN

Rising to a height of 5710 feet, Mt. Wilson is named for the nineteenth-century trapper-trader Benjamin Davis Wilson. The Spanish locals called him *Don Benito*. Once *alcalde* of the old San Bernardino district, Wilson was also elected county clerk, city councilman, and the first mayor of Los Angeles. The largest maker of wine and brandy in the state of California, he owned a portion of real estate whose modern value would be more than enough to make the estate of J. Paul Getty look like the change in the pocket of a Boyle Heights derelict: 2,200 acres near San Bernardino/Riverside; 10 acres downtown that included the present site of Union Station; acreage to the west that included the present site of UCLA; and some 14,000 acres spreading south from the foothills of the San Gabriels and including what is now Pasadena, South Pasadena, San Marino, Alhambra, and San Gabriel.

The principal piece that remains is a tiny, 128-acre fragment of Don Benito's land now termed Lacy Park; it sits in the center of San Marino—a rose-arbored piece of eden below Pasadena, upscale even by local standards, that alone could bring riches beyond the dreams of avarice to any developer who might find a way to wrest it from the hands of the grateful public to whom Benjamin Davis Wilson left it. The famous lawyer, Donald Fell, lives right outside its gates. The late Nate Lasser's liquor store is twelve miles away to the south and west, Lieutenant Bill Bondeson's condo fourteen blocks away to the north.

On the rim of the parking lot at the top of Mt. Wilson stands a weathered plaque commemorating the career of Don Benito, a small tribute to a larger-than-life figure, erected by the Daughters of the American Revolution. It was Benjamin Davis Wilson who had blazed the first trail to the top, in search of wood for his wine casks. And in the garden of the Church of Our Saviour in San Gabriel—the church where his family once worshipped—stands a statue of the now better-known son of Don Benito's beloved daughter Ruth, Benjamin Davis Wilson's grandson.

George Smith Patton, Jr.

Inside the church, opposite the garden, is a piece of glasswork that must be seen to be both believed and appreciated—a combination of myth and symbol and history that could only exist in England or in southern California: St. George on his white mount, vanquishing the dragon of evil, and carrying the insignia of every division and army commanded by the saint's twentieth-century namesake. In one corner, 2 *Timothy*, IV, 7 ("I have fought a good fight, I have finished *my* course, I have kept the faith"); in another—in dark stained glass in an Episcopal Church—Georgie Patton with his helmet, rising out of the commander's cupola of a U.S. Army tank.

Two years ago Chris had taken Tom to see it—a curious bit of local history that was both moving and strange. "They always do something like this to Georgie," Chris said. "Back in the day when I was stationed at Fort Knox, they had Georgie's touring car and field mess kit at the Armor Museum. At West Point he's standing right by the library, clutching his binoculars. The cadets always say that he's trying to *find* the library."

"Well, sometimes we take our monuments where we can get them," Tom said. "Most people don't ever get the chance to do the things that Third Army did. Patton helped put Hitler out of business permanently; that's why all the Latino and Latina kids in Alhambra and San Gabriel are learning English now instead of German. You need people like that."

"People like Hector Campo," Chris said. "I have to say though that he scares me a little bit. I know that he's the sort who's ready to put it on the line during tough times, the times when you most need somebody like that. I'm just a little unsettled by the fact that he seems to enjoy it so much."

"That's the Patton type," Tom said, "What concerns *me* is that in those times when you *really* need Hector you yourself are in very deep kimchi."

FORTY-EIGHT

The skies were unusually clear when Tom drove into the parking lot beneath the shelter house at the top of the mountain. There was a single vehicle there—a dilapidated Ford van driven by the kid who operated the food concession and distributed the maps of local hiking trails from the Big Santa Anita Canyon Historical Society. Tom turned his car around and backed in against the hill about twenty feet away from the van but parallel to it.

He didn't have to wait long. Within five minutes a new, black Buick pulled into the lot and stopped on the west side, fifty yards away. Harris had been parked at the side of the shelter house, next to a utility shed. When he opened the door Tom could hear anthemic, arena rock music blaring from the car. He could also see another human figure in the front seat. Harris was carrying what appeared from a distance to be two small boxes. He was wearing his jacket and cap but had skipped the moustache. He gestured to Tom and pointed toward the south end of the lot, where the asphalt turned to loose gravel and the ground beyond the guard rail was only a few inches wide before it plunged to the canyon floor below. It would be impossible for Hector or anyone else to surprise him there without making *some* noise, no matter how small.

"That's close enough to me," Harris said, "but move your ass over closer to the edge." They were twenty feet apart and standing by the wooden rail, looking toward Mt. Harvard, the Manzanita Ridge, Little Santa Anita Canyon, and beyond to the entire Los Angeles basin.

"This is great," Harris said. "Look at this view. Ocean, sky, mountains, and the whole damn L.A. basin in all its fucking glory. Oh, by the way, asshole, before you get any heroic ideas—I've got a blasting cap attached to the chiefie's chest. To be more specific, it's just above his heart; you can see it move a little as his heart beats. (Actually, his heart's been *pounding* more than beating lately.) All I have to do [he lifted a detonation device that Tom had thought was a simple box] is push this little button under my index finger to blow a nice hole in the center of his chest. I don't think you'd want me to do that. Or would you?"

"What do you want, Harris?" Tom asked, looking beyond him in hopes of seeing some sign of Hector.

"What do I *want*? I'll *tell* you what I want, asshole. Just shut your fucking mouth and be patient. I told you to look at the view and you still haven't done it. Can you see the city? It looks like a set of toy blocks stacked in a nice, neat little package. Can you see Palos Verdes? You can't quite see Catalina, but you can come close. That's really something, isn't it? What would you say—sixty miles? Seventy five?"

Tom didn't answer him.

"I asked you a question, asshole," Harris said.

"Maybe sixty five," Tom said.

"Damned right. You know something—you and your fucking cop buddy tried to ruin everything. You wanted to save your girl friend. So what did you do—you tried to trick me. You used that cheap set-up at the hospital with that phony bitch trying to look like Sarah. Then you brought in that pissant impersonator who claimed to be Loyal. Anything . . . you'd do absolutely *anything*, wouldn't you? You don't care one fucking bit about *my* feelings. You think you're some sort of white knight or something, protecting that slut nurse. She screwed me over good eleven years ago and now you and your goddamned friends won't let me set things right. Well, you'll see, asshole. We're going to set things right after all. And you're going to be sorry you didn't let me do things my way the first time around."

His heart and lungs were racing ahead of his mouth. He paused for a second, then started in again.

"I checked the newspaper files, Deaton. They say you just got promoted to lieutenant. Like you're some kind of fucking hot shot. Is that right?"

"I got promoted," Tom said.

"Perfect. And you solve all the tough cases. Some kind of fucking wizard. At least *you* think you are."

"I wouldn't say that."

"Oh yes you would. You think you're something special. But suddenly things don't look so fucking good for you. Your boss's head and face are all fucked up and he's got a blasting cap strapped to his chest. Meanwhile, you're standing there with your thumb up your ass, wondering how that could have happened. You're not doing so well on this case, are you fuckwad?"

"We haven't closed it yet," Tom said.

"Brave boy. Don't worry, asswipe, you won't."

"We'll see," Tom said.

"Yes, we will. Believe me, we will," Harris said, smiling. "OK, shithead, you've had some basic weapons training. You should know what one little blasting cap will do."

Tom remained silent.

"Well, do you? You fuck with me and you *will* see what it will do."

"Yes, I know what it will do," Tom said.

"It'll blow a big fucking hole in a piece of steel sheeting, won't it?"

"Yes," Tom answered, "it will."

"And you don't want to see your little chiefie's blood and heart and face splattered all over the windshield, do you?"

"No."

"Then listen the fuck up and stop wising off at me, asshole."

"OK," Tom said.

"That's better. You're learning. It's taken you awhile, but you're finally learning. You keep it up and you'll have some real fun today. *I plan to have fun; that's for damned sure. I plan to have more fun than I've ever had before.*"

"What do you want me to do, Harris?"

"I'm getting to that, goddamnit. Now will you shut the fuck up and listen?"

Tom nodded yes.

"Good. Now we can start. Look at that city. Beautiful, isn't it? Especially from up here. You don't smell the odor or see the dirt and the crime or any of that other shit, but from up here it looks damn nice. But you know, it's really not perfect, even though it may look like it is. You know why? Because this is the desert here. Right where we're standing, asshole. The desert. Things get dry and when it rains you have mud slides. Right? And when it doesn't rain you have forest fires. In fact, you have forest fires here all the time. Especially when the Santa Ana winds start blowing. Santa Ana—that's your neck of the woods, asswipe. Those old Santa Anas are a son-of-a-bitch. They lower the humidity and turn everything into tinder. Every year the assholes here lose something—thirty, forty thousand acres. I'm talking about Los Angeles County alone now, not all of southern California. In 1970 they lost 130,000 acres. Oooh and all those little numbnuts lost their homes and their cats and puppy dogs. Terrible, wasn't it?" he said, smiling.

"It takes fifteen to twenty years to get new growth after a big fire. That's why they brought in that wild mustard shit back in the 20's. They use it to reseed after big burns. It's not native like the other crap—the manzanita, sumac, chamise, and stuff. Grows quick though. Isn't that interesting?"

Tom nodded.

"And it's educational too. I told you we'd have fun. You're *learning* things, asswipe. And learning is always fun. That's what my third grade teacher told me . . . at least she did before I put the little sack full of dead things in her fucking purse. She stopped singling me out and talking to me after that. Anyway, this is all about you and me, Deaton. *You're* gonna learn something today. You like to learn, asswipe?"

"Yes," Tom said.

"Good. Then shut the fuck up and listen. Every day the Fire Department measures the moisture in the brush. They call it the 'fuel stick.' They also give out what they call the 'burn index.' That rates the chance of fire on a scale that goes from zero up to two hundred. You know what the 'fuel stick' and 'burn index' are today, Deaton?"

"No," Tom said.

"*I* do," Harris said. "And guess what? The 'fuel stick' is real low and the 'burn index' is real high. It's dry today. And there are no clouds. No rain in sight, Deaton. You know what that means?"

"Yes."

"You tell me what it means, asshole."

"It means that it would be a bad day for a fire."

"Oh no, it would be a *good* day for a fire. It would be a bad day if you owned a house around here, but it would be a *damned good day* for a fire. Did you ever notice—nobody ever sees things from the fire's point of view?"

"I hadn't noticed that," Tom said.

"Oh but you should have. Your daddy and his friends and the fucks that are in charge now . . . a lot of them were in the 'Nam. They started a whole hell of a lot of fires, didn't they?"

Tom didn't answer.

"Well, didn't they, asshole?"

"They used fire, yes."

"You're damned right they did, you prick. Well, guess what. You're gonna have a chance to do that all over again. Here . . . you see this…?" He showed Tom the second metal box; the lid was covered with buttons. "These are transmitters. They set off bombs. I've got bombs all over the place—*incendiary* bombs. Wouldn't you like to know where they are? I'm gonna give you one of the transmitters. It's gonna be yours all alone. Of course, I have one too. Did you take a close look at mine?"

Tom leaned forward to look at it.

"Mine has tape on it, so I don't drop it. You see, if you had made a move on me I would have blown the chiefie's heart right out of his chest. Kaboom! Bye-bye fuckhead! Then, when you were standing there with the shit running down your pants leg, I would have smacked you in the face with the box. Maybe given you a second and third pop too. Aren't you glad you didn't try anything?"

"Yes," Tom said.

"I thought you'd say that. Now . . . let's talk about our little game. I'm going to drive away from here with my transmitting buttons and your fucking cop friend. He's not feeling real good right now. You see, I had to take some of the fight out of him. A couple good swats and he was ready to cooperate. I gave him a couple extra just because I fucking felt like it."

He smiled, baring the brown tips of his teeth.

"Anyway, as I said, I'm gonna drive away and the only way you can stop me is by pushing your buttons and hoping that when you set off a bomb it's somewhere between me and my destination. But you won't know what buttons go with what bombs. You could be stopping me or you could be blowing up some rich cocksucker's house or setting a canyon on fire. You won't know until you try. And if you *don't* try I'll just drive away with my finger in the air. I'll just fucking escape! Doesn't that sound like fun? Of course I've got my own buttons and I know where *all* the bombs are, so I may set off a few just to complicate your life a little. I wouldn't just stand still if I were you. Unless, of course, you're feeling a little cold and want to be warmed up by a nice little forest fire. Did you notice how many buttons there are on your box?"

"Six."

"That's a lot of buttons and a lot of bombs. I've got seven on mine—one for the chiefie, remember? Suppose I told you the bombs were set up all across these mountains. Maybe one above Altadena, one above Sierra Madre, one above Arcadia, one above Monrovia. Maybe one button sets off a whole string of bombs. Twenty or thirty fucking bombs! Do you see what I'm driving at, asshole?"

"Yes."

"What?"

"You could set the whole mountain range and San Gabriel Valley on fire."

"No, no, no," he said. "*That's* not the point. Don't you see the *point?*"

"No," Tom said. "I don't see the point. Why don't you tell me?"

"The point *is*, asshole, you're playing white fucking knight trying to save your chiefie and your cunt girlfriend, but I'm playing something else and I'm fucking in charge. We're playing my game, asshole. We're playing 'Return to the 'Nam'. And you're fucked, because you can't just shoot. You don't know where your enemy is. He may be all around you. The only way to stop him is to start blowing things up, even if that means you have to destroy everything—the whole damned village. *You've got to destroy the village in order to save it.* That was their fucking motto, right? If you *don't* set off the bombs to trap me, I'll set them off to trap you. You don't have any choice, asshole. That's what they told the press, wasn't it? They *had* to destroy the village—all those lying cocksuckers who think they're in charge of us now. Those assholes who push us around and give us orders. They *had to destroy the village.* Well look at *this* village, asshole." He gestured with his right arm, indicating the length and breadth of the Los Angeles basin.

"I see it," Tom said.

"If you fuck up, it all goes. All of it, along with a lot of the assholes who live there. Sound like fun?"

Tom didn't answer.

"It sure as hell sounds like fun to *me*."

Tom still didn't answer.

"Well then, let's play," Harris said. "First you sit down. Then I go put your magic buttons in your car. When I drive out in my car you can move. If you move before I do that, I either blow out the chiefie's chest or cut his throat and see him sitting there gurgling and bleeding all over himself until he dies. Maybe I'll cut slowly, take my time and enjoy the moment..."

Harris smiled at Tom, looking for a reaction while he held up the box and ran the tip of his index finger over the button below it. "Now sit the fuck down, asshole. Right there in the gravel."

Tom sat down and Harris backed away toward Tom's car. When he got to the car he put the other box on the front seat, looked back at Tom, smiled, and then reached into his pocket with his left hand. He pulled out something metallic that gleamed in the sun, plunged it into Tom's left front tire, said "Whoops!" and laughed as the car collapsed. He ran over, got into his own car, and put it in gear. Tom stood up and Harris drove toward him, turning sharply as soon as he got close enough to let Tom see Chris, his forehead bloodied, his eyes swollen and dazed, his mouth covered with furnace tape. "I told you it'd be fun," Harris said, laughing. "Sorry about your tire, asshole; that may slow you down a little bit." Then he hit the accelerator, spraying gravel into the air as he headed out of the lot.

FORTY-NINE

Hector came out of the trees so quickly that he startled Tom. "Get in the van, Lieutenant," he said. "I'll drive."

Hector threw his jacket over the transmitter box on the front seat of Tom's car, locked the door, and hurried over to the van. He put away his hammer when he saw that the door was unlocked. He tossed his green backpack on the metal floor of the van and it landed with a succession of clunks. As he hot-wired the ignition the kid who owned it came running down the hill, yelling and waving his arms frantically.

"Police," Hector said. "Don't call anybody. There's a bomb in that black car that will be detonated if there's any sign of additional officers."

"Wh-what should I do, then?"

"Pray," Hector said.

The kid turned ashen and backed away as the men who had taken his van hit the accelerator and sped off in pursuit of the other man in the Buick. He wondered what could possibly be going on; no more than ten minutes before, he had been sipping hot black coffee and polishing off the remains of a large blueberry muffin, the sort he really liked, the kind with the nice sugary crumbles that covered the top and sort of slid down the sides. Then this guy drove out from the side of the shed and started talking to this young guy who had just pulled into the lot and looked like a plainclothes policeman or firefighter or something—something official. Then this Latino guy came out of the woods. Now, suddenly, someone was ready to blow the top off of Mt. Wilson and him with it. He stumbled momentarily and bumped into the redwood rail leading up to the shelter house as he tried to focus, staring at his van as it disappeared through the trees and down the side of the mountain. He braced himself and looked down at Tom's unmarked cruiser with the dead tire and started running a succession of images through his head: sticks of stacked and bound dynamite, bottles of nitro laying in a box lined with brown excelsior, coils of det cord and neatly-wrapped packs of C-4 or Semtex. As he tried to clear his thoughts he realized that he had suddenly stopped breathing.

"We've got to get right up on him," Hector said, swerving sharply to the right and dodging one of the scientists who had come out of the green building housing the people who operated the Mt. Wilson telescopes. "You see what he's up to, don't you?"

"It's starting to become clear," Tom said. "In the first place, he must have put a little inconspicuous plastic in that transmitter somewhere so he could blow me away any time he wanted or needed to."

"Very likely," Hector said, turning hard to avoid some rocks in the narrow road. "Whether he did or not, we couldn't take the chance. My guess is that the transmitters are real enough but that they're not on the same frequency as the bombs. He'd figure that you had some demolitions training somewhere along the line and would be able to tell the difference between a legitimate transmitter and a toy or phony. What you *wouldn't* be able to know is the frequency of the bombs. The big thing is that he wanted you to have a legit device. That way *he* could close off his escape route or set the forest on fire and make it look as if *you* did it. The point is that there would be no way of knowing whether it was him who had set up the devices or you."

"Right," Tom said. "He could leave the box intact, put the blame on us, at least temporarily, and give himself enough time to drive away into the sunset. Since we knew about the meeting in advance, the press and the powers that be would assume that we set up the bombs in order to trap him. He bolted, we panicked, and accidentally destroyed everything."

"Right," Hector said. "Something like that. He might also be planning to crush you under a mini-avalanche or blow you off the road and down the side of the mountain. Either way there would be a good chance that the detonator would survive in some form and you could still take the fall for everything. In the meantime, I've got to stay right on his bumper. He probably has one or more of the bombs set up along the road so he can pass them, detonate them, and seal his exit. I'm gonna be on him like a dog on a meat wagon. He won't be able to take us out without coming along himself."

"And taking Chris with him," Tom added.

"Yes," Hector said, "but I'm figuring that the only thing on his mind will be his own sweet self. If he thinks the universe revolves around *him,* the chief's presence will be purely incidental. Little Earlon's first priority will be to protect Number One."

The van steered like an unsprung lead box and there were five miles of narrow road between the top of the mountain and the Angeles Crest Highway.

Hector wrestled with the steering wheel. "I've driven vans and half-tons with a mind of their own since I was a teenager," he said, "but I've never driven anything quite like this relic. Hold on." Every few yards of straightaway Hector gunned the motor, moving in slow and coming out fast on the curves. When a station wagon full of people approached him on the mountain side, Hector held his hand on the horn and kept on going. The driver turned into the burn, his face flushed with terror.

"There goes their upholstery," Hector said.

"We can't let him get ahead of us," Tom answered. "That's for damned sure."

They were within a half-mile of the main highway when they saw Harris' stolen Buick.

"Hit it," Tom said. "He's got both of his hands on the wheel. That means he had to put down the transmitter. As soon as he gets on the highway and he sees us he'll be able to use his other hand."

"The chief's still sitting up," Hector said. "Harris won't detonate the blasting cap (if there is one) while the chief's sitting two feet away from him."

"No," Tom said, "but he's also got that knife and he can use it anytime he feels like it."

As Hector accelerated over some loose stones and gravel, they heard the first explosion.

FIFTY

"I can see dust and patches of smoke but I can't see any flames," Tom said.

"Where was it?" Hector asked, focusing on the road ahead as he hit the accelerator.

"Near the top but outside the gate," Tom said. "He's sealing off the crest."

"How many people are up there?" Hector asked.

"I don't know, but I'm sure they're all on their cell phones now, calling the rangers and firefighters and anybody else who'll listen, and screaming for help."

"There's not too much wind," Hector said, swerving to the right and then the left. "Maybe they'll be able to control any fires he was able to set."

"There's the son-of-a-bitch," Tom said, lurching forward in his seat, as Hector came out of a curve and Harris came into view less than a quarter of a mile in front of them.

"I think he's spotted us," Hector said, accelerating again. "Quite a plan, huh? Burn up the whole forest and probably some of the city. He doesn't think small, does he?"

"And he plans to blame it all on us," Tom said. "I figured it would be something big—at least big enough to match his anger over Sarah, but I didn't know just how much anger he had."

The next explosion was just behind and above them.

"I didn't much care for that," Tom said, as dirt and gravel splattered the top of their van. "We've got to get closer to him, Hector."

"Odd," Hector said, momentarily looking in the rear-vision mirror. "He must be thinking *escape* more than *fire*. That one closed the road behind us, but there's so damned little brush around here that I don't think the flames will spread. I saw the flash but I don't think you'll see much else now."

"Hit it," Tom said. "I want the next one farther behind us. If he detonates one in front of us he's out of here and Chris is history."

"I know," Hector answered, coming out of a tight curve and feathering the brake.

"Look, Hector," Tom said.

"What . . . the . . . hell?"

Suddenly the car ahead of them in their lane was a corroded yellow Pinto, not Harris' stolen Buick. The rear bumper was hanging loose and reddish-brown rust was spreading over its fenders like fire ants moving across the south Texas border.

"Where did that rattletrap come from?" Hector asked.

"He must have been driving up the mountain when the first bomb went off. He turned around and as he was headed down Harris passed him," Tom said. "Look…"

In front of the Pinto was a maroon Honda.

"He passed both of them on a blind curve at forty miles an hour," Tom said. "That's a death-wish move."

"He's trying to put enough distance between us to make a run for it," Hector said. "I'm afraid I can't permit that to happen. Not today."

Hector passed the Pinto and came up on the Honda. Tom caught a glimpse of the Pinto driver, who had stopped and was leaning forward in his seat and choking the steering wheel. The Honda driver tried to move to the side, figuring he was being followed by another lunatic, but when he came up on a turnout he was going too fast to take it and maneuver out of Hector's way. Hector passed him anyway and the Honda braked, skidding toward the edge of the mountain.

The driver's head jerked as he brought the car to a sudden stop. Tom turned and saw him pounding the steering wheel, screaming down the canyon in anger and fear.

"They're OK," Tom said. "Just shaken up a little. Well . . . maybe more than just a little."

Hector didn't respond.

"There's Harris," Tom said.

Hector saw him. He was passing a station wagon, no more than thirty yards short of a blind curve.

"Go," Tom said, keeping one eye on Harris and waiting for the sound of the next explosion. "We've got to catch him before he buries us in rocks and flames."

They held their breath but the explosion never came. Suddenly there was no sign of Harris' Buick. "Where the hell did he go?" Tom said, as Hector's eyes searched the road and the ravines.

Suddenly the bombs went off, exploding behind them in parallel lines of fire that obliterated the road and followed them like tracers from a strafing plane. The final blast was thirty yards from their bumper.

"That was too damned close," Hector said.

"They were on each side of the road," Tom said. "He didn't want to miss. It's a good thing you scared the hell out of the Pinto and Honda drivers so that they had to stop to catch their breaths. They're thanking you now. That last set would have taken them out. I'm not so sure about the station wagon."

"What do you think, Lieutenant?" Hector asked. "Was that the whole wad?"

"Who knows?" Tom answered. "It depends on how they were wired. It sounded like several went off separately, but with the echoes it's hard to tell."

"I'm sure as hell not going to wait around for more," Hector said.

They were five miles from La Cañada-Flintridge now and the road was surprisingly empty. They saw two park police outside their cabin, frantically talking on car radios, trying to find out just what in the world was going on, and gesturing at the towers of smoke and flame above them. As they got closer to the bottom of the mountain the number of turnouts and staging areas had increased; several of the open areas were filled with tourists who had given up any thought of attempting the climb as the dust and smoke began to encircle the mountain and close off any possible views of the summit. The main highway itself was suddenly deserted.

"Wait a minute," Hector said. "What if he pulled off back there and switched cars?"

"He could be behind us," Tom said. "We can't lose him, Hector. If we do, Chris is a dead man."

Hector swerved to the left into a narrow turnout and started back up the mountain, accelerating hard. He drove into the first turnout. No sign of the Buick—just a car full of kids, dad pacing the burn in cargo pants, mom offering solace to a baby, and a park policeman waving to Hector to stop. Hector kept going.

The second turnout was an overlook and it was crowded. A dozen cars at least, and on the end Harris' Buick with Chris in the front seat.

"You go take care of Chris," Tom said. "I want Harris."

"Are you sure?" Hector said.

"I'm sure," Tom answered.

Hector slid to a hard stop, frightening the people from the adjoining cars who were trying to dodge the fenders of the van and still look in the window at Chris Dietrich.

"Maybe Chris saw the car he took," Hector said, jumping out of the driver's seat, grabbing his backpack and heading around the back of the van.

The doors of the Buick were locked and the windows were up. There was blood on Chris's head and throat. He was unconscious and there was no time to go through the crowd asking questions. Another five seconds might have been all that Harris needed. Hector turned to the van to wave Tom on but he was already gone, leaving nothing behind him but a thin patch of tire tread from the aging van, and a spray of dust and hard gravel.

FIFTY-ONE

Tom was following a Mercury Sable with plastic sheets stretched vertically across the rear windows. Along the highway on his left he saw the beginnings of civilization—newer homes in the low seven-figure range surrounded by tall palms and thick pines, leaning over the valley, announcing their presence to their neighbors in La Cañada-Flintridge. Suddenly there were four cars ahead of him as he came up to the sign for the Foothill Freeway interchange: a Mercedes 190, a vintage Pontiac Bonneville, a silver, four-door Cutlass, and the Sable.

"*Damn* it," Tom said to himself. "Where did *they* come from?" The Sable abruptly turned into the shoulder lane. Tom slowed and as he passed saw a woman's face behind the wheel. No one was holding a knife to her throat. He accelerated and caught up with the other three cars. The Pontiac was heading southeast toward Pasadena, the Mercedes and Olds northwest, into the Valley.

"Command decision time, Lieutenant," he said to himself, aloud. He was fifty yards from the freeway entrance, his right foot hovering between the brake and the accelerator.

"Take the odds," he said, turning right. He was too far behind and too high up in the driver's seat of the van to get a decent look at the drivers of the other cars and he didn't want to get close enough to any of them to give himself away. None of the cars had made a clear break as yet and all of them could easily outrun and outmaneuver him if they wanted to do so. There was great consolation in the fact that Harris no longer had Chris, but the sobering reality was that if he escaped now he would almost surely leave a new set of victims in his wake. For that matter there was no guarantee that he would actually *leave*. If Tom couldn't find him now they would all have to continue living with the thought of this maniacal psychopath hovering over them, capable of destroying their lives in an act of singular violence. Sarah would, as always, be the most vulnerable target as well as Harris' target of choice and though she might *understand* how hard Tom had tried to protect her it would still be difficult for her to ever bring herself to the point where she would actually be prepared to forgive him.

"If Harris grabbed the Pontiac he's a free man," Tom said, squeezing the steering wheel. He called Bill Bondeson on his cell phone, caught him on the second ring, and briefly explained the situation. It was the longest of long shots. Before anyone in law enforcement could pick up any one of the three cars in question Harris would have a five to ten minute lead, an eternity in southern California traffic. Tom described the Pontiac and gave Bill the license number. He then accelerated and gave him the numbers for the Mercedes and Cutlass.

"Thanks, Tom. We'll give it our best shot," Bill said.

"Thanks," Tom said, knowing the odds. If Harris could switch cars as quickly as he had on the edge of the mountain, what could he do in downtown Pasadena or in the alleys and back streets of La Crescenta?

"I can eliminate the latter possibility at least," Tom said, as each car passed the exit for La Crescenta. In a few moments, however, the Cutlass' right turn signal flashed.

"One in three chances now. Crunch time," Tom said. Suddenly it hit him. *Tujunga. He's going to pick up Lorna.* He cut the Mercedes loose and turned on his flasher.

The Cutlass accelerated as soon as it hit the surface streets. "He's getting anxious," Tom said to himself. Somehow it reassured him to be talking out loud to himself in that fashion. The Cutlass drove eight blocks, turned right, turned right a second time, and eased into a space at the end of a strip mall. Tom followed. Leaning forward in his seat he was able to see the large yellow plastic sign with oversized black lettering: *Crouper's Kitchen World*. Tom pulled in across from the *Hallmark* shop, reached behind him and pulled out the service automatic inside his belt. He checked it, got out of the car, slipped the gun into his pants above his left front pocket, and hurried around to Harris' car.

As far as he could tell he hadn't been seen. He reached into his right sock, took out his Buck knife, and stuck it into the right rear tire of Harris' Cutlass. Nothing happened; the tire swallowed the point without comment. He tried a second time. This time he plunged the blade in harder and it slid in neatly as the car began to collapse slowly over the rim.

Tom went up to the edge of the window of *Crouper's* and looked inside. The air conditioner above the front door was whirring and muffling the sounds from inside. He felt a drop of water land on the back of his neck. Crouper himself was in the back of the store, yelling at Harris and shaking his hands in the air. Tom couldn't see Lorna. Harris picked up a pole of some sort and smashed the side of Crouper's head with it. Crouper collapsed and Tom raised his gun, throwing his shoulder into the steel and glass door.

In the split second that it took to shove open the door Harris was suddenly gone. Tom turned to look for a rear exit and saw one at the side, behind a display of plastic glasses with painted watermelon and sun-umbrella designs. He hurried toward it just as Harris jerked Lorna to her feet. They were just to the side of him. She had hidden behind the counter and Harris' arm was now around her chin, with the point of his knife at her throat. He had bent over to seize her in the instant that Tom had come through the door.

"I'm not going with you, Earlon," she said. "I don't care what you say and I don't care what you do. I'm not going with you."

"The hell you're not," he said, screaming into her ear. "You're gonna come with me now or you're gonna die right here on this fucking spot. You're sure as shit not going with that fucking Roy; that's settled. Now don't make me hurt you, Lorna, because you know I damn sure will do it if I have to."

Harris now felt the presence of the automatic pointing at his forehead. He turned toward Tom.

"What the fuck are *you* doing here, asshole?" he said to Tom. "Drop the gun or by God she's dead where she stands."

Tom paused for a moment and finally dropped the gun into a waist-high floor display of terracotta planters.

"No, no, asshole," Harris said. "Not so close. Take the gun out of the goddamned pot and kick it away from you; kick it as far as you can. And don't even think about fucking with me again."

As Harris watched Tom kick the gun, Lorna looked at him from the corner of her eye. Suddenly she grabbed at his arm, reducing the pressure of the knife against her throat as she drove the steel plate of her heel down his right shin and into his instep. The edge of the knife caught her throat but she managed to free herself and run. Harris screamed in pain, looked at Tom, bolted, and hopped toward the door.

Tom looked for his gun but didn't see it immediately. He grabbed the pole which Harris had used on Crouper, who was now bleeding and moaning next to his imitation teak salad set display, and followed Harris into the lot. Harris saw the flat tire on the Cutlass, kicked the fender with his good foot, and hobbled toward the back of the car.

"How's your foot feel, Earlon?" Tom asked.

"You come near me and I'll slash the shit out of you," Harris said.

"Oh, I'm coming near you all right," Tom said. "You can count on that."

FIFTY-TWO

Harris stood behind the Cutlass, not moving, his eyes fixed on Tom. A late-model blue Chevrolet pulled into the space next to him; the driver was an elderly man with darkened glasses. He was out running errands, not counting on anything like this. He didn't even notice the two men in the lot beside him.

"Don't even think about it," Tom said, the point of his pole directed at Harris' eyes.

Harris stood there, thought for a second, and then grabbed wildly at the door handle on the passenger side of the Chevy. The old man's eyes locked open with fear and he reached to check the passenger-door lock as Tom swung the pole in a high circular arc. The end hit the door handle like a hammer and the shaft split down the center. Harris missed losing another set of fingers by a fraction of an inch. In the process he had dropped his knife. He looked at it there on the ground in the instant before Tom drove the end of the broken pole into the center of his chest. Harris fell backwards and sprawled on the ground. Tom kicked the knife under the door of the Chevy, out of his reach, walked toward him, threw the remains of the shattered pole into the distance, and held out his hands.

"Give me a reason," he said.

Harris' eyes were scanning up and down, looking for an opening. He got under his feet, supporting himself with his left hand, and stood up, uneasily. Suddenly he threw himself at Tom, tearing at his left eye and right ear with his fingernails. Tom grabbed him by the wrists, slipped a knee that was aimed at his groin, held him firmly for a second and then butted Harris sharply in the nose with the top of his forehead.

Harris fell back, his nose shattered and crushed, streaming blood over his lips, down to the tip of his chin and across his chest. He came at Tom again, kicking wildly with his left foot. Tom grabbed his ankle in the air, lowered it slightly, and drove the point of his left shoe into the inside of Harris' knee. Harris fell back against the asphalt, his eyes flashing, his hands clutching his leg in agony. Tom kicked him a second time in the same place to immobilize him and Harris rolled over, biting his lip and trying to hold his leg with trembling fingers.

"If Chris Dietrich is dead, so are you," Tom said. He picked Harris up by the back of the neck and threw him toward the van. Harris stumbled and fell to one knee. Tom picked him up, taking him by the neck and wrist, and guided him across the parking lot. He opened the back doors of the van and looked around inside for something to use to tie Harris' hands and feet.

"So," Harris snarled, "you thought it would be that fucking easy?" He turned and thrust the heel of his left hand toward Tom's nose, trying to drive the bone into his brain. Tom jerked his head to the side and saw the fear in Harris' eye as his open fist slipped by the edge of Tom's right cheek.

"Yes," Tom said, throwing him against the left rear door of the van. "I knew it would be easy. You're not attacking women and civilians now," he said, driving his right elbow into the center of Harris' mouth. Harris howled in pain and Tom crushed his nose a second time with a vicious left jab. The screaming stopped as Tom threw a final blow with his right fist, an uppercut into the center of Harris' sternum. He was coughing and convulsing, his face smeared with blood, his mouth and lips a broken red hole. Tom threw him onto the van floor, trussed him with a piece of clothes line and a set of tire chains, and tightened the knot attaching his feet to his wrists. "It's always easier," he said, "when you're up against a coward. They flail and act desperate once they know that *you* see what they really are and how little they really have. Now relax and make yourself comfortable. Try not to bounce your face against the van too often while we take a drive. If I were you I'd be praying fervently that Chris Dietrich is still alive. If he is, that'll buy you a little more time, but not much. You've got a date with the man with the *big* needle, you little punk. When he sticks *that* in you, you'll notice it. The rumor is that it's so big you can hear it puncturing the flesh. I hope that's true, because I'll be one of those watching from the other side of the window and I'm looking forward to seeing the beads of sweat form on your head and watch your upper lip start to shake."

Harris turned on his side, his face flushed with rage and hate. He caught his breath and spat out the words. "No way, you fuck. I'll plead a psycho. I'll still win." Through the blood and mucus and shattered teeth and bones he was smiling.

"Think so?" Tom asked.

"I know so, asshole," his voice reduced to an ugly whisper.

"Ever hear of a lawyer named Donald Fell?"

"Who?"

"The D.A.'s smarter brother," Tom said. "They work together from time to time. Donnie sits behind him in court, passing him messages. He lives in San Marino, just next to Lacy Park. He's a local legend. And guess what—you're the one who just tried to burn down his town. He carries grudges, Harris, big grudges. The kind that *take*. He used to help Chris Dietrich when he lived up here and he's a buddy of the LAPD lieutenant who's working this case with us. He's very public-spirited. You'll be his pro bono poster child . . . until they execute you. You know what I'd do if I were you?"

"What?" he said, the contempt running from his mouth like a draining sore.

"Look through your old wrinkled Loyal notes and see if there's anything in there about small-time bullies who try to play in the big leagues. Maybe *he's* got some advice for you, Harris, because you sure as hell are going to need it. You go ahead and plead a psycho. We can all use a good laugh. But don't get your hopes up. Donald Fell will bring down the curtain on you, you little twerp, and when he does he'll dot every *i* and cross every *t* so you can't count on a decade of appeals. When *he's* finished *you'll* be finished. Let me tell you something, *Snack*. There are some animals that will only eat live prey; did you know that? The zoo keepers feed them behind closed doors so the tourists don't get frightened or sick at the sight. You think that old lady's Rottweiler was hungry and mean? Wait till this boy takes his bite. There won't be anything left of you to bury but some bloody shreds."

FIFTY-THREE

Two Weeks Later

Over the objections of the Park Police, the Fire Department, the California Highway Patrol, and the American Civil Liberties Union, Chris, Tom, and Hector were awarded certificates from the local chapter of the DAR, recognizing their valor and resourcefulness in bringing a criminal to justice and helping to prevent what might have become a major forest fire. The ceremony was held in the parking lot of the Church of Our Saviour in San Gabriel. In attendance were Sarah, Chris's ex, Laura, Hector's girlfriend, Luisa, the mayors of the surrounding communities, a few hundred kids who were happy to be let out of school and then disappointed that they were forced to attend a ceremony, and an equal number of noisy but relatively disorganized demonstrators. Members of the LAPD had been discouraged from attending because of the already dubious publicity.

A cash gift of $1000 was offered to the three of them, but Chris thanked the assembled officials and told them that their wish was that the money would go to the shelter house attendant on Mt. Wilson, Gary Schlagel, to be used to scour the bloody floor and repair the suspension of his van.

The ceremony was over in less than twenty minutes and the mayors immediately scattered, their assistants at their sides, checking their schedules for their next functions. Laura invited the heroes to the trunk of her car for a drink in celebration of the event.

She opened a large Coleman cooler and exposed a row of caffeine-free diet Cokes. Even with the bandages on his face she could see Chris's twisted expression. "All right," she said, "have it your way." She scooped up the cans and exposed a dozen chilled Tecates and a magnum of Pol Roger champagne.

"The champagne is for Sarah, Luisa and I," Laura said. "We sat patiently in silence while you three went joy-riding around the countryside."

"I think you should have something special for Tom," Chris said. "Like mead or something. The old guy in the Chevy at the strip mall said he was wielding his staff like Robin Hood. I *think* he said *Robin Hood*. It could have been *Friar Tuck*."

"You can see that the Chief's feeling better," Tom said. "His sense of humor is intact again."

"Uh, Lieutenant," Hector said, "did you ever happen to mention what it actually was that you were using to disable that little bastard?"

"No, as a matter of fact I didn't happen to mention that," Tom said.

"Well?" Sarah asked.

"It was a pole, that's all," Tom said.

"That's not exactly what I heard," Hector said. "I spoke to that Crouper character and he told me that it was the base for some kind of garden candle. You put a hunk of citronella on the top of it and it keeps the bugs out of your yard while you're enjoying your picnic or barbecue."

"So?" Tom said. "That's what those in the military call a *field expedient*."

"Crouper called it $19.95 worth of Polynesian bamboo, on sale for $14.95," Hector said, "and he wasn't at all happy that you broke it, Lieutenant. Not that he'll make you pay for it or anything, but he's afraid the neighborhood kids might start jousting with them now and breaking them while they're still under warranty."

Tom smiled.

"How's Lorna doing?" Hector asked.

"Lorna is in high cotton," Chris said. "Since Marie White interviewed her for the evening news and Crouper complimented her publicly for being a loyal employee, the job offers have been pouring in. She told me and Tom that she's decided to start making some major changes in her life. She's going to spend less of her time with sleazy men and less of it driving back and forth from work on the freeway. She said she thought it was high time that she start to carve out more of a life for herself."

"I just talked to her this morning," Tom said. "She told me she was moving to Pasadena and taking a job in Old Town. Bill Bondeson found her an efficiency apartment in his building. She's going to be managing a crafts store. She also told me to say hi to everybody. And her health is fine, Chief. Harris only scratched her. You took a worst shot than she did."

"I think he would have slit my throat and half a dozen other things if he had had the time," Chris said, "but he just smashed me on the cheek and temple with the heel of his knife. I guess he left his transmitters and everything else in the Buick when the Cutlass pulled in and he saw that the driver was a skinny teenager. That's what they tell me anyway. After he hit me I was gone."

"So Tom and Hector were worried sick that you might be blown up," Laura said, "and you were just sitting there asleep."

"The hand I was dealt," Chris said. "If I had had my choice I would have been wielding one of those tiki torches with Tom."

"We were never really worried anyway," Tom said. "Any one of us could have handled Harris easily enough; the only real threat came from Professor Loyal. I thought *he* might be the end of all of us. By the way, Laura, were you serious when you said that that champagne was for ladies only?"

"Deadly serious," she said, popping the cork and tilting the heavy bottle to fill Sarah and Luisa's glasses. "Well, maybe just a few short ones," she said, lifting a blanket and revealing extra glasses.

Hector smiled, passed, and opened a Tecate using the opener chained to the side of the cooler. "Were you afraid we might take this?" he asked Laura.

"Ask the kid with the van," she said. "Next time the three of *you* are in the area he'll be sure to remember to bolt *his* things down."

Chris took a long sip of the Pol Roger and looked up toward the San Gabriels. It had rained that morning and the wild mustard had turned the mountains a translucent yellow. "They're still there," he said. "There wasn't enough fire to keep the department busy for more than an hour and a half. You have to have wind, not just fuel and flame. We were lucky. Damned lucky."

Just then a small boy tried to tap at Hector's back, but barely reached his belt. Hector turned around.

"Officer Hector?" the boy said, "my mother said that you and your chief and that other white man saved all of our lives and all of our homes and that I should say thank you."

"What's your name, son?" Hector asked.

"Manuel," the boy answered.

"Manuel," Hector said, "tell your mother that we were all saved by the white man with the wooden staff. Tell her that he's a legend around here and that he takes from the rich and he gives to the poor. You ask him nicely and he'll show you how generous he can be."

"I can't do *that*," the boy said. "My mother would *kill* me."

"Here," Tom said, giving the boy a $20 bill. "Tell your mother to buy something special for dinner tonight to celebrate the Chief's recovery, and tell her that as soon as he's completely well he's going to ask Officer Hector to take you and at least twenty of your closest friends on a hike up the side of the mountain and that the rest of us will all meet you at the top."

"Really?" Manuel said.

"Really," Tom answered.

"All *right*," he said, as he ran off skipping and cheering and waving the bill in his hand.

☙☙☙